Al Capone

AND HIS AMERICAN BOYS

Al Capone

AND HIS AMERICAN BOYS

MEMOIRS OF A MOBSTER'S WIFE

WILLIAM J. HELMER

*Including the never-before-published
manuscript by Georgette Winkeler*

INDIANA UNIVERSITY PRESS

Bloomington & Indianapolis

This book is a publication of

Indiana University Press
601 North Morton Street
Bloomington, Indiana 47404-3797 USA

iupress.indiana.edu

Telephone orders   800-842-6796
Fax orders   812-855-7931
Orders by e-mail   iuporder@indiana.edu

Manufactured in the United
States of America

Library of Congress Cataloging-
in-Publication Data

Winkeler, Georgette.
  Al Capone and his American boys :
memoirs of a mobster's wife /
[edited] by William J. Helmer.
    p. cm.
  Includes bibliographical
references and index.
  ISBN 978-0-253-35606-2 (cl : alk. paper)
  1. Murder—Illinois—Chicago—
History—20th century. 2. Crime—
Illinois—Chicago—History—20th
century. I. Helmer, William J. II. Title.
  HV6534.C4W56 2011
  364.1092—dc22
  [B]
                                    2010038264

1 2 3 4 5   16 15 14 13 12 11

For Robert Smith, Mario Gomes, John Winkeler, Chriss Lyon,
Joe Bergl, Daniel Waugh, and Belinda Marcum

In memory of Rick Mattix

CONTENTS

FEATURES

FOREWORD

I contacted Bill Helmer several years ago after reading his book on the St. Valentine's Day Massacre. I was more than a little surprised to learn that he was working on the memoirs of Georgette Winkeler, the woman who married my cousin Gus. At that time, I was trying to track down details and fill in gaps for ancestral purposes, and so was he. This led to much collaboration that I've greatly enjoyed while helping on this project. "Cousin Gus" was the best-kept secret in our family, and rightfully so, because of the notorious life he led in the twenties and early thirties. This work provides the family with long-buried history in the words of Georgette, who, one way or another, came into contact with nearly every memorable crook in the Midwest and who otherwise would never have gotten them in print.

John Winkeler

FOREWORD

That a gangster's wife would ever think of writing her personal memoirs, or that they would be found buried in files of the FBI some fifty years later—this must be the first, and I suspect the only, occasion such a manuscript could be found. That it was found at all, in the course of other research, amounted to quite a stroke of luck.

Women don't usually play a guiding role in organized crime. Gangsters' wives are typically silent, obedient, and deliberately kept ignorant of what their husbands do. An outlaw's "moll," on the other hand, may actually participate in his crimes. Georgette Winkeler fits somewhere in between.

She knew Al Capone, Frank Nitti, and other prominent mobsters of the day. She knew of the robberies and killings by her husband, Gus Winkeler—who became one of Capone's little-known crew of "American boys"—but not until he and his cronies discussed their crimes afterward. That was how she met many armed robbers of the twenties and thirties, and learned about the gangland killing of Frankie Yale and the St. Valentine's Day Massacre.

On February 14, 1929, seven members of Bugs Moran's North Side gang, whose war with Al Capone had kept Chicago in a state of siege since 1924, were lined up against the wall of a freezing garage at 2122 North Clark Street and dismantled with machine-gun fire. Moran escaped death only because a barbershop appointment caused him to run behind schedule. He arrived in time to see the killers, two of them dressed as cops, make their escape after leaving five of his top lieutenants,

along with the garage mechanic and an optometrist who liked hanging
out with gangsters, lying in a bloody jumble on the greasy floor.

Capone had finally won. Briefly.

The mass slaying shocked the public out of its decade-long com-
placency toward gang violence and drew the attention of the federal
government to Al Capone and his underworld empire. In 1931 Capone
stood trial for tax evasion, a charge easier to prove than murder, and he
was sentenced to eleven years in federal prison.

Georgette Winkeler says that the "American boys"—her husband
Gus, Fred "Killer" Burke, Bob Carey, Ray "Crane Neck" Nugent, and
Fred Goetz, most from St. Louis—were the Massacre shooters. She recalled watching them suit up and strut about in the police uniforms
meant to fool the Moran gangsters into thinking they were headed for
the station house instead of the morgue. It was the last job the crew ever
pulled for Capone, who reportedly raged over their failure to include
Bugs Moran in the Clark Street body count. After Gus Winkeler was
murdered in October 1933, the distraught Georgette attempted suicide
and then tried to publish her memoirs, ostensibly to dissuade other young
women from falling for gangsters. When her manuscript was found "too
hot," and presumably too dangerous to the Chicago mob, she gave it to
the FBI, which then had no authority to deal with "local" crime.

Independent corroboration exists for much of Georgette Winkeler's
account. When I was researching my first book, *Guns and Roses: The
Untold Story of Dean O'Banion, Chicago's Big Shot before Al Capone,* I interviewed an elderly Kansas resident, Edward Barnett, who had worked
for the North Side gang under its first leader, Dean O'Banion. After
O'Banion was murdered in 1924, Barnett sought a safer profession, but
he maintained a casual acquaintance with the Northsiders for years
afterward. He recalled meeting George "Bugs" Moran in a Waukegan
tavern in 1932, and hearing a boozy Moran say that he'd just gotten back
from "the coast," where he'd settled an old score with someone named
Bob Carey. The name meant nothing to Barnett (or to me, at the time),
but it turns out that Bob Carey was one of the "American boys," and he'd
recently been found dead in a New York City apartment.

Several years later I wrote a biography of Bugs Moran: *The Man Who
Got Away.* Research included interviews with Moran's relatives. They

informed me that the aging gangster never discussed the Massacre in detail except to say he'd called the meeting himself, but over the years he dropped the names of the men involved, usually accompanied with a bitter epithet. They included Gus Winkeler, Ray "Crane Neck" Nugent, Fred Goetz, Fred Burke, and Bob Carey, which tallies with Georgette Winkeler's story.

In the eighty-plus years that have passed since February 14, 1929, writers and armchair detectives have postulated any number of theories about the Massacre. The primary questions have been, Who did the shooting? What brought it on? And under what pretext were the Moran gangsters lured to the garage? In 2004, William J. Helmer and his co-author, Arthur J. Bilek, provided definitive answers in *The St. Valentine's Day Massacre: The Untold Story of the Gangland Bloodbath That Brought Down Al Capone,* which was the first book-length treatment of the subject. In this new offering, Helmer revisits both the Massacre and the years leading up to it. "Too hot" to print in 1934, Georgette Winkeler's memoir is too hot to miss in 2011.

Rose Keefe

ABOUT THIS BOOK

This memoir was written by the wife of a St. Louis gangster, recruited by Al Capone, who took part in the killing of New York mobster Frankie Yale and participated in the St. Valentine's Day Massacre. When her husband was shot to death in 1933 on orders of Frank Nitti, she attempted suicide but was saved by the wife of Fred "Killer" Burke, the only one identified as a Massacre gunman and by then in prison for an unrelated murder. The following year she tried to expose the workings of the Chicago Syndicate.

The Indiana publisher who bought her manuscript was threatened by the mob and canceled the contract, declaring her story "too hot" to print and even recalling the galleys that had been sent to book reviewers. She then contacted Melvin Purvis, Chicago's chief federal agent, and gave her manuscript to the FBI in the mistaken belief that the U. S. Justice Department would or even could crack down on the city's racketeers.

The writer was Georgette Winkeler* and her manuscript—literate, if less than literary, and sometimes melodramatic—describes her life with Gus Winkeler, a St. Louis hoodlum who moved to Chicago in 1927 and became one of what she called Al Capone's "American boys." They included first her husband, then Fred Burke and other gunmen, most from St. Louis, who acted as a special-assignment crew unknown to either the Chicago police or to Capone's rivals.

---

* The name was spelled Winkler by the press, and some of the dates and language likely came from an earlier version researched by a mysterious Dr. Hollenberger, mentioned in her FBI interrogations and in the biographies.

Some of them soon traveled to New York with Thompson submachine guns (the first use of such a weapon in that city) to kill top mobster Frankie Yale on July 1, 1928; then on February 14, 1929, Capone's
"American boys" used their Tommyguns to kill seven of the Bugs Moran
gang in the St. Valentine's Day Massacre. Georgette's personal account
of that crime was independently supported by a Massacre lookout later
captured for other crimes, as well as by Chicago detectives and journal-
ists who had stayed on the case. The FBI wanted nothing to do with it.

While Georgette's story tries to diminish Gus Winkeler's role as a
robber and killer and no doubt exaggerates her efforts to reform him, she
candidly describes the crimes he committed, the fears she experienced,
and her stress of being "on the run."

It professes to be a cautionary tale that warns other young women
against taking up with gangsters, but in retrospect it is a painful account
of her life in the late twenties and early thirties—and it appears to be the
only memoir by a person who personally knew Al Capone, his successor
Frank Nitti, and other high-profile mobsters and that gives an insider's
account of the St. Valentine's Day bloodbath that confirmed Chicago as
the gangster capital of the world.

Gus Winkeler's murder made banner headlines in Chicago and
reached the front page of the *New York Times,* but by 1933 Capone was in
prison, Prohibition had been repealed, and Kansas City had a "massacre"
of its own that provoked the new FDR administration into declaring the
first national "War on Crime."

Practically overnight public excitement shifted to a new breed of
federal agent that a little-known but extremely savvy J. Edgar Hoover
soon transformed into Dick-Tracy-style "G-men." They were wrongly
portrayed as an "American Scotland Yard," but it became their job to
pursue, capture, or kill "interstate" kidnappers and bank robbers with
such catchy monikers as Machine Gun Kelly, Pretty Boy Floyd, Baby
Face Nelson, and the Dillinger Gang. (The Dillinger outlaws had broken
out of an Indiana prison on September 26, 1933, the same day Machine
Gun Kelly was captured in Memphis and only two weeks before Winkeler himself was killed.)

Winkeler's death on October 9, 1933, was ordained when the Chicago
Syndicate discovered he was secretly cooperating with federal agents in

their search for the fugitive Verne Miller, a former Winkeler accomplice involved in the Kansas City killings earlier that year. And in the month after Winkeler was murdered John Dillinger engaged police in a wild shoot-out that landed him the title of Chicago's Public Enemy Number One. (Hoover had flatly rejected the Chicago Crime Commission's offer to create a national Public Enemy list, although he didn't object to newspapers applying "Public Enemy" to any criminal who became the G-men's main target.)

Winkeler, using aliases, had eluded Massacre investigators largely because Chicago police ignored its then-independent detective division's leads that pointed at St. Louis. Instead they arrested only the "usual suspects," whom they later had to release.

Chicago's gangland killings were old news by the time Winkeler began opening nightclubs and casinos on the city's Near North Side, previously the turf of the Bugs Moran mob. Also, the St. Valentine's Day Massacre belonged to the prosperous Roaring Twenties, and by 1933 the public, in the throes of the Depression, more than welcomed the new and incorruptible G-men, not realizing that the Justice Department had to treat the Massacre as strictly a local crime for local police to solve and not an "interstate" offense.

It was during Gus Winkeler's secret cooperation with federal agents that Melvin Purvis came into possession of Winkeler's nickel-plated and pearl-handled .45 automatic with which he later killed himself.

Georgette Winkeler wrote "A Voice From the Grave" in the spring and summer of 1934, while hiding with a personal friend in northern Indiana. The names and crimes she discusses are well enough known to researchers on twenties and thirties lawbreakers, but most also are included in the list of brief biographies.

As it happens, her conversations with FBI agents in Louisville over a year later either substantiate or elaborate on the crimes and individuals described in her memoirs.

William J. Helmer

ACKNOWLEDGMENTS

Georgette Winkeler's memoirs were found, virtually by accident, during one of several visits to the FBI's Reading Room in Washington, D.C. Much of the historical and biographical material has been provided by Mario Gomes, John Winkeler, Joe Bergl Jr., Chriss Lyon, Rick Mattix, Rose Keefe, Daniel Waugh, Brad Smith, Richard Lindberg, Jeff Gusfield, Larry Wack, Abraham Lincoln Marovitz, and Ellen Poulsen, as well as many dozens of books, newspapers, detective magazines, and other periodicals of the period. All photos are from the author's collection unless otherwise credited; many of the newspaper reproductions were provided by Mario Gomes.

My special thanks to Robert Smith for his fact-checking, proofreading, and, most of all, his laborious work of indexing this project.

Al Capone

AND HIS AMERICAN BOYS

A NOTE ON GEORGETTE
AND GUS WINKELER

August Henry Winkeler was born in St. Louis on March 28, 1901, to Mary and Bernard Winkeler, following six older brothers and sisters. Gus apparently moved his birth date back to March 28, 1900, so he could join the army and serve overseas as an ambulance driver, after which he returned to live a life of crime.

Georgette's birth date has been harder to pin down. According to a "delayed" birth certificate issued many years later, as well as her death certificate in 1962, she was born in Louisville on August 10, 1898, to Thomas and Mary Bence. However, she evidently shaved a few years off her age, since a John Thomas Bence and his wife "Mollie," her presumed parents, died in the mid-1890s.

About the only thing known of Georgette is that she and her two brothers, Andrew and Henry, and two sisters, Bertha and Minnie Belle, probably were raised by relatives who moved to St. Louis.

At a fairly early age Georgette and one of her sisters (probably Minnie) opened a boarding house that attracted a rowdy crowd—including young military veterans associated with the Egan's Rats gang, who graduated from burglary to bootlegging and other crimes. That she and her sister were running with an unsavory crowd can be inferred from the card playing and whiskey drinking that went on in their parlor in spite of Prohibition, which became the law of the land in January of 1920.

There she met Gus Winkeler. It was after his first stint in the St. Louis Workhouse that she and Gus took up with one another and supposedly were married by a St. Louis minister in the early twenties. Georgette conveniently neglects to mention that on January 21, 1920, Gus had been

1

Gus Winkeler.

Georgette Winkeler.

married to one Pearl Hays, whose possession of a stolen fur coat already had landed him in jail, and that at the time of Georgette and Gus's wedding, Gus possibly still was married to Pearl.

Georgette remained devoted to Gus even as he advanced from hooligan to hoodlum. When many of the "Rats" had either fallen in battle or gone to prison the survivors began migrating to other northern cities, where anyone from the battlefields of St. Louis could find gangster employment in one capacity or another.

One of Gus's early cronies, Fred Burke, had graduated from robber-at-large to Detroit kidnapper and hit man, and by 1927 had a $27,000 price on his head. That same year Gus and Georgette arrived in Chicago and Gus began collaborating with Burke in what was called the "snatch racket"—the low-rent kidnapping of rival gangsters and illegal gamblers who were usually released unharmed (and unreported) after payment of a modest ransom.

The snatching of one of Al Capone's Detroit friends, whom Winkeler had sequestered in Chicago, led to an uncomfortable meeting with Capone, who recruited Gus, Bob Carey, and Ray Nugent as a special-assignment crew that Georgette called the "American boys" because they were unknown to rival gangsters or Chicago cops. With them came Burke, who had worn out his welcome in Detroit.

Gus distinguished himself by killing Brooklyn's notorious Frankie Yale on his first major assignment and then participating in the St. Valentine's Day Massacre. After lying low for a year he took the name Michael Rand (which gave rise to his nickname "Big Mike") and rose to prominence as the owner of fashionable nightclubs in Chicago's Gold Coast district. The St. Valentine's Day Massacre, however, ultimately proved to be Capone's undoing. Following that bloodbath Capone was summoned to a so-called national gangster convention in Atlantic City, after which he began a ten-month sabbatical in a Pennsylvania prison that lasted into 1930 and was followed by his conviction for tax evasion in Chicago on October 24, 1931.

Two months later, to fulfill his mother's wishes, Gus and Georgette were married in a Catholic ceremony at Chicago's Notre Dame Church on December 16, 1931. The wedding was conducted by Father Edward Dwyer, a priest and confidant of Georgette and Gus, who either didn't know of his Frankie Yale and St. Valentine's Day indiscretions or was extremely forgiving.

By this time Gus's business acumen was earning him major concessions in what had been Bugs Moran's North Side territory, and with Capone's blessing he already had negotiated the return of loot stolen from a bank in Omaha, Nebraska. Once Capone was in prison, however, his other "American boys" began leaving the reservation and were being replaced by Italians loyal to Frank Nitti, whose suspicions about Winkeler only deepened when Gus was seen visiting the Chicago offices of the Bureau of Investigation after the Kansas City Massacre in 1933.

Nitti already resented Winkeler's increasing independence and did not know what Syndicate secrets he might be spilling. Federal agents later believed that Gus's cooperation with the Bureau was what led to his murder on October 9, 1933.

Before Gus Winkeler's body was moved to St. Louis for burial, many friends (and also his enemies) attended services that were held in Chicago. And after Gus's interment at Park Lawn Cemetery in St. Louis, also attended by a crowd, and the placement of an impressive gravestone, Georgette returned to Chicago to find that "burglars" had hit their apartment for six sable coats and other valuables. Evidently the doorman and any observant neighbors decided it was not in their best interest to notify the police.

On October 22, 1933, Georgette attempted suicide by stove gas after making a phone call to Bonnie White, Fred Burke's Missouri wife—the one he'd married in Centerville, Iowa. Georgette liked Bonnie and had set her up in Chicago after Burke's conviction for a murder in Michigan. Bonnie deduced from Georgette's obvious state of depression that it was her way of saying good-bye, so she called a neighbor in Georgette's building who summoned a rescue squad.

By October 26, and after counseling from Father Dwyer, Georgette began moving out of their six-room apartment at 3300 Lake Shore Drive to stay in northern Indiana with Martha Grabowski, a personal friend who apparently had not figured in Gus's mischief.

Meanwhile, several family members from St. Louis tried to locate Gus's holdings, most (and perhaps all) of which had been owned in the names of other mob members or front men and had been taken over by the Nitti Syndicate. By her account, Georgette was left without the support that usually was granted to gangland's widows. She had money to live on, however, possibly secreted in safe-deposit boxes or otherwise hidden from the mob.

The following August 28, 1934, Georgette resorted to a séance that was attended by several people, one of whom turned out to be a reporter. A wispy "Gus" supposedly appeared, as requested by the medium, but did not have much to say beyond encouraging her to continue writing her memoirs. When Georgette raised other issues, Gus vanished, to the disappointment of the already skeptical reporter, who years later devoted a short and sarcastic feature to the experience.

It may have been in some connection with the séance that Georgette met Walter Marsh, a seventeen-year employee at a Chicago construction firm who had two children from an earlier marriage. They soon moved to Louisville, where Georgette still had family, bought a house at 113 South Western Parkway, and opened the Triangle Restaurant at 1605 Bardstown Road (the FBI mistakenly lists this address as 1804 and 1805). According to FBI agents, Walter was a multi-talented husband, their house was more than comfortable, and in keeping with his Good Samaritan impulses he evidently became ordained and established a small Episcopalian Spiritual Church, using part of their home for services.

Walter had no problems with Georgette's previous lifestyle and wholeheartedly approved of her travels to St. Paul to testify about the political corruption surrounding a Barker-Karpis gang kidnapping. She then returned to Louisville to resume an apparently normal life, for she and Walter's children became fond of one another, and one step-grand-child bears her name.

About 1938 they bought a farm in the nearby town of Westport, Indiana, and eventually moved to Indianapolis, where they lived at 521 East 29th Street. There Walter opened the Sacred Science Church, where he remained pastor for another sixteen years. He retired about 1957 and died in 1961. Georgette died on February 14, 1962—ironically the same date as the St. Valentine's Day Massacre—and both are interred at Crown Hill Cemetery, the resting place of several prominent Indiana citizens, including John Dillinger.

"A VOICE FROM THE GRAVE": THE MEMOIR OF GEORGETTE WINKELER

Traced through the career of one man, it is written in an effort to show the reader how the modern criminal is born—and why. It undertakes to show methods, and above all, motives.

In the person of Gus Winkeler, this book will attempt to give the reader an intimate insight of the life of a man who sought to rule by blood, not for the sake of money, but for the power and influence money would give him.

With as little offense as possible, this book undertakes to show the wreck and ruin he leaves in his wake, not only in the lives of those nearest to him, but the lives of those with whom he comes in contact.

Without pointing directly to a moral, by a recital of bare facts I hope that the reader may draw some profitable moral conclusions, and at the same time become better acquainted with the ramifications of crime as it exists today.

In spite of that, this book is not offered as an expose, although by the mention of certain names, it may appear to be essentially an exposure of a few who still live.

The names of some have been written across the pages of crime history. Most have gone the way of all criminals. Others still flourish, and have yet to reap the reward of all those who live by crime.

In some respects this book may appear malicious, but not intentionally. In honesty to myself I have been forced to point out some facts that on the surface might appear to be unnecessary.

In any case those facts are related in an effort to further demonstrate the methods of big business in crime.

I have often alluded to my reactions, believing that in so doing I may more fully reveal to all women, what any women in the same circumstances might feel.

The only direct message I feel qualified to give is directly to girls and women, who by accident or choice become the wives or companions of criminals.

I have made no effort to varnish the facts, for they speak for themselves. Although the subject of this book was my husband, I made no effort to conceal his true character, or present him as a hero.

In dealing with organized crime in these pages, I fully realize that I take my life in my hands. But as this book will reveal, it is the fulfillment of a pledge.

The book is not offered as a literary work, but as a recital of plain facts by one who knows.

Mrs. Gus Winkeler

1

THE SEVENTH CHILD

From the adjoining room came the smart slap of a hand on bare flesh, followed by a smothered, quavering wail which steadied and grew in volume.

The waiting man smiled in satisfaction. Judging from the experience of six previous similar occasions the child was normal.

The doctor came out of the room, his coat under his arm, rolling down his sleeves as he advanced.

"Boy," he said briefly.

Ben Winkeler rubbed his hands. Fine. He'd call him August Henry, an old name in the family. He'd be the pride of the family, for wasn't he the seventh child?

Concerned about his wife, who had been home hardly a year from a sanitarium where she had been treated for mental and physical collapse, Ben Winkeler waited impatiently until summoned.

Under the deft ministrations of the nurse the wails from the other room gradually subsided.

Had the father had the ear of prescience, he would have heard in those halls the voice of "Big Mike," which in thirty years would assume the tone of authority in Chicago's racket land. Honest, God-fearing man that he was, he might have hoped that that voice had been stilled at birth.

It was March 28, 1901.

The mother recovered and the child thrived in an atmosphere of mother love and sister affection.

Mrs. Winkeler lavished her entire attention on her last child. He was the pet of the household, which under the mother's dominion denied him nothing.

Little Gus flourished physically, learned what it was to have his own way, and become a dominant personality in the home. The same influence followed him into parochial school, where records show he was a normal pupil.

During early school age he became obsessed with the same mania for guns that most normal boys fall heir to. On the playground Gus could be seen almost any day flourishing a wooden pistol and leading his mates in the old game of "cops and robbers."

But his mania was not confined to play pistols. He found his father's revolver, and in a vacant field near the school experimented until he learned how to operate it. Since his father rarely touched the gun he failed to notice that it was in use, and to save him from Ben Winkeler's wrath the mother bought cartridges to replace those used by her son.

In the face of reprimands from the sisters, Gus carried the gun to school, and entertained his fellows with his rapidly improving marksmanship.

Gus was graduated from the eighth grade, none the better so far as moral education was concerned. The mother's indulgent fondness outweighed the influence of the sisters. Gus got whatever he wanted, and like most youngsters learned the power of tears, which he turned on in volume as a last resort to gain his ends.

I sincerely believe his mother's pampering was a dominant factor in Gus Winkeler's later life.

School days left behind, Ben Winkeler felt it high time that Gus go to work and become a useful member of the household. Mr. Winkeler was sexton of a nearby cemetery, and grave digging was one of his duties.

Gus was far from pleased the first time his father took him to the cemetery to aid in digging a grave. Returning home he exhibited a blister, which threw his mother into such a rage at what she termed "abuse of the tender lad," that his father was glad to end it then and there.

From then on Gus' time was his own. Mrs. Winkeler saved every cent she could get to buy him silk stockings, silk shirts and other fineries unusual for a boy at his age. She became a virtual slave to her favorite child, unwittingly contributing more and more to his natural strong will and obstinate character.

When Gus was sixteen his sister Anna got him a minor position in a furrier's shop where she was employed, but Gus didn't make money fast enough to meet his increasing requirements. With no childhood influence to curb him, he committed his first offense against established order.

One day he gained possession of a one hundred dollar check payable to the firm, forged the name of the proprietor and cashed it. A few days later it was discovered and Gus was accused.

When brought before the management he pleaded to such good advantage that it was agreed to drop the matter if he would make the check good. Mrs. Winkeler came to the rescue, but her son's second job was ended.

Another year of leisure followed for Gus, with his mother providing the money. During that time he made the acquaintance of a number of doubtful characters. However, the telling announcement of the drums that this country had entered the war changed the course of his life for a time.

Gus was too young to be affected by the draft, but caught in the fever that gripped the nation he volunteered for service.

Ben Winkeler stormed when he saw his boy in uniform and refused to let him go, but Mrs. Winkeler as usual insisted that he have his way, so with persistent pleas and diplomacy Gus won his father over and went to war with the blessing of both parents.

Overseas the young soldier was assigned to the 362nd ambulance corps under Captain Herbert E. Wheeler. It was his duty to transport the wounded from the battlefield to the field hospitals. What he saw and heard had, perhaps, a lot to do with his future career; for it was there he saw murder legalized.

After the first fear wore away he became hardened to cries of anguish, blood and death. Whatever noble sentiments he may have had were buried deeper and deeper with every carload of wounded or dead men. His nerves grew cold, and the vision of blood became as common-place as breakfast.

The armistice was declared, and at the little home in St. Louis Gus' mother prepared to restore him to his old life. She saved every penny she could get, but a few weeks before her son returned she lost the money from the top of her hose.

Ben Winkeler found it, and knowing for what it was intended, planned not to return it. But Mrs. Winkeler became so frantic over her loss that fearing a recurrence of her previous breakdown he gave up the money.

Home again and encouraged by his mother, Gus slipped back into his pre-war existence, and resumed his life of idleness. Instead of seeking work to occupy his mind and time, he sought the companionship of his old associates.

Gus was big, fearless, and friendly, and with his war experience behind him, was looked up to by his cronies.

It was through one of these "friends" that Gus met a girl named Pearl Hays who proved to be his first nemesis.

She was a shoplifter and associate of those a little farther along the road to crime than his companions up to that time. Gus was flattered by her attentions and proud to be seen in public with a woman he described as a "swell dressed dame."

Gus was serious in his attentions, but knowing her background and habits hesitated to introduce her to his parents until he struck the idea as presenting her as the daughter of a prosperous St. Louis family.

Through her acquaintance Gus met many of that notorious gang of hoodlums known in St. Louis and East St. Louis as "Egan's Rats." Pearl Hays flaunted these men as models for Gus, showing that they always had money and didn't work for it.

So it was not extraordinary that when they passed a furrier's window while out walking one night, and the woman admired a coat displayed on a wax figure, Gus smashed the window, stripped the coat from the form and fled. The coat became a present to Pearl Hays.

A few weeks later she was identified wearing the coat, and violating the law of the gang, she "squealed." Gus was arrested and sentenced to two years in the workhouse.

During his term the girl visited him occasionally but after his release Gus learned that she always came to the workhouse with another of his old gang.

In his first rage he planned to kill them both, but having had a taste of the law, decided on a less severe judgment rather than decorate a hangman's noose.

Through underworld grapevine channels Gus learned that Miss Hays was staying in a cheap Chicago North Side hotel. Borrowing enough money to get to Chicago he sought her out and gave her a severe beating.

Serving his two year workhouse sentence Gus got what he later termed: "a postgraduate course in crime." What he did not previously know about robbery and murder he heard discussed calmly and viciously in the prison. He learned about entries, getaways, concealed identification and other gang methods.

He was never again the same. He was a man with a record. He was under continual suspicion by the police. He was picked up and questioned concerning every unsolved crime.

He learned to hate the law—the attitude acquired by every seasoned criminal.

2

"FOR BETTER OR FOR WORSE"

The circumstances under which I met Gus Winkeler should have warned me that any association with him would never be sound and normal.

With the aid of my sister I operated a rooming house near the downtown district in St. Louis. We had many friends in the vicinity and were members of a card club that held meetings each month.

It was customary for the girls entertaining the club to have something to drink, so when they met at my house it was not unusual that I had a quart of whiskey in my ice box.

Before there was any demand for highballs there was a knock at the door and I admitted Gus, a stranger to me then, who was calling on Isadore Londe, a roomer at our house. I showed him to Londe's room.

About an hour later one of my guests discovered Gus sound asleep in the tub in the bathroom. We all rushed to the room when she screamed that there was a dead man in the house. Not only did we find Gus "passed out cold," but Londe as well, stretched across the foot of his bed. Our emptied whiskey bottle was on the table in his room.

We hauled Gus out of the tub and placed him beside Londe. Apparently ashamed, he slipped out of the house after recovering, but came back the next day and apologized to me for drinking the whisky and for the scene he had created.

He called frequently after that, but it was weeks later before he revealed that he was coming to see me instead of his friend.

I will never forget the first time Gus invited me to what he called "a party."

"I'll take you to the swellest cabaret in St. Louis County," he said by way of persuasion.

I consented to go and he called for me in a car. We went to "Jerry's Place" which any amusement seeking St. Louisan will remember. The decrepit old building gave me the shivers, and when I entered I was really frightened.

The plain walls and ceiling were perforated with bullet holes, which Gus said was a result of "target practice."

The place was crowded with all types, from the rich seeking relaxation or a new thrill, to the fledglings and full-fledged members of the underworld. The place fairly swayed with people. Bowery dances, the bunny hug, Negro hip swinging and other dances moved on to the accompaniment of "lowdown" music, yells from the men and shrieks from the women. Smoke from cigarettes, pipes and cigars filled the room, and the atmosphere became heavier and heavier. Money flowed freely and I could readily understand very little of it was earned by hard work.

My disgust was so evident that Gus and some of his friends decided to leave. We drove away at top speed, with the men occasionally firing a revolver in sheer recklessness. I was afraid not only of an accident, but of arrest, and decided before we got home that I would never go out with Gus Winkeler again.

The next day my sister was angered at my story of the previous evening and threatened to throw Gus out if he ever came to the house again. But he did come again, talked to my sister and won her over, and not many days later we were married, "for better or for worse."

At my pleading Gus promised to give up his old habits and companions and attempt to find honest employment. But a short time later while I was in Michigan attending to some business a telegram informed me Gus was in the St. Louis County hospital with a bullet wound in his arm.

I rushed home in a panic and found Gus still in the hospital recovering from blood poisoning. I insisted on knowing how he had been wounded and he explained he was shot in a quarrel with a taxi driver over the amount of fare.

But before leaving the hospital he confessed to me that during my absence he had met some of his old companions who prevailed on him to aid in the holdup of a dice game in a roadhouse outside St. Louis.

Instead of getting silver they got a hail of bullets, one of which lodged in Gus' arm.

Fred Burke, a St. Louis hoodlum, later to be known as "Killer," was a member of the holdup party. Since it would have been courting arrest to go to a doctor, Gus said Burke removed the bullet from his arm with a safety razor blade.

"The wound refused to heal and hurt like the very devil," Gus said. "The boys were afraid to take me to a doctor and also afraid I'd die, so finally they found a quack who agreed to care for my arm and keep mum. But he didn't know much and I got blood poisoning."

Gus said the police must have got a line on him in some way for they came to inquire about his wound and arrested him, sending him to the County Hospital where he was under guard. However, they failed to make a case and Gus was released.

As a result of Burke's operation on my husband, from that time on, he was known to his friends and associates as "Doc."

Again I pleaded with Gus to go straight, for I was just beginning to learn what it meant to be married to a man involved with a gang. I felt that if I sold the rooming house and got a private home it might aid Gus in his avowed intention of dropping his old friends. And it was while I was attempting to dispose of the house that I had another experience that added to my growing fear.

I returned from making a deposit at the bank one day and found the house locked. No one answered my knock. I was not alarmed for my sister had intended to go out for a while although I expected her to be back.

I called a neighbor and asked him to climb in through a window and unlock the door for me. No sooner was he in than he stuck his head out and the window saying: "Good lord, Mrs. Winkeler, your house is an awful mess."

I ran in as soon as he opened the door and found the house ransacked from front to back. A faint thumping led me to a closet where I found my sister bound and gagged, and half suffocated. When she was released she said someone had broken in and searched the place after binding her.

I supposed it was a plain case of daylight robbers and called the police, who found no clues, but I did not learn the truth until Gus came home.

He explained that a gangster named "Sticky" Hennessey had aided some others in holding up a bank in Illinois, and had left his share of the loot with his sister Irene, who lived at our house. The satchel containing the money proved to be missing. Gus judged someone who knew of it had stolen it.

But Egan's Rats had a different opinion. They believed that since Gus knew where the money was, and had not been a member of the bandit party, that he had taken the satchel. The leaders ordered Gus to report at Jerry's place, and knowing gangland methods, my husband feared he would not come back.

He went to Jerry's, but he was accompanied by Fred Burke and myself. Burke was a respected member of the St. Louis underworld and acted as spokesman for Gus. He told the gang that Gus had been with him when the robbery was committed at our house.

But the gang was not satisfied with Burke's explanation so he went directly to Dinty Colbeck, then leader of the Egan's Rats, their chief, and presented Gus' alibi. Colbeck was convinced and issued orders that Gus was not to be molested further.

But Gus knew how narrowly he had avoided being "taken for a ride," and told Burke at that time that he would have no further dealings with any of Egan's Rats.

The gang finally learned the truth about the stolen satchel, when the grapevine revealed that a brother of one of the bandits, angered because he had not been included in the holdup, had stolen it to "get even."

While Gus' escape still was fresh in his mind we sold the rooming house and moved to 4545 Delmar Avenue, where Gus had decided to open a beer distributing plant and sever connections with his old associates. Gus was able to operate the place through an arrangement with police. He told none of the gang where he had moved, but naturally they found it out and started making themselves at home in our new quarters. They often split loot in our place, and as a result it was not long before police were making regular visits. Gus had told them he had quit the gang, but now they were suspicious. They told him specifically that unless he kept Art "Fagin" Wilson, a notorious crook later killed in Detroit, away from the place they would have to close it up.

Gus begged Wilson to stay away but the gangster only laughed. One day, while being followed by police, Wilson came in the back door while the officers were coming in the front. He made his escape, but the police lost faith in Gus. They confiscated his beer by the truckload, and tried repeatedly to hang holdups and robberies on him.

On one occasion when a girl and her escort had been robbed of jewelry and money, Gus was arrested and the girl positively identified him as the bandit. Even after the real bandits had been arrested and confessed she insisted Gus was the man.

Harrowing by the police and loss of beer shipments were bad for business, but Gus was determined to stick to it rather than go back to the gang.

It was an accident that made things really difficult. On a cold winter day while the pavements were covered with ice, Gus and I started to a place to buy a gallon of whiskey.

Driving carefully down Washington Boulevard toward Pendleton Avenue, another car tried to pass us just as a matron from an orphanage started a line of children across the street. Unable to stop the car on the icy pavement, and prevented by the passing automobile from making a turn, Gus' only course was to twist the wheel and whirl the car about. The car skidded into the line of children, throwing three little girls onto the pavement and injuring them, while the other machine drove through the breach he had made in the line.

The police told Gus to report at headquarters after he had taken me home. Gus was badly shaken by the accident and I urged him to take a small drink to steady his nerves. In the meantime the matron had found our empty jug, which had fallen from the car.

At the police station the examiner decided Gus was "drinking but not drunk," and this fact, added to the empty jug, made a case against Gus. With the dwindling income from the beer business Gus employed an expensive lawyer and began to fight the charge of felonious wounding filed against him.

So pressing was the need for money that Gus began to cast about for additional income. A Jew I knew only as "Sam" frequented the Weber Rental Garage which operated on the main floor below our beer plant.

Gus learned that Sam was the ringleader of a "hot" car ring, and made a deal whereby he became one of its operators.

A lad called "Smitty," not yet twenty years old, spent considerable time at the garage, and Gus got him to help with operations of the ring. The business in stolen cars thrived to such an extent that the federal government started an investigation. The entire gang withdrew when the trail got hot.

At a council of war the leaders agreed that as long as Smitty lived their secrets would not be safe. When Gus came home after the meeting he told me that when Smitty telephoned for his usual instructions to order the boy to meet him at a pre-arranged place. I gave Smitty the message.

Gus came home late. He was nervous and excited and could not sit still. He paced back and forth through the house and the veranda. At the edge of the porch I saw him take a gun from his pocket and toss two empty cartridges over the railing.

I felt a crawling sensation at the pit of my stomach.

"Gus," I demanded, "where's Smitty?"

"How should I know?" he said shortly.

Then I knew. The crawling sensation spread to my heart.

"Gus," I insisted, "did you kill Smitty?"

He made a few more turns of the room before replying, one hand thrust deep into his pocket, the other stroking the back of his bent head in a customary gesture. At the end of the room he turned and spoke.

"I helped," he said in a faint voice.

"Oh, Gus," was the only answer I could summon as I sank into a chair.

My horror did not help my husband. He finally begged that we go for a drive to clear his head. We drove all night, and I pleaded with him to give up crime. I pictured the horrors of hanging, and a life in prison.

Early in the morning we came home after buying a paper that told of Smitty's death. He had been "taken for a ride." His body was found beside the road.

"Somebody said we had a flat tire," Gus explained. "Smitty and I got out to look—then we killed him. He never knew what happened."

The St. Louis police never found the murderers.

Fred Burke and Egan's Rats

Few men dedicated themselves to crime with more gusto than Fred Burke. He was a brainy and elusive bank robber involved in the so-called snatch racket and also an alcoholic womanizing contract killer. From a good home.

The crime for which Fred Burke is best remembered is Chicago's St. Valentine's Day Massacre. Why he became an immediate suspect is not entirely clear, unless it was because he already had earned himself top billing among midwestern police departments as early as 1927, and a witness had noticed what he took to be a speeding detective cruiser whose driver was missing some teeth. However, Chicago police persistently refused to follow up its detective division's leads that pointed to shooters from St. Louis, and the reason for that is also unclear, unless Detective Chief Stege was on Capone's payroll, as Byron Bolton later claimed.

Burke's birth name was Thomas Camp, the fourth son born to the respected farm family of Warren and Martha Camp outside the village of Mapleton, Kansas, on May 29, 1893. According to researcher Dan Waugh (*Egan's Rats*), the Camps later were taken to the cleaners by a gregarious Texas land salesman peddling phony property deeds, but not before he had recruited Thomas into the scam. When the sheriff finally closed in, the salesman split and left young Tom to face the music. And after his mother died, the seventeen-year-old Thomas left the family farm and headed to Kansas City, where he frequented poolrooms and saloons and started picking up arrests for disturbing the peace, burglary, and rob-

Police raided Fred Burke's house in
Stevensville, Michigan, and found
two "Massacre" submachine guns.
Burke, a.k.a. Dane, had left behind his
"paramour" (in FBI parlance), Viola
Brenneman, to take the heat. Hiding out
in Missouri under the name of White,
Burke legally married a student nurse,
Bonnie Porter, who would later interrupt
Georgette Winkeler's suicide attempt.

Fred Burke.

bery. He walked away from half-hearted prosecutions, or maybe jumped bail, and ended up in St. Louis about 1915.

Now the family black sheep, Thomas Camp made one trip home at Christmas of 1916, more or less to demonstrate the rewards of life in the Big City—he was dressed to the nines and had money to throw around—but the reunion was tense. After wishing his family well he went back to St. Louis and never saw them again.

In St. Louis the twenty-two-year-old Camp now called himself Frederick R. Burke and found his way into Egan's Rats, a gang whose hundred or so members fenced stolen goods via saloonkeeper Tom Egan and his brother Willie, meanwhile doing any dirty work for the St. Louis Democratic machine. Burke's style and fashionable dress allowed him to win the hearts and ultimately the pocket books of older lonely ladies staying at the nicer hotels.

At some point early on he hooked up with Robert Carey, and by the end of the summer of 1917 Burke was indicted for forgery. With Carey and Johnny Reid, he jumped bail and made for Detroit. There Burke and Carey were indicted for burglary and again jumped bail to return to St. Louis, where they eluded the law by enlisting in the military in May 1918.

Burke found himself in the army's fledgling tank corps just in time for the Meuse-Argonne campaign. It probably was there that he met Raymond Nugent, a small-time hood from Cincinnati who also would end up in St. Louis as a friend of Burke's buddy, Bob Carey.

With the 1917 forgery case still hanging over him, Burke headed back to Detroit and looked up Johnny Reid, who had just been acquitted of a murder. He also went back into the phony land deed business in 1919 until a bilked investor squawked, sending him to Michigan's state prison. He was paroled a year later, only to be extradited back to Missouri, where the old forgery charge landed him in that state's prison at Jefferson City.

Upon his release in 1922, Burke returned to St. Louis, where his "Rats" had lost their original leaders, Tom from an illness and Willie from a bullet. The new gang boss was William "Dinty" Colbeck, who had begun enlisting younger "red hots." Burke considered them too reckless, but he respected Colbeck, a fellow war veteran.

Meanwhile, the old Rats were confronting a new group of bootleggers calling themselves the Hogan Gang, who were suspected of killing

Willie Egan. The Hogans were led by Edward "Jelly Roll" Hogan, who had been kicked out of the state legislature over a fistfight with another lawmaker, only to become the deputy Missouri state beverage inspector.

The extent to which Burke engaged in the escalating gang warfare isn't known, but by 1923 he was hanging out at a roadhouse called the Sharpshooters Club and there met another young hood who would become his closest friend.

Gus Winkeler had been born in Lemay, a south suburb of St. Louis. He was a few years younger than Burke but knew many of the hoods and wannabes in both camps, and like Burke he was a World War I veteran. He may have been a part of Burke's "personal crew" when Burke, Carey, and others hit a federal warehouse on April 25, 1923, making off with $80,000 worth of "medicinal" whiskey. Apparently this was the first time Burke donned a police uniform to gain entry. The idea may have been Carey's, but it later became a Burke trademark.

By his thirtieth birthday Burke knew every major hoodlum in the St. Louis area and had expanded his operations into southern Illinois, where he acquainted himself with the Birger and Shelton gangs before they had their falling out. Working out of East St. Louis, he and some fellow Rats targeted small-town payroll messengers, who stood little chance against well-armed robbers. It was while consorting with the Birgers and Sheltons that Burke picked up his first Thompson submachine gun, No. 2347, which the Auto-Ordnance Corporation had legally if unwittingly sold to Marion County Deputy Sheriff Les Farmer in November 1924. Farmer had affiliated with the East St. Louis hoods, and in 1929 this Thompson would be one of the two submachine guns used in the St. Valentine's Day Massacre.

After having knocked over the United Railways offices for $38,000 on July 3, 1923, Burke figured he'd be questioned about a major mail robbery the previous April. He quickly vacationed back to Detroit, where he linked up with Bob Carey and Isadore "Izzy" Londe, who likewise had fled St. Louis. Strapped for cash, Burke and his friends robbed a Detroit jewelry store on March 10, 1924, but two nights later Burke got so drunk that the bartender called the cops, who found part of the stolen jewels in his car. That charge was later dismissed, but he was shipped back to the prison in Jackson as a parole violator.

Burke walked out of Jackson on October 22 and into the arms of St. Louis detectives, who arrested him as a suspect in the United Railways robbery the previous year. Less than a month later, on November 15, 1924, nine members of the Rats were convicted of that robbery and sentenced to twenty-five years in Leavenworth—thanks largely to one of the Rats who ratted out the others to save his own skin. Egan's Rats, as they still were called, never quite recovered from that calamity. Burke, charged separately, jumped bail, and joined up with several survivors of the St. Louis mob bust that virtually ended the reign of the Rats.

Burke's principal cronies during this period were Gus Winkeler, a superb getaway driver, probably from his experience driving ambulances during the world war; Bob Carey, who used such aliases as Robert Newberry, Harry Davis, and Robert Sanborn; Raymond "Crane Neck" Nugent, a Cincinnati-based war buddy of Burke's who followed Carey to St. Louis; Milford Jones, a seemingly psychopathic triggerman credited with killing something like twenty people; and Charles Maginness, otherwise known as Raymond "Shocker" Schulte. Some rejoined Fred Burke in Detroit and later in Chicago. Byron (variously spelled) Bolton, a young navy veteran from downstate Illinois, lived near enough to St. Louis and Chicago that some accounts have him as one of Burke's drivers.

Before Burke left St. Louis, police there spotted him, Gus Winkeler, and Milford Jones driving along a downtown street on June 5, 1925. They gave chase, nearly ending Burke's career when a bullet passed through the left shoulder pad of his suit coat. The car slammed into a Mack truck, and while some guns already had been tossed out, the police found a German C-96 "Broomhandle" Mauser semi-automatic pistol with a wooden stock, which they erroneously labeled a "submachine gun." Charged with carrying concealed weapons, Burke and Jones presumably jumped bail, while Winkeler was returned to the city's workhouse to complete a term for felonious assault. (He and Georgette, whom he'd met earlier at her and her sister's rooming house, had skidded their car into a group of children.)

Around this time Burke was back in Detroit perfecting what had become known as the "snatch racket." Fred and his pals would abduct a wealthy bootlegger or illegal gambler and then call the victim's friends, telling them they could have their man back upon payment of a modest ransom. It didn't matter if the victim was protected by the East Side Sicilian mob, the Polish mob on the Southwest Side, or even the notorious Purple Gang, for bootleggers and gamblers alike lived in fear of what was dubbed the "St. Louis Gang." Over a period of about three years Detroit police estimated that Burke and company had raked in more than $300,000 in ransom payoffs from at least nineteen gamblers and other underworld characters.

The most brutal event involved three out-of-towners who thought they could muscle in on Burke's snatch racket and also had killed a Purple Gang member. Two months later, on March 28, 1927, the Purples commissioned Fred Burke and two colleagues to lure the kidnappers into a trap at the Milaflores Apartments, where they were machine-gunned in what became known as the Milaflores Massacre. One, who was fatally wounded, when asked if he knew his attackers, said no but added: "The machine gun worked. That's all I remember."

Georgette later explained that Gus had been collaborating with Burke in the kidnappings when he, Bob Carey, and Ray Nugent were in Chicago and holding a snatch victim who turned out to be a friend of Al Capone. Capone summoned them to a meeting where he not only put a damper on Burke's snatch racket, of which Capone personally disapproved, but ended up recruiting Burke into what Georgette would call his "American boys."

3

HEIST GUY—EGAN'S RATS AND THE CUCKOO GANG

With the auto ring dissolved and the beer business operating at a loss, we decided to move. Our next home was outside of the city.

But bad companions, like bad pennies, always show up. Gus made the acquaintance of Charles Crow, a member of the St. Louis "Cuckoo Gang," rivals of Egan's Rats.

Crow resembled anything but a gangster. He had wide friendly eyes, a genteel manner, and a bashful air. He had not been married long and was very fond of his wife and children.

On December 23, 1923, the Sunday preceding Christmas, friends of ours invited us to dinner, and during the course of the meal Crow dropped in. We urged him to eat with us. At first he refused, but finally sat down, then seemed too shy to ask for anything to eat. He amused everyone.

After dinner Red Honacker and Lou McConroy, two St. Louis gangsters, arrived and Crow and Gus excused themselves saying they would return shortly. Midnight came and they had not returned, when the sound of a stopping taxi took me to the front door. Gus came up the walk nervous and excited, and I knew at once that he had gone back to his old habits.

He hustled me into the taxi, where I immediately accused him. He denied any crime and we quarreled all the way home.

A few minutes after getting home Gus went out and brought back an "extra" edition of the paper, handing it to me without a word.

The headline told the story. Crow was dead—shot in an attempted holdup of the Abeln Brothers Tobacco Store, 3928 Broadway.

The Abeln Brothers had resisted the holdup and Harry Abeln had been wounded in the gun play. The papers said four bandits attempted the robbery, and that all four had escaped in an auto in a fusillade of bullets fired by Officer Frank J. Hurt, who was rushing to the scene after hearing the shots.

Sitting at the table Gus told me that Honacker, Crow, McConroy, himself and two others had attempted the holdup, which was undertaken in a stolen car.

"One of the officer's shots punctured the gas tank," Gus said, refusing to look me in the face. "We had to ditch it. We separated and took to our heels. I went down alleys, over fences, through vacant lots and back yards until I was sure no one had followed me. Then I caught a taxi and came straight to you."

"I'd rather take a beating than do what I've got to do now," he said as an afterthought. "I've got to tell Crow's wife."

I was sick at heart for Mrs. Crow, but told Gus to go at once. When he came back he had nothing to say except: "She took it like a man."

I helped Mrs. Crow sell her furniture and move to a different neighborhood, but the stigma of gangland followed her children.

Several days later I told Gus that I heard that the neighbors would not allow their children to play with Mrs. Crow's three-year-old daughter.

Gus thought about that for several minutes and then reached a conclusion.

"We won't have any children," he said. "Poor little devils, they can't help what their fathers do."

A year from the date of her father's death the Crow child was killed by an automobile.

Not many days after the frustrated holdup the police arrested Gus on information of a corner newsboy that he had several times seen Gus and Charles Crow together. Gus was held for the lineup but the Abeln brothers could not identify him.

That is as near as the police ever got to "making" the case.

"I'm quitting," Gus said following his release. "There's no percentage in it."

We moved to his father's home on Gravois Avenue, and Gus went to work for Ben Winkeler, who had charge of a construction gang.

I helped him in every way possible, confident at last that he intended to make good his promise to "go straight."

Gus Winkeler.

4

THE BAD PENNIES

Gus Winkeler always envied those whose station in life was superior to his own. In his own words he liked to "put on the Ritz," but lack of money prevented him from improving his acquaintances.

Although he associated largely with the criminal element he resented their uncouthness and was disgusted with the complete lack of refinement in most of them.

So when I planned his twenty-third birthday party for March 28, 1923, I decided to invite only his very best friends—those I felt would have enough respect for him to conduct themselves properly.

Homebrew, the almost universal beverage at that time, had been ageing for weeks in the basement of our home on Gravois Street in St. Louis County. I had arranged for a small orchestra, a canvas had been stretched across the grass as an improvised dance floor, long tables flanked the canvas, and the trees were festooned with Japanese lanterns to light the scene.

I spent the entire day preparing chickens, sandwiches, salads, sweetmeats and dozens of other dishes identified with the party lunch.

Knowing only a few of Gus' friends I took Tommy O'Connor and his wife, Jack Britt, and Lou McConroy into my confidence. [Not the same "Terrible Tommy" O'Connor who, three days before his scheduled hanging, escaped from Chicago police in 1924 and was never found.]

"You know who Gus' friends are," I told them. "I'm going to trust you to invite some nice people."

The hour for the party arrived, and the guests I had invited personally arrived with it. The lanterns were lighted, the orchestra played, and as Gus and I stood arm in arm viewing the scene I was proud of my work.

But I was not prepared to reap the whirlwind, which drew up at the curb in front of our house in the shape of a rickety old car decorated with all the known wisecracks. The car was followed by others.

Britt, McConroy and O'Connor had done their work too well. The word had gone out that there was a "blowout" at Gus Winkeler's house.

Out of the cars poured safecrackers in boiled shirts, pickpockets in checkered suits, bank robbers with bristling hair, holdup men with furtive eyes—in fact, the cream and the skimmed milk of St. Louis' gangland. All were accompanied by women—most of them gaudy, some shoddy, and all of doubtful character.

"Good lord, Gus!" I cried aghast. "Are these ruffians friends of yours?"

The newcomers had taken possession of the place without greeting the hosts. They shouted, cursed, and jostled each other as they made for the tables where the beer was ready to serve.

Bottle caps popped. The overflow of guests could not find enough glasses. They dashed into the house and brought out stew pans, soup bowls, flower vases and anything that would hold beer.

While Gus and I stood helplessly by they wrecked our party. Most of them were partly or completely drunk and becoming more and more objectionable. They brawled on the dance canvas and indulged in all kinds of vulgarity.

All I could do was wring my hands and say: "My party, oh, my party."

The life had gone out of Gus. He leaned dejectedly against a tree, his shoulders slumped and his hands in his pockets.

"This is the work of Lou and Jack," he said. "I'll show 'em."

As the party fever mounted Gus moved over to me and dropped his arm around my shoulders. "I'm sorry, honey," he said. "I'll make this up to you. I'll quit this gang of riff-raff. I'll be somebody if I have to go straight to do it. All I want is ten years, just ten years, honey, and we'll give a party that'll wipe out the memory of these damned hogs."

"We'll have friends that are somebody, and that's a promise."

"Bring out the eats and let's get it over with."

I started carrying the food from the house. There were not enough forks and spoons. Hardly before I could put the bowls, baskets, and plates on the table the food was scooped out by the hands of the guests and devoured standing. There was a general rush, centered at the tables. The lunch disappeared as if by magic.

The visitors were too far into their drinks to care to dance. Gazing around and finding nothing else to eat, someone shouted: "Let's go where there is some excitement, gang," and the whole crowd staggered away, and departed boisterously down the street in their flivver.

What a scene they left behind. The dance canvas and yard was ankle deep in napkins, bottles, dishes, discarded food and other rubbish. Tables and chairs were broken. The music of the orchestra was a mockery.

I leaned on Gus' shoulder and sobbed.

"Never mind, honey," he said softly, patting me. "You're too good for this filth. It won't happen again. I made you a promise and I'll keep it."

I prayed he would.

5

AFFAIRS WITH THE POLICE

Gus Winkeler's decision to quit the gang did not end his affairs with the police.

He had been found guilty in St. Louis courts of the felonious wounding charge growing out of our motor accident. He had appealed the case, but the decision was upheld and papers were issued for his arrest to start serving a nine months sentence in the workhouse. Throughout the trial and rehearsing of the evidence, Gus' reputation and his relations with gangland were brought up repeatedly as a weapon for his conviction.

But the police had failed to locate him.

Not long after the birthday party a telephone call came to our house for "Billy," Tommy O'Connor's wife.

It was a fine spring day and I decided to walk to the O'Connor home on Hamburger Avenue, a short distance from our house.

I knocked on the door fully expecting Mrs. O'Connor to open it, and was shocked when a policeman opened it and demanded: "Who're you and what do you want?"

Before answering I looked over his shoulder and saw four or five other officers lounging about the sitting room. Apparently they had made a raid in search of Tommy.

"Why," I stammered, "I came for a fitting for a dress Mrs. O'Connor was sewing for me."

"Come in here," commanded the officer, grabbing my elbow and pulling me inside.

Seeing that none of the officers recognized me I started to "put on a scene," but when I refused to give my name they decided to take me to the station.

I sobbed and pleaded, and finally pointed out that I could not go with them in the house apron I was wearing. To give due credit to my acting, I deceived them. Their attitude changed and they suggested that I borrow a dress from Mrs. O'Connor. Fortunately several of my own dresses were in her clothes closet, and I was soon properly attired.

But I continued to be aggrieved, and finally their gruffness turned to downright pity. With apologies they loaded me into their car and took me to the station.

Being unable to identify me they took me directly to Chief Kaiser.

As I was led into the room the chief's head lowered, he thrust out his chin and turned to his officers: "Where in the hell did you pick that up?" he demanded. "Do you know who this is?" Then answering his own question: "It's Gus Winkeler's wife."

The chief cursed them all, and the men who had treated me so politely glared at me balefully. They had been duped—and in front of the chief, too.

"All right hussy," said the chief turning to me, "come clean. Tell us where you live."

I knew the truth meant Gus' arrest so I answered, "I don't know."

The chief blustered, wheedled, and cursed. He called me names so vile I could not think of answers. But I wouldn't tell where I lived.

"Won't talk, eh?" he said finally. "Well I'll find out in thirty minutes."

He mumbled an order into the telephone and a short time later Gus' brother and sister were marched into the room. Gus' sister was a girl of fine character who worked every day, and should not have been made to suffer such embarrassment, but all three of us were thrown into jail.

She spent the night with a cell full of prostitutes and streetwalkers and went through the police lineup the next morning as if she were a police character.

We were released after the show-up, but Gus' sister lost her position as the result of her arrest.

I hurried home and found Gus involved in moving. He had learned of my arrest and did not know but what the police would locate him. He felt that not his act but his reputation had convicted him in the accident case, and he was determined to avoid serving the sentence if possible.

We moved to a new subdivision on the West Side near Delmar Boulevard.

6

FUGITIVES ON THE LAM

A few blocks from our new home lived Mrs. Lawrence Daugherty. Her husband, in gang vernacular, was "on the lam" as the result of the holdup of the Portland Bank at Louisville, Kentucky.

Gus soon learned that the holdup was staged by Lawrence Daugherty, his brother Chester, Paul and Baskal Farina, Red Honacker and Louis McConroy.

At this writing Chester Daugherty has not been apprehended but Lawrence and the Farina brothers are serving time in the Kentucky penitentiary for the holdup.

Gus explained that there was such a stir in Louisville over the $2,190 robbery that Lawrence Daugherty was afraid to try to get out of town with the gold.

So he undertook to mail the bundle to his home, addressed to himself. However, the postal clerk stumped him by asking if he wanted the package insured and for how much. Daugherty was afraid he would give himself away and on the spur of the moment could think of nothing to tell the clerk except that the package contained shirts.

"Do your shirts rattle?" asked the clerk, shaking the package.

"There's a shaving mug in there," was Daugherty's lame excuse.

But the clerk was suspicious and after accepting the parcel turned it in for postal inspection.

The coins were identified immediately and when the package went to St. Louis federal officers rode the same train. The parcel went through the regular channels and was delivered to Mrs. Daugherty's door. She did not want to accept it, but the messenger urged her to sign for it.

The minute her signature went on the delivery receipt federal officers stepped across the street and took her into custody.

She was at a complete loss. She knew nothing about the Louisville robbery. She had been married only a short time and was not even aware that her husband was a gangster. She had lived in the country, had no acquaintances with police methods, and her admitted ignorance made the police even more suspicious. She was held in jail in St. Louis, then moved to Louisville, and weeks later released when officialdom was convinced she did not know her husband's whereabouts.

Gus and I were sincerely sorry for her. She had no money, no friends, and did not know which way to turn. We gave her money from time to time, and once gave her money to get to Detroit to visit her husband who was hiding there.

We received letters from both Mr. and Mrs. Daugherty swearing undying gratitude. I clearly remember one phrase from Daugherty's letter: "If I ever get the chance I will repay you for your kindness."

How he repaid us will be related later.

In the meantime Mrs. Daugherty, like many other women, had found a way to make money—on the streets. She went from bad to worse. She met Daugherty's friends and became their companion.

In disgust at her conduct Gus finally ordered me to have nothing further to do with her.

Since we did not know at what minute the police might locate us, Gus deemed it advisable to take another residence to make a quick move possible. So while we retained our home in the West End suburb, we took a cottage on Creve Coeur Lake, a well known hideout for those evading the police.

The adjoining cottage was occupied by Deputy Sheriff Adam Hoerner, now dead, an old friend of Gus' who held a warrant for his arrest on the accident charge. Mrs. Hoerner and I became very good friends and spent many pleasant afternoons while Mr. Hoerner, Gus, and the other boys at the resort played cards and drank beer.

One of the frequent participants in these card games was Louis "Cokie" Walsh, a narcotic fiend and a gangster.

The day after I first met Walsh, Gus and some of his friends were at a bar operated at the resort by James Duffy, now dead. Someone came to our cottage and asked for Gus and I ran over to the bar to get him.

I opened the door, saw Gus in the room, and started toward him. I had taken only a few steps when someone struck me, nearly hurling me to the floor. Gus leaped to my side and steadied me by the arm. He rushed me out of the room by another exit.

"Listen Honey," Gus said as soon as we were outside, and before I had time to recover from my anger at being struck, "you don't know how close you came to being killed just now."

"Cokie had just drawn a gun on Lou McConroy and you walked right between them. Cokie is full of 'snow' and when he's that way he'll kill in a minute. The fellow that struck you was just trying to save your life."

Later I had further evidence of Cokie's viciousness.

Not many days later Gus got word the police had located him and were at Duffy's bar attempting to locate which cottage he was in.

Gus ran for his car, jumped in, and started to roar away right under their noses. The police heard the motor, and uttering cries of "halt" scrambled through the door toward their auto. The entire settlement had heard the commotion and everyone was watching.

The police fell over each other getting into their cars as Gus started down the winding resort road toward St. Louis.

Gus was an expert driver, and had the advantage of knowing the bumps and curves. For a time the watchers could not tell if Gus was gaining or losing ground, owing to the turns, but most of them felt that Gus would be caught on "Deadman's Curve," a dangerous corner just before reaching the main highway.

To many anxious eyes it appeared that Gus was slowing down, but a second later I heard the mounting roar of his motor as the police car drew near just before entering the turn. There was an explosion of dust as he went into the curve, and my heart jumped for I thought he had wrecked his car. The police squad was lost in a cloud of dust.

Then out of the fog came Gus, bearing down into the highway. The dust settled and the police cars were soon seen beside the road—the officers clearing the dirt out of their eyes. They had been afraid to make the turn.

"They'll never catch that Dutchman 'till they learn to drive an automobile," someone in front of Duffy's bar remarked as the knots of spectators broke up.

As soon as he found quarters in the city Gus sent for me. Confident that the police would not credit him with enough audacity to return to the cottage, Gus outsmarted them by doing that very thing.

There was celebration at Gus' safe return. One night a few days after his escape a number of the boys were gathered in one of the cottages playing cards. Every one of them was wanted for some crime or other, so all were on the alert.

When a strange car drove into the grove someone peeped through a crack in the blind then warned: "Fade, gang. It's the bulls."

The party scattered like chaff before the wind. Some dashed through doors. Gus, Lou McConroy, and Fred Burke went out through the window and started through the undergrowth with Burke leading the way.

Up to this time Fred Burke had not distinguished himself as a criminal, although he claimed to be one of the last official members of Egan's Rats. He had served time for minor offenses such as confidence games, but had never been connected with major crimes.

On this occasion he proved himself to be something besides an arrogant killer.

As he fled through the brush he heard Gus and Lou crashing along behind him. His fear distorted mind could imagine nothing but police in pursuit, so when he came to the margin of the lake he did not stop running. When he could run no farther he plunged.

Gus and Lou stopped and concealed themselves in the bushes along the bank. Neither of them could figure Burke's plan. However, when they saw his head break the pathway of moonlight on the water then disappear again they caught the idea.

The next time Burke raised his head Gus whispered: "Duck, Doc," and Doc did. As soon as he came to the surface again Gus called, "You're right in the moonlight, they'll see you."

They kept Burke bobbing up and down in the water until he was entirely exhausted. His dives were more brief each time. His gasps for breath were plainly audible to the two men on the shore, who by this time had lost all thought of the police and were convulsed with laughter.

Whether Burke heard them and "got wise," or whether he came to shore with the intension of surrendering to the police they never learned. At any rate, when he saw his two friends rolling in mirth, he swore to get even.

About that time others came from the cottage and said the alarm was false, and that did not help Burke's temper for he had made himself ridiculous without cause.

The scare caused Gus to consider that since so many people were coming to the resort to escape the terrific heat in the city, it might be safer for him in St. Louis, so we returned to our West End home.

Both of us were afraid to venture out so we kept to the house, suffering intensely from the heat.

Finally Gus suggested we go for a ride to get relief. I begged him not to take the chance, pointing out that if arrested he would be in the workhouse during some of the hottest days of the summer.

"It can't be any hotter in jail than out," Gus said decisively. "I want some beer, let's go."

No sooner had we stopped at the roadhouse than the entire police department appeared to have cultivated a sudden taste for beer. The place was full of cops, who took Gus into custody immediately.

But the roadhouse was in the county, and when Deputy Hoerner stepped over and claimed Gus as his prisoner the officers were forced to give him up. But they explained the arrest by phone to my very dear friend Chief Kaiser, who, when told that I was with Gus, told his men to bring me in.

So Gus went to town with Hoerner, but before he left told me he was glad he could quit running. I went to town with the officers, and became the brunt of their indignation at not being able to bring Gus.

I never found out why Chief Kaiser wanted me, but I am certain it was merely to "get even."

To avoid the twenty-hour "holdover" law, and to prevent my friends from finding me and affecting my release, he had me moved from jail to jail, technically releasing me and re-arresting me each time, until forty-eight hours had elapsed.

Then I was allowed to return to our vacant flat to make my way the best I could until Gus' nine months term had been served.

7

WORKHOUSE WIDOW

When Gus went to the workhouse he was faced with a $500 fine, payable before his release.

He left me with just $600, out of which I was determined to save enough for the fine. However, shortly after Gus was imprisoned his attorney came to me saying he could "fix" the case and "spring" Gus for $500. I gave him that amount, took the rest of the money and paid our bills, then sat down to wait for Gus to come home.

Gus did not get out and I heard nothing more from his "mouthpiece," so in a few days I became desperate. Tommy O'Connor knew I was in financial difficulty, and asked me what became of the money. I told him about giving it to the attorney.

He was white with anger at the story.

"That damned lip thinks he can get away with that just because Gus is on ice," Tommy said. "Just sit tight baby, I'll get that sugar back."

A few days later the money was returned. Tommy told me that the gang had informed the lawyer that, unless he sent it back, they would pay him a personal call. Knowing gangland methods the attorney wasted no time in drawing a conclusion.

Grateful to Tommy for his aid, and knowing that he too had no work or money, I rented a small apartment on Enright Avenue and invited Mr. and Mrs. O'Connor to share it with me until our circumstances improved.

On the first workhouse visiting day Gus learned that I was saving the money for his fine. He became angry and insisted I use the money to live on, saying he would have the fine added to his term.

But Gus was in and I was out, and my own boss, and I told him flatly the fine would be ready.

I never missed a visiting day. From my meager supply of money I bought him tobacco, food, magazines and other articles. But worry exacted its toll, I became ill, and was bordering on a nervous collapse.

Eventually Tommy O'Connor found a job and moved to a new locality with his wife, while my sister came to live with me.

None of Gus' friends could go to see him for the most of them were either sought by police, or were heckled to such an extent they did not care to risk being seen. Even his relatives avoided him while he served his sentence.

However, as the end of the term drew near the boys planned a celebration for him. Lou McConroy, the practical joker, and Tommy O'Connor were the schemers.

Their idea was to kidnap Gus as he came out of the workhouse, and take him to their cottage on the Merrimac River outside St. Louis, before I could get to him.

A workhouse guard tipped me off to this scheme, and the warden told me that if I would come a half hour early he would turn Gus over to me—that is, if I could pay the fine.

I was on the dot with the money, and had Gus at home a half hour before three cars filled with the party crowd drew up in front of the workhouse.

They were sighted immediately by a police squad, which ran them down on general principles. One car was stopped and the boys taken to jail for twenty hours. However, the other two cars stopped at our house, and the boys started roughing it up to such an extent Gus told me to get my dog and we would go with them.

The cottage had been converted into a jail yard scene. In the middle of the floor was an immense boulder, surrounded by many smaller stones. The boys presented Gus with a big sledge hammer, bearing a tag "To our pal, so he will feel at home."

The carousing finally reached such a point that Gus told me that if I would take the dog and slip out to the car, he would follow me and we would escape.

Gus came out as soon as the motor started, but the rest of the boys piled out too, got into another car, and started in pursuit. None of them could drive as well as Gus, so when they were sighted by a cruising police car, they were crowded into the curb, and the whole gang taken to headquarters and held for the lineup.

In spite of my condition, when I saw a card in a Childs restaurant window seeking the services of an experienced night waitress, I went in and lied expansively about experience I had never had. I got the job.

Frankly, if the restaurant had not served on trays I would have broken every dish in the place. Mr. Lee, the night manager, wasn't long in noticing that I was a novice.

When he called me to him I fully expected to be discharged.

"Georgette," he said kindly, "where did you ever learn to wait table? I can see you're trying hard to make the grade but don't try to kid me."

So I told him the whole story including the fact that I was not well.

After considering for a moment he said: "You've got guts. Stick around."

After that he paid particular attention to my work. He gave me little tips on how to lighten my burdens, and when he saw me making mistakes took me aside and told me the proper method.

I rewarded him by doing my best to become a good waitress, and before long became the most tipped girl in the restaurant.

The work was hard. Sometimes I put in twelve hours a day and more because I needed the extra money. On nights before workhouse visiting days I would be so exhausted I was afraid to go to bed for fear that I would awaken too late. I would sit up all night and bathe my swollen feet.

Even then I was hardly strong enough to push my way through the crowds of visitors until I could get to the screen which separated me from my husband. I often was so exhausted and nervous after reaching Gus that I would be hysterical.

Gus was filled with remorse.

"I'll make it up to you," he would say over and over again.

The workhouse warden finally noticed me, called me aside, and I explained my difficulties. He kindly allowed me to come a half hour before the doors were opened so that I could talk to Gus alone and avoid the jostling. I will never forget that act of kindness.

8

GRATITUDE—AND MURDER

"I hope that someday I will be able to repay you for your kindness."

These were the words contained in the letter from Lawrence Daugherty while he still was being sought for the Portland Bank robbery in Louisville.

Daugherty was captured by police and started to "repay" us immediately.

Gus had been out looking for work all day, and returned with disgust written all over his face.

"We're hot again," he announced, as he started to pack a few personal articles into a traveling bag.

"Lawrence Daugherty had pleaded not guilty and says that I held up the Portland Bank."

This report was a bombshell to my happiness. With the serving of his sentence Gus had wiped his slate clean, and I had every reason to believe that he was going straight. The shattering of my illusions made me suddenly ill.

"It just looks like you can't quit," I said helplessly.

"No, I guess not. Not as long as I've got pals like Daugherty," Gus replied bitterly.

So again we were poised for flight.

It was about this time that the papers were full of the mysterious murder of Benny Tessmer, gangster, gunman and dope peddler, and his sweetheart, Dorothy Taylor, known as "Toots" and "Trixie" Clark.

Their bodies had been found September 6, 1925, in the Valley Park clubhouse just out of St. Louis.

We were much interested in the case because we knew both of them. Although the newspapers attributed the shooting to either jealousy over the woman, gang reprisal, or a narcotic war, Gus was convinced it was not gang work, and began to make inquiries.

He learned the truth from Lou McConroy, whose girlfriend was a sister of Mrs. Louis "Cokie" Walsh, the same Walsh who had nearly shot me at Duffy's bar on Creve Coeur Lake.

Tessmer and Toots and Cokie and his wife had been spending several days at the park, Gus learned. Cokie had been drinking and was in his customary vicious mood. He and Tessmer argued, but apparently Cokie was afraid of Tessmer on account of his reputation as a killer, and did not carry the quarrel to a showdown.

After Tessmer and Toots had retired Cokie saw his opportunity to settle the score, and slipping to the window, fired four shots into Tessmer's body. Dorothy Taylor screamed and tried to get out the door, and in his anxiety to wipe out all clues, Cokie shot her down. Mr. and Mrs. Walsh escaped in a car.

The police were never able to solve this case.

But gangland was anxious to settle with Walsh for "eliminating" one of its most trusted members. A widespread undercover search got underway, but Walsh was not located.

However, later they heard that Walsh had gone blind from use of alcohol, and was living in some small town in Indiana. [During Prohibition the government's deliberate doctoring of a patent medicine called Jamaican ginger extract, which contained drinkable ethanol alcohol, caused "Jake-leg" and other types of paralysis or blindness that affected an estimated 30,000 to 50,000 people.]

Due to activity of the police in the Tessmer investigation, the gang was afraid to venture into any of the customary hideouts, but after the ardor of the search had cooled, decided to throw a party at the Creve Coeur Resort.

The boys had been "laying low" for so long that their funds were exhausted, and they did not know how to finance the party. A gangster known as "Snorting Whitey," who earned that name because he couldn't talk plain, offered a solution.

He said he knew a man in St. Louis who stored his homebrew under the porch of his lake cottage. He explained that the man lived in St. Louis and spent only the weekends at the lake.

Tommy O'Connor, Lou McConroy, Jack Britt, Fred Burke, Red Honacker, Gus and several others pooled their money, rented a cabin, bought ice and drove to the lake.

Under cover of darkness they invaded the cache and took a hundred bottles of homebrew.

They had been in hiding in the city for so long they now broke all bounds of restraint, and when the card game became too tame, they started wrestling, and before long stuttering Whitey was bare to the skin.

Of course McConroy would think of a prank. He suggested to the boys that they climax the evening by taking Whitey into town, and pushing him out of the car at Grand and Olive Streets minus his clothes.

On the way into town McConroy conceived a better plan.

He began to mimic Whitey's manner of speech, knowing that Whitey was very touchy about his handicap, resulting from a battered nose and lip. He mixed his mimicry with abuse.

Whitey snorted a challenge to the joker, and with a wink at the boys McConroy agreed to get out in the road and fight him. Leading his victim a distance from the car, McConroy took to his heels. Before they could drive away Whitey succeeded in climbing onto the spare tire carrier.

The boys made a spectacular entry into the city, much to the amusement and mystification of motorists and pedestrians.

Gus told me they finally were sighted by a police car, and it was fortunate for the whole gang the officers were personally acquainted with them.

"Get that naked ape under cover before we run the bunch of you in," the officers ordered as they drew alongside. So Whitey was allowed to get in the car.

9

FLIGHT FROM ST. LOUIS

A few days later Gus ventured out to the barber shop and during his absence Lou McConroy, Red Honacker and several others came to the house.

Learning that Gus was gone they asked if I had a sharp butcher knife.

"Sure," I said, inviting them in. "Go on back in the kitchen and help yourself."

As they filed through the sitting room I noticed they carried a large satchel. I heard them talking in the kitchen for a time, then they returned to the sitting room, told me goodbye, then left.

When Gus came back I told him the boys had been there.

"What did they want?" he inquired suspiciously.

"A butcher knife," I replied laughing, "can you imagine that?"

Gus jumped out of his chair and ran to the kitchen.

I heard him swearing and followed.

On the kitchen table was the satchel, slit across the side.

"Put on your coat while I wrap this thing up," Gus ordered as he gathered some old newspapers. "We've got to get it out of here. Board a street car and take it as far away as possible. Ditch it someplace—it may cost me another jail term."

Gus' anger and anxiety frightened me, and I knew automatically the bag had contained loot of some kind, and was a clue that the boys had deliberately passed on to Gus.

By the time I got out the door with the package under my arm I was a bundle of nerves and sick with apprehension. I imagined that I was the focus of all eyes, and as a matter of fact did not know if the police were trailing me.

As I got to the street I broke into a cold sweat of fear. In spite of my coat the perspiration trickled out of my hair and ran down my back. I was so weak with fright my knees wobbled under my coat.

I stopped at the corner to wait for a street car which I never thought would appear. I considered abandoning the satchel then and there, but second thought told me that it was too close to our home.

When the car arrived I could hardly climb aboard. I felt that my newspaper-wrapped package was as transparent as cellophane. After riding a couple of blocks I signaled for a stop, got up and started down the aisle, leaving the package in the seat. I got to the door, it was opened, and I was just drawing a deep breath to omit a sigh of relief when I felt a hand on my shoulder and heard the words, "Just a moment lady." I nearly fainted.

An old lady sitting across the aisle had noticed me. I mumbled incoherent thanks and stumbled from the car, still possessor of the package.

As I started down the street my flesh prickled. I walked on aimlessly, losing all sense of time and direction. The sudden shout of "extra" by a newsboy I was passing gave me such a start I nearly collapsed.

Eventually I found myself on a narrow side street. I pretended to be waiting for a cab and set the package at my feet. I would venture a little distance away, then return. Each excursion took me further. At last I continued walking, and when I turned the first corner I ran until I was exhausted. When I reached home I was ill.

The newspapers of date October 20, 1925, told me the rest of the story. Four masked bandits had held up and robbed Orville H. Stewart, assistant secretary of William R. Warner and Company, at Fourth and Spruce Streets in broad daylight, escaping with a satchel containing a $6,000 payroll. The robbery was never solved.

The following two years were a nightmare. The police still were looking for Gus in connection with the Louisville robbery, and knew he was in the city although they couldn't find him. We moved from place to place, hardly ever going out during the day.

On May 2, 1927, we were invited to dinner at the home of Red Honacker. Shortly after we arrived, Harry Bostleman and William F. Davis, ex-convicts, and a third gangster I knew only as "Little Jackie," came to the house and asked to talk to Gus and Red.

We heard them whispering in a back room. My suspicions were aroused by their apparent excitement, and when Gus came out with them and said he was leaving for a few minutes I knew something had happened. I smelled burning paper when they opened the door.

They all hurried out but thirty minutes later Gus and Honacker returned. Gus was nervous and suggested we go home at once.

At home Gus paced the floor and kept me running for papers.

Finally an extra was on the street and in glaring headlines I found out what had happened.

Clifford M. Hicks, ex-minister, lawyer and gang confidant, had been found murdered on a road outside St. Louis, a victim of gangland. All his papers and $3,000 he was known to have carried were missing. I knew the papers had been burned at Honacker's and suspected Gus got some of the money.

"But where did you come in?" I asked Gus in bewilderment. "We were at Honacker's when the killing occurred."

Gus explained that Hicks had been handling stolen bonds for the gang, and had "pulled a fast one" which merited justice.

"The boys pulled the job in a stolen car," he said, "and got to thinking someone might have caught the license number so they abandoned it. After they got away they figured they might have left some fingerprints on it, or they might have been seen by the police. They didn't have the nerve to go back after the car, so I disposed of it myself."

"But Gus," I said, "aren't you afraid of getting mixed up in it?"

He turned slowly until he faced me: "Gus Winkeler don't leave fingerprints," he said. "Nevertheless, it's time to move again."

In the annals of the St. Louis police the Hicks killing is an unsolved crime.

We took the second floor of a house on Page Boulevard occupied by a wealthy family. Gus never went out, and as an excuse I told our landlords that he was suffering from [wartime] shell shock.

We felt comparatively secure in these surroundings until Red Honacker came late one night while we were listening to radio reports of Charles Lindbergh's flight across the Atlantic, and warned us that the police were coming.

We hurriedly packed some clothes and went to Honacker's house. We understood that a few minutes after leaving the police arrived.

"What's this all about?" Gus asked when he was settled in front of Honacker's radio listening to Lindbergh reports.

"It's the heat on that Louisville job," Red explained.

"Yes, and they're getting too much dope on that Hicks killing, too," Gus came back. "I ought to scram out of this town, but the minute I stick my nose out of the house the cops will cut it off for me."

Gus was discouraged and both Honacker and I could tell it as he continued: "These damned cops have got the Indian sign on me [which invited 'bad luck']. Every time there's a job pulled around here the first thing they think of is, 'Go get Winkeler.' I can't go out on the street without being 'tailed' or dragged off to the station. They won't let me hold an honest job. Why, a man couldn't go straight in this town if he wanted to."

His harangue was interrupted by the radio announcement that Lindbergh was crossing the British Isles. Gus listened intently, for he was an aviation enthusiast.

Suddenly his face lighted. "Say," he declared, "there's a St. Louis boy who has more guts than I have. Here he's braving the weather and the ocean and I'm afraid to cross the river. Say, by God, if Lindbergh can get to Paris in an airplane surely I can get to Illinois in an automobile. I'll do it, and right now."

He jumped to his feet and grabbed his luggage.

"Get out the car, Red," he ordered. "I'm off to Chicago. I'll telegraph you when I get there, Honey," he said turning to me, and out he went.

Gus and his baggage were jammed under the turtleback of an old roadster, and the lid was closed.

As Lindbergh safely crossed the English Channel Gus Winkeler made a safe passage over the Mississippi River via the toll bridge, and as Lindbergh landed at Le Bourget, my husband got to Belleville, Illinois.

When Red Honacker pulled him from beneath the turtleback Gus was unconscious from the monoxide gas from the exhaust, but water and fresh air revived him.

May 20, 1927, was a red letter day for the police of Chicago, although they didn't know it.

"Big Mike" Winkeler had arrived.

10

MEET AL CAPONE

A few days after Gus' escape from St. Louis I received a letter from him saying he was at the Alcazar Hotel, under an assumed name and to come at once.

As soon as I arrived I told Gus I expected him to keep his promise and try to find work, and since our money was low, that I would seek employment for myself.

I telephoned a sister who lived in Chicago, and told her I was coming to her house for a few days, because I felt she could help me find work.

A few days after we made this arrangement Gus came to the house and told me he was going to East St. Louis for a few days.

"I don't think there's much chance of getting caught," he explained. "The cops won't be expecting me back."

"It's okay with me if I can go along," I said. "I'll go down and visit friends." Gus consented.

During the week I was in St. Louis I saw very little of Gus, but one evening he came in with two men I did not know, and told me to pack my grip and go to Chicago on the morning train. He said he would drive through with his friends.

When I objected he went into the bedroom and packed my grip himself.

"Don't open this thing until I see you in Chicago," he warned as he placed it beside my chair. "Watch it every minute—and what I mean, watch it."

The cold hand of fear which I had dared hope was a thing of the past again gripped my vitals.

"Please, please Gus," I begged, "what have you done now? Tell me what's wrong."

Gus looked sullen and said: "Do as you're told or we're all in a jam."

Of course I would do as I was told, I always had, but my heart was sick.

When I boarded the morning train I was a nervous wreck. I kept the grip between my feet. When the porter reached down to put it in the trunk rack I pushed his hand away. I was afraid to leave it in the seat when I went to the washroom. In my anxiety to guard the grip my conduct was so suspicious that everyone was watching me.

When I arrived at our rooms in Chicago Gus met me at the door and took the grip out of my hand with a smile of relief. He had driven up the previous night. As I removed my wrap he opened the bag, and as I sat down he reached under some of the garments and tossed a bundle of paper money in my lap.

I thumbed through it. It totaled $4,000.

For the first time I felt completely defeated in my efforts to turn Gus Winkeler from a career of crime. I knew he could never have earned $4,000 honestly in one week. I knew the money represented a crime— probably bloodshed.

I was too disappointed to ask questions. I just pushed the money to the floor and sat quietly with my hands over my face.

Apparently Gus had found good hunting in his home town. He made two or three more trips to St. Louis or East St. Louis and each time he came back well supplied with money.

After one of his excursions he brought back a man he introduced as Bob Newberry, but who I later learned was Bob Carey, known to his friends as "Gimpy," due to a slight limp. I mention him here because he played an important part in our lives from that time on.

Gus wanted to move to the North Side, so we took quarters in the Leland Hotel, where I met more of his new acquaintances. Prominent among them was Ray "Gander" Nugent.

Carey, Nugent and Gus were inseparable, and often were out of town together for weeks at a time. During their absences I was always uneasy, but I was resigned to the fact that Gus' companions and the urge for easy money exercised more control over him than I did.

I tried to question my husband about these trips but he seemed changed. He was quiet, his eyes were steely, and he did not talk to me with the same freedom he had in St. Louis.

When I pleaded with him that I was lonely he would say: "You've got plenty of money, go out and enjoy yourself, take in shows and have a good time."

It was true I had plenty of money, more than enough, but no woman can wipe away the bitter tears of worry and anguish with thousand-dollar bills.

Often I got down on my knees beside my bed and prayed that something would happen to change Gus. Then he would come home from a trip, apparently himself again, and for a few days I would think that my prayers had been rewarded.

On these occasions he would go to my sister's home for dinner, and often Bob Carey and Ray Nugent would accompany us. I spent most of my time in my sister's beauty shop, but always went home when Gus would telephone he was back in town.

One day I happened to be at home, and Gus and his two friends came in. They were so excited Gus barely greeted me, then immediately plunged into argument and conversation as if they were alone. This was unusual for they never talked their business in my hearing.

From their conversation I learned they were maintaining an apartment somewhere on Grace Street, where they were holding a Detroit Jew named Henry Wertheimer for ransom.

Finally they seemed to reach a conclusion for I heard Gus say he would go to the Congress Hotel and collect the ransom from Wertheimer's Detroit friends. He did—$35,000.

I read of this kidnapping in the papers, but it was never solved by the Chicago police.

It was evident Gus could see a change in me, for sometimes when he returned from a trip he would appear to get confidential. He would make about the same kind of a speech he made at his birthday party in St. Louis, for he knew I held his words close to my heart.

"I know these boys are a bunch of thickheads and common as dirt," he would say. "I know you don't like to be seen with them, and you de-

Capone at ease. Clockwise from lower right the men are Al Capone, Frankie LaPorte, Rocco DeGrazia, Louis Campagna, Claude Maddox.

serve a better break than you're getting. But give me time. I'll make big dough and be somebody yet."

The "snatch" racket was ended for a time when Gus learned that one of his friends in Detroit had been shot by someone who had a connection with Wertheimer. This led them to believe they were known, and they remained under cover for awhile to see if the Detroit men would invade Chicago. But when nothing happened they went back into the racket.

Naturally, they made a mistake, as all schemers do. They kidnapped a friend of Al Capone. Of course Capone had little difficulty learning the identity of the kidnapers.

But Gus didn't know they had been found out until Capone sent for all three of them.

They knew the Chicago crime czar only by reputation, and Gus, Carey and Nugent were awestruck and frightened at the summons, but in Gus' favor I must say he seemed the least concerned of the three. Nugent and Carey considered "taking it on the lam," but Gus convinced them they could not evade the gang chieftain wherever they went.

"I'm going to talk turkey to you guys," he addressed Nugent and Carey when they had gathered in our rooms a few hours before their appointment with Capone.

"This fellow Capone is a big shot," he continued. "He's bigger than the police in this man's town, and that's something. Now you guys act like gentlemen."

For over a half hour he drilled them like a school teacher. He told them how to hold their hands, their hats and their tempers. He told them how to answer the questions he thought Capone would ask, and had them repeat the answers until he was convinced they had memorized them.

All I knew of Capone was what I had learned from the papers. I pictured as a fiendish killer, and felt that Gus would never come back alive.

"Never mind, Honey," my husband said as he went out, "this was bound to happen and I'm prepared for it."

In an agony of suspense I paced the floor all night, clasping and unclasping my sweat soaked palms.

About five o'clock in the morning I heard Gus' key rattle in the door, and he walked in as unconcernedly as if he had been at a night club. He looked at me in surprise.

"Say, what're you doing up?" he said. "You look like hell. You better start getting some sleep. You'll have gray hair if you keep carrying on like this every time I go out."

"Capone," I said in a strangled voice. "What did he say, what's he going to do?"

Gus' face lighted. "You've got him all wrong," he said. "Al Capone is a swell fellow. He didn't even get rough. He talked to us like a Dutch uncle trying to show us we were in the wrong racket and couldn't last long at it. He told us snatching was a rotten business and begged us to quit. Then he set up the drinks and took us to a swell feed."

Then his face darkened. "Do you know what those two dirty bums of mine did? They got drunk—and after that preaching I gave them. There I was, trying to act like a gentleman crook, and those damn fools had their feet on Al's desk. I was ashamed for a big shot like Capone to see what kind of company I was in.

"Then he offered us some money, and I refused in a hurry so Bob and Ray would take the tip. But can you beat it?—both those monkeys took what he offered them."

Gus said after they got to the door Capone called him back and took his hand, saying: "Cut it out, Gus. If money is so hard to get you have to go in a bum racket like the one you're in now, drop in and see me."

"I told him I would quit," Gus said, "because he's the main spring around here and a regular fellow. He's making money and keeping his nose clean, and so can I."

So Gus retired from kidnapping and shortly afterward we moved to 52nd and 25th Avenues in Cicero. Gus loafed in the Greyhound Hotel saloon on 22nd Street and became friendly with Fred Goetz, a Capone man better known as "George."

Nugent and Carey stuck with Gus, apparently accepting him as their leader.

One evening Gus came excitedly into the house and I could tell by his expression that he had news.

"Guess who I saw," and before I could ask him he continued: "Fred Burke."

To my knowledge this was the first time he had seen Burke in two years. Gus said Fred had been in the west with some wealthy St. Louis woman he had married. He left her as soon as her money did.

Since then, however, the newspapers and police have said that Gus and Burke were inseparable during those two years. They attributed many crimes to the pair. Furthermore, Lawrence Daugherty also had linked Burke with Gus in attempting to give them the "rap" for the Portland Bank robbery in Louisville.

Some time later Gus said we were invited to the Goetz home for dinner. They lived in an extravagantly-appointed Cicero bungalow furnished by Al Capone. In the same house lived Bryant [Byron] Bolton and his wife, known to the gang as "Dumb Dora." She was not popular but I liked her and her two children. Not long after that I also met Louis Campagna, known in New York as "Lefty Louie," as I called him, and in Chicago as "Little New York." He was a trusted Capone henchman, one of the many Italians he employed. I also met Charlotte, the girl he later married. I never liked either one of them and made no effort to conceal it.

Gus Winkeler (*left*) and
Fred Burke (*right*), 1925.

Al Capone

Alphonse Capone was born in Brooklyn in 1899, and during his early teens he joined a street gang whose leaders came to the attention of local mobster John Torrio. Torrio had hooked up with another up-and-coming gang leader, Frank Yale (Americanized from Ioele to Uale and thence to Yale), owner of a dive pretentiously called the Harvard Inn.

About 1912 Torrio was summoned to Chicago to help a relative, Big Jim Colosimo, deal with Black Hand extortionists. He did so by killing three of them in a Southside railroad underpass and became Colosimo's associate in operating brothels and low-rent restaurants in Chicago's Levee, the Near South Side's Red Light district.

Meanwhile, Capone had gone to work for Yale as a bouncer/waiter at the Harvard Inn, where a knife attack by a boozed-up customer earned him the nickname "Scarface." When police sought him for attempted murder, Capone departed for Chicago and became Torrio's young bodyguard and assistant at the Four Deuces, a combination office, gambling parlor, and brothel at 2222 South Wabash. Torrio had since risen to management level under Colosimo, who had opened a prospering new restaurant nearby called Colosimo's Café.

Capone turned 21 the same day that national Prohibition went into effect, and meanwhile had risen in the ranks with Torrio. But Colosimo's increasing prominence as a restaurateur, combined with his infatuation for a young songbird named Dale Winter, blinded him to the opportunities that a Dry America would soon present, especially in a city already racked with so much graft and corruption—its street gangs could abandon low-rent crime and mobilize for honest bootlegging.

Torrio had foreseen this and, in partnerships with others, would soon begin buying up or fronting for breweries otherwise fated to produce "near beer" (which, conveniently enough, required brewing real beer and then removing the alcohol, but which also could be "needled" back up to proof). His only obstruction was Colosimo, a pioneer vice lord whose yearnings for respectability and longing for his songbird persuaded Torrio that he had to go. On May 11, 1920, two weeks after

Colosimo married Dale Winter, someone stepped out of his café's cloak-room before the place had opened and shot him to death. Torrio's old friend Frankie Yale was believed to be in town at the time and presumably did Torrio and Capone the favor.

This advanced Capone farther up the corporate ladder, while Torrio organized the various gangs into a more-or-less peaceful syndicate with allocated territories. This became known as the Pax Torrio, and lasted until Mayor "Big Bill" Thompson lost his third-term election to reform mayor William Dever, who began closing bars and brothels and drove Torrio and Capone to the neighboring town of Cicero. Following a violent election there in 1924 that compelled the Chicago police to intervene, Capone forces prevailed and quickly turned Cicero into a wide-open city of sin. Dever proved to be no match for Chicago's and Cicero's hoodlums, the politicians who were in their pocket, and any city cop who could not resist graft that far exceeded his annual salary.

Thomspon, also known as "Clown Mayor Thompson," who threw extravagant parades and named rats after his adversaries, was reelected four years later with the tacit understanding that the Levee district, if it turned off some red lights, could return to normal.

During the Dever period Torrio and Capone were mistakenly regarded as Cicero hoodlums, but that would soon change. In 1924, Chicago's only notorious bootlegger was Dean O'Banion, who also controlled politics in the elegant Gold Coast neighborhood and on the Near North Side from his flower shop at 738 North State Street, just across from the Holy Name Cathedral. That year he feigned retirement from the rackets and sold his share of the Sieben Brewery on North Larrabee to Torrio, just in time for it to be raided while Torrio was inspecting the property.

With Torrio facing jail time for his second Volstead Act conviction, O'Banion wisely chose to vacation at a Colorado dude ranch owned by fellow Chicago hoodlum "Two-Gun" Louie Alterie, and on his return he stocked up on weapons in Denver in anticipation of a bootlegging war. Included in his arsenal were three Thompson submachine guns, which "security personnel" in that state and in the South had been using to discourage striking miners. Those were the first Thompson guns to reach Chicago, but they were still on the shelf when O'Banion was murdered in his flower shop on November 10, 1924, probably by Frankie Yale again, still doing favors for Torrio and Capone. The banner headline in the *Chicago Tribune* read:

KILL O'BANION, GANG CHIEF

O'Banion's murder opened the Chicago Beer Wars as various gangs scrambled to affiliate with the Northsiders, the Southsiders, or battle each other, and full-scale shooting began. What had been a relatively polite racket, with booze dependably rolling in from Canada, New York, and hundreds of secret small distilleries (often turning out rotgut that was artificially flavored, giving rise to "highballs" to mask the flavor), became a deadly game of maneuvering truckloads of beer and booze through enemy territory. Off-duty police officers sometimes rode shotgun, which also discouraged hijackings by hoodlums too lazy to make their own.

Within two months after O'Banion was killed, the Northsiders shot up Al Capone's touring car (he wasn't in it) and nearly killed Torrio in the front yard of his apartment building. Seeing his relatively peaceful "business" splintering into warring factions, Torrio turned his operations over to Al Capone and retired to New York as gangster emeritus.

Although Capone's family home was on Chicago's South Prairie Avenue, Capone was still considered a Cicero mobster, headquartered at the Hawthorne Hotel on that city's main drag. And it was Hymie Weiss, O'Banion's successor, who pulled what must still be the mother of all drive-by shootings. He and his men, in a daylight motorcade of several cars, poured something like a thousand rounds into the Hawthorne and surrounding stores on September 20, 1926. That stunt amounted to a fitting valedictory for Weiss, for three weeks later he was ambushed by a machine gun and shotgun firing from the window of a neighboring apartment as he and others stepped out of a car in front of the Holy Name Cathedral.

Which left Capone to deal with "Schemer" Drucci, whose reign was cut short in April 1927, when police did "Big Al" (as he was becoming known) the favor of plugging Drucci when he was resisting arrest. Inheriting Drucci's North Side throne was George "Bugs" Moran, who teamed up with his neighbor in Little Sicily, Joe Aiello, to do battle with the Capone "Outfit." That ended two years later with the St. Valentine's Day Massacre of 1929.

The machine-gun murder of seven Moran men in a garage at 2122 North Clark Street made news all over the country as the gangland "crime of the century," and it resulted in the so-called first national gangster conference in Atlantic City the following May. Capone presumably was called on the carpet, for when he left Atlantic City he and bodyguard Frankie Rio went to Philadelphia, where they attended a movie and then obediently surrendered to two handy detectives on a gun-carrying charge.

When he and Rio (spelled Reo by Georgette and in some books and documents) were released some ten months later, Capone would make the cover of *Time* magazine while facing income tax charges that in 1931 would end his reign as the country's most famous gangster.

11

THE TOLEDO KILLING

There is no honor among thieves. I can prove it, although much has been said and written about crooks refusing to take advantage of each other. If there is a code I have never seen it work.

Thieves distrust each other. I do not mean "thieves" in the specific sense of the word—I mean racketeers, gamblers, and all the other professions coming under the general heading of crime.

Take for example the underworld attitude toward "squealing." Any criminal who "talks" to the police knows that he is losing the respect of his gang. He knows what the result probably will be. He knows his act may send his friends and companions to prison for life. The word "squealer" is the acme of contempt in gangland vernacular.

But the majority of criminals will squeal in the hope of beating a rap, and will not hesitate to try to pass it on to someone else. Lawrence Daugherty proved that point in his accusations against Gus and Fred Burke which on top of everything else were utterly false.

Gangsters will shoot each other down. Why? Distrust. Many organized gangs are caught after "pulling a job" because they didn't separate. In fact they didn't separate because they didn't have time to split the swag, and risked capture rather than take the time.

Distrust turned one of the biggest robberies in the world into one of the most ridiculous "boners" known to gangland.

I refer to the American Express Company robbery in Toledo, Ohio, on April 16, 1928, in which $2,000,000 was stolen but recovered.

For a time it appeared that Gus had given up crime as a means of livelihood, although he seemed to have plenty of money.

When I asked how he managed it he explained that it was borrowed money and amplified that with: "We're in debt plenty, too, and don't think we're not."

Whether the money was the proceeds from past crimes or the result of Al Capone's largess I did not learn.

However, I chose to believe the boys really were having hard times when Ray Nugent announced he was going back to Toledo, Ohio, to live with his wife and two children.

But I was too complacent, for not long afterward Gus went on one of his trips. One evening, while having dinner at the Goetz home, I asked why George was not there.

"Why, he and Bob Carey went with Gus. Didn't you know?" was Mrs. Goetz' reply.

No, I didn't know, and immediately the old sick feeling came back. Three weeks went by. The first keen edge of fear had worn away, and I had settled into a state of dull uneasiness.

One evening I sat reading when Gus came rushing into the house, and without greeting me broke out with: "What the devil are you doing here, didn't anyone tell you to leave?"

Before I could say no he rapped out: "Pack your bag and make it snappy, there's no time to lose."

In a fever of excitement I threw a few articles into a grip while Gus telephoned a taxi, and a few minutes later we were installed in a West Side rooming house.

To my surprise both Mr. and Mrs. Goetz were there, and before I could find out what it was all about, Ray Nugent and Bob Carey arrived. Then I knew without being told that whatever had happened had taken place in Toledo.

Gus, Carey and Nugent were at each other's throats in bitter argument. I never saw my husband so angry, and after hearing the abuse he heaped on the other two I expected someone to draw a gun at any minute.

"Of all the dumbbells I ever saw, you guys take the cake," Gus said during the argument. Then they were at each other again, each blaming the other for a slipup in some plan. When the first heat of anger died out they began to discuss the matter with more composure. They seemed oblivious of the fact that Mrs. Goetz and I were present.

I learned what the argument was about. It was the $2,000,000 Toledo holdup. From what I overheard, and from what I was told later by Mrs. Goetz and my husband, here is what happened:

Shortly after arriving at his home in Toledo, Ray Nugent had been informed of money shipments by the American Express Company. His source of information I never learned, but judged he must have had an "inside" connection.

Nugent informed Gus, Bob Carey, and George Goetz and two others, who went to Toledo immediately. They made their headquarters at Nugent's home and kept a close watch on the express company's activities, determining the locations, getaways, guards and all other obstacles. When the job was thoroughly "cased" they made their plans—to culminate when the big shipment came through.

They planned what streets to take out of the city so they could avoid as many traffic stops as possible. Nugent was delegated to bring the explosives to blow open the money box so they could split the loot and separate.

Two cars were used in the holdup. One parked near the place where the money was to be loaded, and where the occupants could signal the second car, parked farther down the street, where the boys waited with "tommy" guns between their knees.

When the signal was given the "heist" car came up so casually the job was pulled before the guards were aware of it.

The two bandit cars roared down the street in a clean getaway, the car with the money chest driven by Gus and leading the way—the lookout car following closely, and ready to repel pursuit.

Gus was the expert pilot, and wheeled the car safely through heavy traffic and so rapidly that the gang was in the country before the customary police blockade could be thrown around the city.

At a pre-arranged place they drew off the main highway, drove through a field and into a thicket. They were burning with glee over their successful conquest, and itching with anxiety to see $2,000,000 in gold.

In the gathering dusk the heavy chest was unloaded and placed on the ground, to be blasted open.

"Well, don't stand around, let's get going," said Gus. "Who's got the explosive?"

"Ray brought it," said George Goetz, turning to Nugent.

Ray Nugent was standing perfectly still with a dazed expression on his face.

"Come on, come on," said Gus, snapping his fingers. "Don't stall around. Hand the stuff over."

Nugent pushed his finger around the inside of his collar. Perspiration stood on his face.

"I—I—I forgot it," he stammered.

The air was blue with curses, and Ray Nugent cringed in fear of his life. Probably the only thing that saved him was the danger of attracting someone with a shot.

For a while the boys were insane with rage, then they were cooled by the emergency they faced.

"Let's bury it and scatter," someone suggested. "We can send back after it when the heat cools off."

Everyone turned and looked at the speaker suspiciously. "Yeah," said Goetz, voicing an opinion for them all, "you mean you can come back and get it as soon as the rest of us are out of sight."

"Hell, we can't stand here and argue all night," said Bob Carey. "Let's get back into town and force it open in Ray's garage. If we hurry maybe we can make it before the bulls get organized."

In frantic haste the chest was put back in the car. It was too large to lay flat, and had to be stood on end.

In the excitement George Goetz, an old lady at driving a car, got under the wheel instead of Gus, a driver trusted by all of them. But with the sole idea of getting their fingers into the money, they did not take the time to shift. So Gus took the wheel of the other car.

The cars slipped into town, Gus trailing. Police cruisers were patrolling the city, but took no notice of the gang.

They might have reached Nugent's garage without mishap if Goetz had not made a clumsy turn, causing a wheel to strike the curb. The money chest, balanced on end, toppled over and its corner struck a door, knocking the glass into the street.

A police car was cruising down the street not far way. The officers were attracted by the shattering glass and started to drive after the machine. The gang was in panic, but all were determined to guard the loot with their lives.

Then Bob Carey made his mistake. He got up on his knees in the back seat, his machine gun in hand, and smashed out the back glass to get a better play with his gun.

He might as well have advertised in the paper that he had the loot. The broken glass was all the police needed to convince them.

The race was on. Goetz twisted and turned through alleys and side streets, and after minutes the gang was sure the police had been "shaken." Only then did they turn towards Nugent's garage.

While a man was left on guard, the others went to the house after tools. They had just started to work on the box when the lookout, peering up the dark alley, whispered: "the cops."

Now all were as anxious to get away from the cash as they previously had been anxious to get away with it.

There was a mad scramble for the door. They ran toward the house to get their coats, which might be used for identification. George Goetz was the last man out.

Just as he cleared the garage a policeman came in from the alley and opened fire. Cornered, Goetz whirled and returned the fire. Officer Zimmerman rolled dead. [The policeman's name actually was George Zientara.]

Having lost time, Goetz abandoned the idea of getting his coat, rushed around the house and fled with the others.

That was his mistake. The coat contained bills and other papers bearing the address of Bryant Bolton with whom Goetz lived in Chicago.

The boys were afraid to undertake to leave town, since Carey's car also had been identified by police and they felt they might be known.

They hid in a shack on the river bank, which they had arranged for in case anything went wrong, and were smuggled out of town one by one in a small cart.

This crime has never been entirely solved.

Toledo Bank Robbery

The Toledo express truck robbery made banner headlines throughout Ohio, largely because police officer George Zientara was killed following the wild chase described by Georgette, who mistakenly calls him Zimmerman. Police said they obtained no useful information from the two women questioned afterward. They claimed they knew nothing of the bandits or, as some papers reported, "refused to talk."

Despite the likelihood that Nugent's garage was at his residence, and that one of the women probably was Nugent's wife, the cops apparently did not pursue the matter, but they did assume that because machine guns were used the bandits must be from Chicago. Georgette doesn't mention that they commandeered the Toledo police car in making their escape, and apparently the police who visited Chicago returned empty-handed.

Gus Winkeler and his friends were new to Chicago at the time and were not yet on Capone's payroll, but Capone made it clear that he did not want his prospective shooters engaging in armed robberies that would only bring down heat on his Chicago rackets.

The Ohio papers filled in many details of the robbery itself. The Elyria *Chronicle-Telegram* reported:

BULLETIN

Toledo, April 16—Five bandits kidnapped an express messenger and three guards here today, seized loot valued at $2,000,000 and thirty minutes later were surrounded in a garage by police.

Abandoning the loot, the robbers fought their way to freedom with sawed off shotguns after shooting Patrolman George Zientara, perhaps fatally.

The messenger and guards had just left the union station with a valuable consignment of cash, securities and travelers cheques when the robbers, riding in a sedan, forced their truck to the curb. The robbers leaped onto the truck and each taking apparently prearranged positions, menaced the messenger and guards with the shotguns.

The chauffeur was forced to follow a circuitous route to a lonely spot near the University of Toledo where two other machines drew alongside.

The messenger and guards were gagged and their hands were bound behind them with tape. While three of the bandits transferred the loot to the other cars, the other robbers dumped their victims into the truck.

The robbery was discovered by a university student. He liberated the four men and police and federal officers were called out.

PATROLMAN SHOT

Two patrolman were first to respond. One of these was Zientara. The officers, in a police emergency car, chased the robbers several blocks to a garage into which the bandits' cars were driven.

As Zientara and his fellow officer approached, the bandits opened fire, then fled through the rear entrance.

Zientara pursued them, firing as he ran. As he emerged thru the rear entrance, he was felled by bullets, fired by a machine gun, from a nearby house.

The bandits swarmed out of the house, and behind a shotgun and machine gun barrage, leaped into the police car and fled leaving the loot in one of their machines....

The bandits apparently had studiously prepared for the kidnapping and theft. Miniature arsenals were mounted in their cars, and they worked with precision throughout.

The university student, John White, was looking out a window of his home nearby when the express truck was brought to a halt. He ran into the street as the bandit cars sped away.

Several guns, a large quantity of ammunition and explosives and fuses were found later in the robbers' garage.

The holdup occurred shortly after 9 A M.

C. E. Mitchell, driver of the truck and the guards were proceeding toward Broadway when the first bandit car forced them to the curb.

The truck was loaded with a weekend accumulation of cash, checks and securities, the exact amount of which has not been determined, but would easily aggregate to $200,000.

Seated in the rear of the trucks with rifles across their knees were the guards, Herman Steinman, Paul Stewart, and George Baldwin.

Mitchell failed to notice the bandit car as he reached the Broadway intersection. The first intimation of the holdup he had was when one of the bandits, garbed in overalls and jumpers, leaped onto the truck's running board.

The guards were disarmed and Mitchell was ordered to drive to a place near the university. The men were bound and two safes taken from the mail truck were transferred to the bandit cars.

The bandits sped to their garage closely followed by Zientara and Patrolman John Biskupski [in another account Biskupski's first name is given as Joseph].
The gun battle and the escape followed.

The day after the robbery the city council posted a reward of $1,000 for the slayers of Zientara and authorities continued turning over every rock in the local underworld, without result. A week later the Toledo finance committee said it would authorize $2,700 to equip the local police with submachine guns and ten bulletproof vests.

Meanwhile, the Toledo robbers had scurried back to Chicago, where they became Capone's special-assignment squad of "American boys" until he was convicted on tax charges in 1931.

CHAPTER **XII**

Frankie Yale

The Capone crime syndicate was not built on robbery. Strictly speaking Capone was not a gangster, rather he was a racketeer.

This definition may seem like splitting hairs, but as a matter of fact the entire Capone enterprise was based on illegitimate business, and not the cruder forms of crime.

So when the word came to him that George Goetz, one of his most trusted lieutenants, had participated in the Toledo holdup, he sent for him at once.

And for the second time he sent for Gus.

Underworld Chicagoland looked wise. More than one thought it was curtains for the pair of them, for Capone would not stand for any crime business that would involve his intricate syndicate.

Goetz felt that the summons was his death sentence.

"Don't be a fool," Gus told him, "Capone is a square with his men. You tell him you're sorry, and that you won't do it again, and if you mean it he'll know it."

So Gus let George Goetz make his apologies to Capone, and when Goetz was finished Gus said simply: "And that goes for me too."

When the interview was terminated Capone called Gus back into the room, and for a second time took his hand.

"You're a smart lad," he said to Gus. "You've got too many brains to be in the kind of rackets you've been in. Now I'm putting you on my payroll for $200 a week. From now on you're my man, and you're quitting that other stuff. You stick with me and I'll stick with you, and everything will be okay."

"Ray Nugent and Bob Carey are good boys and they'll do whatever I tell 'em," Gus replied.

"I've no faith in 'em for they haven't any brains, but if it'll do you any good, and if they'll keep their noses clean, I'll have them put on the payroll too," Capone conceded.

COPIES DESTROYED
3⅔ JAN 19 1973

A page from Georgette's typescript.

12

FRANKIE YALE

The Capone crime syndicate was not built on robbery. Strictly speaking Capone was not a gangster, rather he was a racketeer.

This definition may seem like splitting hairs, but as a matter of fact the entire Capone enterprise was based on illegitimate business, and not the cruder forms of crime.

So when the word came to him that George Goetz, one of his most trusted lieutenants, had participated in the Toledo holdup, he sent for him at once.

And for the second time he sent for Gus.

Underworld Chicagoland looked wise. More than one thought it was curtains for the pair of them, for Capone would not stand for any crime business that would involve his intricate syndicate.

Goetz felt that the summons was his death sentence.

"Don't be a fool," Gus told him. "Capone is square with his men. You tell him you're sorry, and that you won't do it again, and if you mean it he'll know it."

So Gus let George Goetz make his apologies to Capone, and when Goetz was finished Gus said simply: "And that goes for me too."

When the interview was terminated Capone called Gus back into the room, and for a second time took his hand.

"You're a smart lad," he said to Gus. "You've got too many brains to be in the kind of rackets you've been in. Now I'm putting you on my payroll for $200 a week. From now on you're my man, and you're quitting that other stuff. You stick with me and I'll stick with you, and everything will be okay."

"Ray Nugent and Bob Carey are good boys and they'll do whatever I tell 'em," Gus replied.

"I've no faith in them for they haven't any brains, but if it'll do you any good, and if they'll keep their noses clean, I'll have them put on the payroll too," Capone conceded.

In the meantime the Toledo investigation had extended into Chicago, and on Capone's advice Gus took a cottage in Calumet City, and took Goetz, Nugent and Carey with him. Mrs. Goetz and I took furnished rooms in Hammond, Indiana, where the boys often visited us.

When the police appeared to have given up the Toledo investigation, Gus and I moved to Riverside, near Cicero.

Shortly after that Gus told me he had received orders from the Capone syndicate to take "Lefty Louie" Campagna and George Goetz to New York "on a job."

"I can't tell you what it's about, and don't expect to hear from me until I get back," Gus said. "Capone has given strict orders that no one of us communicate with Chicago. What I mean is, we're on our own."

It was Lefty Louie, held highest in Al Capone's esteem, who violated the order. He started telephoning his girl long distance, and at his example, Goetz telephoned his wife.

Often Lefty's girl would telephone me saying, "Come over tonight, Georgette, Louis is calling me and you can say hello to the boys."

One morning while Mrs. Goetz and I were together, Lefty's girl called and told us the boys would be home soon. When I asked her how she knew, her only answer was: "Read the papers."

Mrs. Goetz went out for the paper, and it was headlined with the murder of Frankie Yale, properly spelled "Uale," a former Chicago crime king. The Yale killing took place on July 1, 1928, in New York City. [Yale, or Uale, from an original spelling of Ioele, lived in Brooklyn but visited Chicago. Georgette makes no mention of Burke, although he was later suspected of this crime.]

"If she knows what she's talking about it's because Lefty told her," I informed Mrs. Goetz, "and if she's right the boys will be home soon."

And three days later they did come back.

Late on the evening they arrived I was sitting on the porch when Bob Carey drove up. Gus took him into the front room but I could hear every word they said.

"That fellow Louie burns me up," Gus told Carey. "The damn fool telephoned his girl from his mother's home in New York. Telephone calls are easy to trace, and already the girls know as much about the deal as we do."

After Carey left I told Gus I had overheard him. I had taken my usual cry out on the porch, and was curious to know how the Yale killing was accomplished.

"You didn't know him," I said. "How did you locate him?"

"Well," Gus began, "I had been given some photographs of Yale in all kinds of poses and studied these for hours. I learned the slant of his brows, the wrinkles around his eyes, and the lines in his face.

"I'll show you how well I got to know him. We had located his hangouts and were waiting around for a chance to spot him. One day when we were driving through a crowded corner trying to catch a glimpse of him I looked over in another car and turned to the boys, saying, 'there he is.'

"Louie and Goetz were in the back seat and right then and there they took out their guns and wanted to let him have it.

"That corner was so jammed up we never could have got away, but I had a hell of a time to keep them from taking him right there. It's a good thing we didn't because we'd be in the jug right now. If those two guys have got any brains I'd like to see the stuff they're made of. It's not safe to go out with them."

Gus later took both Lefty and Goetz to task over that very thing, and after the argument Gus never felt the same toward either of them.

Later I asked Gus why the syndicate wanted Yale killed. He explained he didn't know much about it but understood that he had killed both "Big Jim" Colosimo and Dion O'Banion, two of Chicago's original "big shots," and [Yale] thought he was as big as Capone.

"He should have known better," Gus said, "nobody is."

[Georgette, Gus, or both were mistaken with regard to the 1920 murder of Colosimo, who had objected to John Torrio's efforts to expand into bootlegging, and to the 1924 killing of O'Banion (often called Dion, his baptismal name), who had swindled Torrio in a major brewery deal. In both cases Yale had been in Chicago at the time and presumably killed the two "troublemakers" as favors to his former associates from Brooklyn. Yale himself was not killed until 1928, when his steady supplies of East Coast liquor "just off the boat" had stopped reaching Chicago with any regularity, and he also started backing Capone's rival, Little Sicily's Joe Aiello, for control of the Unione Siciliana. Yale's shooting is usually blamed on Jack McGurn, who lived in New York as a child, but Georgette pins it on her husband and Fred Goetz, Capone's "American boys," led by Campagna, who had close relatives then living in Brooklyn. Later it was blamed on Burke because of submachine guns seized at his house in Michigan.]

The police did trace the phone calls from New York to Lefty's girl's house in Cicero, and from there to our house in Riverside. [Evidently both Goetz and Campagna made telephone calls to Chicago.]

However, the first I knew of it was when Lefty's girl telephoned and told me that sometime during the afternoon the police would raid her house and ours.

To say I was panic stricken would be putting it mildly. Here was an emergency in which I was entirely on my own, for Gus was not at home, Mr. and Mrs. Goetz were not at home, and I did not know how to reach them.

I was afraid to stay, because I knew if the police came, they would wait until Gus walked into their trap. I was afraid to leave for there would be no one to warn Gus.

Sobbing frantically I told my sister to pack everything and be ready, and I would wait on the corner to stop Gus before he could get to the house.

I took my post at four o'clock in the afternoon. I paced nervously back and forth on the corner, trying to act composed, but catching myself every few minutes twisting my fingers and wringing my hands.

Gus pulled up at the curb in about an hour saying: "What are you doing out here?" I told him and he squeezed my hand in silent gratitude. "Good girl," he said, "stick right here until Goetz and his wife come along. Don't let them get home."

A few minutes after Gus pulled away rain clouds gathered, and a slow drizzle turned into a steady downpour. In the gathering darkness I kept at my post, shivering with cold, and peering up and down the street.

At seven-thirty a car pulled up at the curb and a man leaned out. It was Bryant Bolton.

"What in hell are standing out here in the rain for?" he said disgustedly.

"I'm waiting for George and Irene Goetz," I replied through jaws so stiff with cold I could hardly speak. "Gus told me they would come by in a short time but that was two hours ago."

"That's funny," Bolton said, perplexed. "Didn't they come by?"

By this time I was angry. "Do you think I'd be standing here in the rain if they had?" I half shrieked.

"I don't understand it," Bolton continued. "Gus saw Goetz two hours ago and told him to drive by and send you home. He sent me over to get you and your sister."

I was half sobbing in futile rage as I went back to the house and got my sister, who was sick with worry. We were just driving away from the house when the police squad pulled up to the curb behind us. Fortunately, they did not see us, or we all would have been taken to jail.

Bolton took us to his house, and by this time I was sneezing and coughing with a heavy cold. Gus swore bitterly when he heard that Goetz had allowed me to stand in the rain.

Early the next morning I sent my sister home and Gus and I drove to Kansas City, Missouri, and located in a downtown hotel for a week. I was too ill to go out, and Gus was hearty in his condemnation of Mr. and Mrs. Goetz.

The Thompson Submachine Gun

The Thompson submachine gun made its debut in New York City when Brooklyn's top mobster, Frankie Yale, was riddled by two of them on July 1, 1928. The shooters, contrary to most accounts, were not Jack McGurn, Albert Anselmi, and John Scalise, but rather two of Al Capone's "American boys," Fred Goetz and Gus Winkeler, led by former New Yorker Louis Campagna, who still had family in Yale's Brooklyn neighborhood. When one of the guns was left in the getaway car and traced to a dealer in Chicago, New Yorkers worried that Chicago-style violence might be coming to their city. Which, in fact, it did.

General Thompson with his gun.

13

MURPHY'S TOUGH SKULL

When I was well enough to travel we went back to Chicago, and Gus promised he would grant my oft-repeated request that I be allowed to keep house. We had been jumping from one furnished flat to another, with a sprinkling of hotel rooms thrown in between. This had been far from satisfactory to me.

I wanted a secluded little place where we were not likely to be bothered and where I could entertain a few friends.

We bought furniture and located in a roomy flat at 61st Court and 22nd Street in Cicero. Gus was at home much of that time and I was comparatively happy.

Shortly afterwards, the papers were filled with the slaying of Tony Lombardo, whom Gus described as Al Capone's "left bower" [right-hand man].

"Somebody's getting even with Snorky [originally the nickname for a spiffy dresser] for that Yale killing," he said.

While the underworld was making an elaborate pretense at mourning for the departed gangster, Mrs. Goetz met me downtown and we went to lunch at the Garden of Italy at 22nd and 48th Street.

Across the room I noticed a man dining alone. Something about him attracted my attention. From pictures I had seen in the paper I recognized him as Al Capone. We had the waiter call him to our table.

Capone had an unconcealed case of the blues, and mentioned the death of Lombardo.

"If you'll have Gus send me some dark glasses I'll go down and have a last look at him," he said.

Mrs. Goetz laughed and said: "I guess our boys will be going back to New York now." With that remark she disclosed to Capone that George Goetz had been talking out of school.

I kicked her so hard on the shin that she wore a blue mark for days, and seeing her mistake, Mrs. Goetz clamped a hand over her mouth as if to stop the words already spoken.

Capone had gone rigid in his chair. His eyelids tightened, and his eyeballs gleamed. Mrs. Goetz was panic stricken. Capone did not say a word, just stared at her a minute, then got up and walked out of the restaurant. George Goetz was given a severe panning by Capone and ordered to "keep his lip buttoned."

Ray Nugent had brought his family to Chicago during the Toledo holdup investigation, and it was at dinner at the Nugent home shortly after my meeting with Capone that I was introduced to Jimmie "Swede" Moran [also spelled Morand], who at this writing still is a hireling of the Capone syndicate. I mention him because he played an active part in subsequent events. Gus told me later Moran was a "brainless flunky who makes $50 a week."

The winter was comparatively peaceful and the boys believed the police had given up the search for the Toledo slayer.

But undercover detectives had been diligently searching for the bearer of the name found on the bills in the coat George Goetz abandoned in the Nugent home in the getaway. The bills were addressed to Bryant Bolton.

Mrs. Bolton had been visiting her father in central Illinois, and when she prepared to return to Chicago a coat of hers was still at the cleaners. So she left orders that it be sent to her by express. Probably it was slips like this that earned her the nickname of "Dumb Dora."

The coat bore her aunt's address in Chicago. It was followed by police, who apparently kept a watch on the aunt's home, after throwing a scare into her and forcing her to aid them. Mrs. Bolton telephoned her aunt who informed her that the package had arrived, and asked specifically that Bryant Bolton be sent for it.

Something about this request sounded "phony" to Mrs. Bolton who went to George Goetz with the story.

"It don't pay to take chances," Goetz told her. "We'll send someone else."

So he sent a southern negro named Murphy, who worked at Clark's Garage where all the boys kept their cars.

Murphy no sooner left the house with the package than he was surrounded by policemen. The arrest was a complete surprise to him, for he did not know what he had let himself in for.

When the police asked him who sent him for the package he said a man he didn't know had offered him a dollar to bring it to him.

Murphy told the police he was to meet that man at 52nd Street and 22nd Street. He later explained he felt sure that if they sent him to that particular corner some of the boys would see him.

So the police stationed him at the corner, and awaited results from places of concealment, but of course no one came, although Murphy stood there all day.

The police tipped their own hand by giving up that plan and going to Clark's Garage, where the word soon got out that Mrs. Clark was telling all she knew.

"That nigger can tell you where every one of that gang lives, he takes them home every night," Mrs. Clark told them and it was the truth.

They took Murphy for a "dressing" but he stuck to his guns, and was held in jail all night. However, an officer told him the boys knew his whereabouts and to keep "mum." He was released the next morning and came straight to our house.

He worshipped Gus, and wanted to tell him all about it.

He said the detectives beat him so viciously before they took him away from the corner that some women passing by insisted they stop. They told him they were a rival gang, and would not hesitate to kill him. They described the morgue to frighten him.

"Dis niggah got tough skull, but them police mighty powerful," Murphy said, exhibiting a head that was a mass of knots and gashes.

Gus was so impressed by Murphy's faithfulness that he said after he left, "He's better than most white men. I'll do something for him some day." He did. He hired him as a chauffeur.

14

THE ST. VALENTINE'S DAY MASSACRE

Due to the frequency of violent deaths in the ranks of those who live "below the deadline," the average newspaper reader had learned to drop one eyelid when "just another gang killing" comes to his attention.

The general public doesn't seem to mind, for it means one less gangster.

But occasionally there appears an underworld crime so atrocious that even the most apathetic individual is startled for a moment out of his habitual calm, and forced to wonder if, after all, criminals are making their own law.

Such an event was the St. Valentine's Day Massacre in 1929, a wholesale killing so vicious it shocked the entire nation.

It was in 1928 that the growing syndicate of "Bugs" Moran began to threaten the dominance of the Capone enterprises. An occasional minor killing was the only indication however that violence was breeding in the underworld.

Those who knew Capone sat back with watchful eye, curious to know if he would submit to the encroachments of his rival, or what course he would take to force the matter to a showdown.

However, everything was quiet in our home until the latter part of January, 1929, when Gus told me it would be necessary for him to be away from home a great deal, and not to worry about his absences.

He tried to appear casual, but as he talked I got the same uncomfortable feeling that always came to me when Gus was undertaking some enterprise, either for himself or the syndicate.

Some days later Gus brought George Goetz to our house, and shortly afterward a stranger arrived, bearing a bunglesome package. I ushered him into a back room where Gus waited, and I heard the three of them talking for some time.

A few minutes after he left I looked up from my chair in the sitting room and out of the corner of my eye caught a glimpse of a uniformed man standing against the wall. I screamed in fright, certain the house had been raided, but a burst of laughter caused me to look a second time, and I saw George Goetz, garbed in a perfectly fitting police uniform.

Goetz enjoyed his costume, and strutted about the house imitating a policeman making a raid. He lowered his voice, talked out of the one corner of his mouth, and impersonated several officers he knew, much to Gus' amusement. Goetz had such a good time Gus insisted on trying on the uniform, and since it was too small for him and made him look ridiculous, he took the role of a Keystone cop. Some of the boys came in later in the evening, and George and Gus repeated their show.

Gus rarely came home after that until February 14, 1929, when he and Bob Carey came in about noon. They had little to say, but in a short time sent me out after papers.

Before I got back to the house I was sure I knew what had happened. The sheets were devoted to the massacre that morning.

The papers said the killers wore police uniforms and more than one hinted the police actually had engineered the slaying.

Six of Moran's gang had been wiped out, in addition to a friend of theirs who was not a member of the gang. The killing had occurred at a garage at 2122 North Clark Street.

When I got to the house I threw the papers in Gus' face and went into my own room. I was too sick with horror to shed tears.

Gus and Carey spent most of the afternoon sitting in front of the windows. They said very little that would give me an inkling of how the mass killing was executed, but naturally in time I got the complete story from hearing Gus, Carey, and Goetz discuss the mistakes that were made.

Bryant Bolton and Jimmie "Swede" Moran [sometimes spelled Morand] had been assigned to watch the garage from a room Swede had rented across the street. The syndicate was well aware that the Moran gang held frequent meetings there, and had instructed the spies to give the "high ball" when Moran and his gang had gathered.

Gus, Carey, and other American boys in the Italian syndicate were staying nearby in the home of Rocco DeGrazia.

While the Italians could plan a job with criminal skill, they never actually took part in the dirty work.

The first blunder was made by Bryant Bolton. He had contracted tuberculosis, and during the time he was on lookout, he was under a doctor's care. On the morning of February 14 he was feeling particularly bad, and had a bottle of prescription medicine in the room. When he and Swede vacated the room Bolton left his bottle.

However, they watched the Moran gang assemble, then gave the signal to Gus and the other boys waiting at DeGrazia's house.

The boys came in an automobile, garbed as policemen, entered the garage, lined the gang against the wall, and shot them down.

When the smoke from the machine guns cleared away they discovered the fly in the ointment that kept the massacre from being a complete coup—Bugs Moran, the man they had been sent to get, was not one of the seven. How Swede and Bolton failed to notice his absence I never learned. But the backbone of the Moran gang was broken.

Notwithstanding the abandoned medicine bottle, the boys felt secure when none were approached by the police.

It was Lefty Louie Campagna who gave the first warning.

On Easter Sunday while I was preparing to go to early mass, Lefty dashed up the steps completely out of breath asking for Gus.

"He's still in bed," I told him.

"In bed?" he gasped. "For God's sake get him out of here. The police think he and Fred Burke pulled the Moran killing and are coming after him." Then he brushed past me and dashed into the house.

Lefty was badly frightened, but when Gus got up and began to don his clothes as if preparing for a late breakfast, he became panic stricken. He begged and pleaded for Gus to hurry.

It was just such excited warnings as Lefty gave Gus that caused the gang to dub him "Paul Revere," for every little report sent him charging around town warning the gang.

Under Lefty's constant urging Gus finally was dressed and accompanied him to his home in Cicero, where Lefty said he would be safe.

However, the warning was more serious than either Gus or I believed, for when I returned from church Mrs. Campagna was waiting for me.

She said we were to bring a package which Gus had hidden in a closet. Strangely, in spite of frequent cleanings, I had not seen a package, but we finally found it and took it to Lefty's house.

"Cheer up, Honey," Gus said, "this'll blow over. We're safe here." But it wasn't five minutes before a telephone call from the syndicate office advised us to move at once.

Lefty and Gus, Mrs. Campagna and the two children and I immediately left the house, with Mrs. Campagna and myself still custodians of the package.

We took the children to the home of Mrs. Campagna's mother, and attempted to leave the package, but she refused to accept it. I cannot blame her for she did not approve of her son-in-law's activities and did not want to become involved.

The package, which Gus was so anxious for us to dispose of, became a trial. We took it to the home of some Italians Mrs. Campagna was acquainted with, but they too refused to hide it.

The only thing to do was take it back to her mother. She would not allow us to leave it so in desperation we called the syndicate office. Frankie Reo [Rio], a Capone man, and several others from the office, came after it immediately.

Then we learned the cause of Gus' anxiety. When the package was opened a police uniform and two bulletproof vests were revealed to our startled eyes. Possession of those articles would have convicted any member of the Capone syndicate.

Frankie Rio gave us specific directions. He told us to go to a hotel and to communicate with Mrs. Campagna's mother so Gus and Lefty could reach us through her. We had no baggage so had to go completely across town to the South side to borrow a handbag from Mrs. Campagna's sister-in-law. We also borrowed two night gowns.

A heavy storm had broken over the city, and the cab in which we started for the hotel stalled in a few minutes. We got soaked to the skin finding another cab, but eventually reached the Paradise Hotel.

Federal Bureau of Investigation

United States Department of Justice

Washington, D. C.

MEMORANDUM FOR MR. JOSEPH B. KEENAN,
ACTING ATTORNEY GENERAL

August 27, 1936

With reference to your inquiry as to information furnished by Bryan Bolton concerning the identity of the persons perpetrating the St. Valentine's Day Massacre in Chicago, Illinois in 1929, you are advised that Bolton was questioned concerning this offense. Bolton stated that the persons who actually perpetrated this massacre were Fred Goetz, Gus Winkler, Fred Burke, Ray Nugent and Bob Carey. Bolton stated that he personally purchased the Cadillac touring car which was used in this massacre, having been furnished with the money to make this purchase by Louis Lipschults. Bolton claims that he purchased this car from the Cadillac Company on Michigan Avenue in Chicago sometime before the massacre happened and assumed at the time that he purchased the car that it was to be used in hauling alcohol. Bolton believes that he used the name James Martin in purchasing the car. The object of this massacre, according to Bolton, which was planned by members of the Capone organization, was for the purpose of eliminating "Bugs" Moran from the bootlegging racket in Chicago. Bolton claims that the plot to perpetrate this killing was initially developed at a place on Cranberry Lake, six miles north of Couderay, Wisconsin, where one George operated a resort. Al Capone, Gus Winkler, George Zeigler, Louis Campagna, Fred Burke, Bill Pacelli (reported to be an Illinois State Senator) and Dan Saratella are reported to have been at the resort operated by George on Cranberry Lake at the time the killing was first planned, this being in October or November of 1928. Bolton states that Jimmy McCrussen and Jimmy "The Swede" Moran were selected to watch "Bugs" Moran's garage, since they both knew Moran by sight, in order to learn his movements.

when the killing took place the persons actually perpetrating therein did not know the identity of each of their victims but rather than risk the possibility of missing Moran, killed all of the persons found in the garage.

RECORDED & INDEXED

As indicated above, Bolton states that Fred Goetz, Gus Winkler, Fred Burke, Ray Nugent and Bob Carey were the actual perpetrators of the Massacre. According to Bolton, Claude Maddox of St. Louis, Tony Capesia of Chicago and a man known as "Shocker" also of St. Louis, burned the Cadillac car after the Massacre.

In discussing this matter, Bolton has informed Special Agents of this Bureau that at the time of the St. Valentine's Day Massacre, Chief of Detectives Stege of the Chicago Police Department was on the payroll of the Capone Syndicate, receiving $5,000 per week, and kept the members of the syndicate informed as to the whereabouts of Bugs Moran.

Respectfully,

John Edgar Hoover,
Director.

Mrs. Campagna registered us as sisters. Since she is large and dark and I am small and blond, and since we had only one very small and very light handbag, the bellboy winked maliciously as he led us to the elevator, carrying the bag by his little finger, and took us to the eighth floor.

The next day a voice I did not recognize ordered me to go home and pack my belongings and store them. I followed out this order, sending furnishings to a storage company and bringing our clothes back to the hotel. The bellboy was aghast at the array of bags.

Since Mrs. Campagna had received no such orders, we went out to buy her some new clothes. When she prepared to pay her bill I was horrified to see a gun in her purse.

"Oh, it's nothing," she explained lightly. "I always carry one when I'm with Louie."

"Well, you're not with Louie now, and hereafter leave that thing at home when I'm along," I said.

But I kept to the room all week rather than go out with her again.

The St. Valentine's Day Massacre

Although Georgette briefly describes what occurred at home on the morning of the Massacre, and describes it in more detail in later interviews with the FBI, the crime remains officially unsolved.

The nearly universal account has it engineered by Capone's right-hand man, "Machine Gun" Jack McGurn, who supposedly tricked the Moran Gang into assembling at 2122 North Clark Street, their Near North Side booze depot, to take delivery of a load of Old Log Cabin whiskey hijacked from Capone. This turns out to have been reckless speculation based on the remarks of a Prohibition official who had learned of a recent hijacking. (The same official also blamed the killings on rogue members of the Chicago police. He later backed off from his initial headline-making remarks, but he was banished from Chicago and then lost his job.)

That account also has the crime labeled a "Valentine from Al Capone" in which a car, tricked out to look like a detective cruiser, pulled up to the front door of the garage, let out two men in police uniforms who disarmed everyone inside, and then let in two men in overcoats who machine-gunned the seven occupants. Afterward the killers supposedly handed the machine guns to the uniformed men, marched with hands up back out to their car, and sped south on Clark Street.

In fact the victims, except for a mechanic and an optician, were gang royalty, dressed in their best; and Moran himself dismissed the hijacked-liquor story. According to Rose Keefe, author of the carefully researched book *The Man Who Got Away*, Moran later told a relative that he had personally called the meeting to deal with an assassination attempt the

The St. Valentine's Day Massacre.

previous month outside the Chez Pierre nightclub (later remodeled by Gus Winkeler into the Chez Paree).

Also ruling out the hijacked liquor story is the discovery that surveillance of the garage had begun some two weeks earlier and that the shooters had to spend time with Rocco DeGrazia, waiting until they were called into action. Capone himself probably regretted the mass murder and the fact that the killings took place on St. Valentine's Day, forever making it Capone's Valentine gift to Moran.

In any case, about 10:30 A M on February 14, 1929, the Moran lieutenants were drinking coffee in their unheated garage (innocuously identified as the S.M.C. Cartage Co.) when they were interrupted by two men in police uniforms who (contrary to other accounts) had parked in the alley and entered through the back door. Annoyed but not particularly worried at what they assumed would be a routine shakedown, the Moran men surrendered their weapons and were ordered to line up facing the north wall, about the only area not crammed with the trucks and cars used in their particular line of "cartage."

Presumably one of the supposed cops then let in two more men whose overcoats covered their Thompson submachine guns. After wend-

Illustrator's reconstructions of the SMC Cartage Company garage on Clark Street, scene of the St. Valentine's Day Massacre. *Above,* back alley entrance; *below,* front entrance, showing the suspected activities of killers posing as cops.

ing their way past several cars and trucks, the men raked the Moran group with seventy bullets from two Thompsons, plus a couple of shotgun blasts, before leaving in the manner already described.

Little attention was paid to the two youngsters, George Brichet and a friend, who said they had seen the phony cops enter through the alley door; and Bugs Moran, the primary target, survived only because he arrived a few minutes late, saw the bogus detective car parked in front of the garage, and (supposedly) ducked into a corner coffee shop.

Police immediately rounded up the "usual suspects"—those they could find—but had to release them for lack of evidence. Later they found Jack McGurn in a room at the luxurious Stevens Hotel on Michigan Avenue (now the Hilton Towers), but his girlfriend, Louise Rolfe, whom he later married, would always stick to her story that Jack had been with her all morning. After a short time in jail, he, too, was released.

To fill in other gaps in Georgette's brief account:

On February 22 a car exploded in a small alley garage behind Wood Street, and police found the burned-out remains of a Cadillac that had been disguised as a detective cruiser. They soon traced the renter of the garage to an address next door to Claude Maddox's Circus Café, 1857 West North Avenue, which by now had closed its doors. In the adjoining building, however, they found a Thompson submachine gun drum and several overcoats, as though the occupants had bailed out as soon as they learned of the gasoline explosion.

The police soon picked up Maddox, who, as luck would have it, happened to be in court the morning of the Massacre, perhaps leaving Fred Goetz (at whose lodge the killing of Moran had been discussed about three months earlier) to step in with his shotgun and more poor judgment. A later FBI document, quoting lookout Byron Bolton, said nobody knew what Moran looked like, so they killed them all.

The consensus seemed to be that the killers had headquartered at the Circus Café and Rocco DeGrazia's, but instead of putting Maddox through the wringer, or following the leads that pointed to St. Louis, detectives went to Bolton's family farm near Thayer and found an empty machine gun crate. And the investigation apparently ended there.

Police scuttlebutt did make it into the newspapers, in unattributed articles, speculating that the shooters were gangsters from St. Louis.

And Fred Burke quickly was named a chief suspect, but by then he, Gus Winkeler, and the others had decamped.

A witness from across the street, who had been shown pictures of the Keywell brothers from Detroit, partially identified them as lookouts but later changed her mind. However, both have remained identified by most subsequent writers as the Massacre lookouts, thanks to initial newspaper accounts.

A week after the gasoline explosion led police to the Circus Café, a second car was blasted with dynamite in the suburb of Maywood. That indelicate effort to destroy evidence brought local police rushing to the scene, where they found another wrecked automobile rigged to look like a detectives' squad car. Not only did it possess a gun rack and other police accessories, but they also found a notebook belonging to Albert Weinshank, one of the Massacre victims. That event was reported for only a day or two before the matter was dropped, except by a few annoyed detectives who kept investigating on their own.

The murders made the front page of every daily paper in the United States and in many foreign countries, becoming the "gangland crime of the century." Chicago police launched a great crackdown on the city's several thousand speakeasies, which cost Capone's Outfit a fortune and landed him a personal summons to a national "gangster conference" held in Atlantic City three months later. Before returning to Chicago, he and his bodyguard, Frank Rio, allowed themselves to be arrested in Philadelphia for carrying guns. The one-year sentence they received (reduced to ten months) annoyed Capone, who was expecting thirty or sixty days, but he still was treated like royalty at the Pennsylvania prison.

Capone's arrest and instant conviction was applauded in Chicago newspapers, all of which marveled at Philadelphia's swift and sure justice compared to Chicago's inability to nail Capone for anything. Before the Massacre, Chicago's press had tiptoed around Capone's political dominance and his anti-hero popularity (baseball fans often applauded him), but now that the Big Fellow was safely locked up in Pennsylvania the papers decided they could attack him personally.

Meanwhile, two wealthy and civic-minded citizens had put up funds to hire the services of New York ballistics expert Calvin Goddard, who had attracted national attention through his work on the Sacco-Vanzetti case. Goddard was anxious to get the new science of forensic ballistics more widely recognized as admissible evidence in courts, and he immediately set up the first full-service crime lab—the Scientific Crime Detection Laboratory—under the auspices of Chicago's Northwestern University Law School. Local police, it seems, not only were dubious about mixing crime with science, but still were not trusted to supervise much of anything.

During the year a dozen sessions were held before a coroner's jury, and the bullets and casings picked up in the Massacre garage established that two submachine guns had been used—one with a fifty-round drum and the other with a twenty-round box magazine. But efforts to track their sales mainly revealed how recklessly various dealers had been trafficking in submachine guns, how little their records revealed, and how one dealer, Peter Von Frantzius, had supplied the guns to a "reseller" who, in some cases, wanted his machine-gun crates to be filled only with bricks and shipped to a hotel in nearby Kirkland. It also turned out that Von Frantzius would have his gunsmith grind off serial numbers for an extra two dollars.

The guns actually used in the Massacre did not turn up until December 1929, when Fred Burke, going by the name Frederick Dane and apparently drunk, managed to sideswipe another car in St. Joseph, Michigan. When Patrolman Charles Skelly tried to intervene, Burke shot him to death and then tried to escape. Burke wrecked his own car on the outskirts of town, commandeered others, and eventually escaped. Papers found in his wrecked car led police to the house of Frederick Dane in nearby Stevensville, where a search yielded an arsenal of weapons.

Berrien County sheriff's officers and St. Joseph police soon figured out that Dane was in fact Fred Burke, and the guns and ammunition were immediately taken to Calvin Goddard's new crime lab in Chicago. Goddard was particularly interested in the two submachine guns, both of which fired test bullets matching those taken from Massacre victims. In addition, New York police brought Goddard several .45 bullets recovered from the body of Frankie Yale. Goddard established that slugs from one of the two submachine guns used in that killing matched those from a machine gun used in the Massacre. This led police to believe that Burke also was involved in the Yale murder, although he isn't named by Georgette.

In fleeing St. Joseph, Burke left his ostensible wife, Viola, to deal with the authorities before she returned home to Kankakee, Illinois. Meanwhile, Burke made his way to a farm near Green City, Missouri, owned by relatives of Harvey Bailey. He was not captured until March 26, 1931, after he had officially married a young student nurse named Bonnie White. She moved to Chicago and became a good friend of Georgette Winkeler.

Burke Is Sought as Leader in Massacre St. Valentine's Day

FUGITIVE SLAYER, HIS WIFE, ARSENAL FOUND IN HOME

ARSENAL FOUND IN HOME OF FRED DANE.

ACCUSED OF UALE MURDER

Declared by Chicago Police to Be Most Dangerous Criminal Alive.

FACES MANY CHARGES

Participated in Cincinnati and Hamilton Bank Robberies, Claim.

By FRANCIS F. HEALY.
(I. N. S. Staff Correspondent.)
CHICAGO, DEC. 17.—The killer of seven members of George "Bugs" Moran's gang here last St. Valentine's day.

The slayer of Frankie Uale, boss of Brooklyn Sicilian gangsters.

Murderer of a St. Joseph, Mich., policeman.

Directing general of the Farmers' and Merchants' bank robbery at Jefferson, Wis.

Toledo $100,000 mail robber.

Robber of banks at Louisville and Lexington, Ky.; at Peru, Ind.; at Hamilton and Cincinnati, Ohio, and former terror of the Egan's Rats gang in St. Louis.

HAS MANY ALIASES.

In this manner today did police describe Fred R. Burke, with many aliases, sought by police of the nation as the most desperate criminal alive today.

Since his latest known killing, that of a traffic policeman at St. Joseph, Mich., Burke has been swallowed up by the haunts of gangland and no trace of the man has been found

15

HIDING OUT

I heaved a sigh of relief when Gus telephoned me the following Monday and instructed me to check out and meet him at an address in Melrose Park.

The address proved to be an inn operated by Louis "Doc" Stacci who made a business of harboring syndicate men sought by the police.

Gus transferred our luggage from my taxi to his car, and when I was in the machine announced: "We're going to Michigan until this heat cools off."

We drove to a summer home near St. Joseph, Michigan, which was occupied by the father of Phil De Andrea [D'Andrea], Al Capone's paymaster. Lefty Louie Campagna, Mr. and Mrs. George Goetz, Phil De Andrea, and Bob Carey already were there. But the next day Lefty returned to Chicago, much to the relief of everyone, for Lefty was not popular.

In the meantime the strain of running, hiding, and waiting had been too much for me and I became ill with another of my increasingly frequent nervous attacks. Gus was compelled to take me into town several times for treatment, although everyone at the De Andrea home tried to avoid being seen in St. Joseph.

I learned the place was a hideout for Italians sought by police in Chicago and other northern cities. Sometimes there were as many as ten there at one time.

Since no one knew how long they might have to stay at the resort, they avoided going out as much as possible to prevent exciting the suspicion of neighbors and casual motorists. There was nothing to do but play

Phil D'Andrea.

cards, but at no time did they fail to keep a lookout around the house, both day and night.

Being housed up so closely was a strain, and this was augmented by the fact that everyone was constantly on the alert. So guarded was the atmosphere of the place that often I caught myself listening intently for sounds that did not exist.

Naturally, at the end of a month, nerves in the De Andrea hideout were on the ragged edge. Good humor was infrequent, and the men snapped at each other and argued over trifles that otherwise would not have been noticed.

It was about this time that I witnessed one of the most striking examples of what it means to be hunted.

It was late at night. The men were in the kitchen playing cards while Mrs. Goetz, old Mr. De Andrea and I were in the front room.

The distant hum of a motor drew closer, and as the sound mounted, I could hear the conversation over the kitchen card game gradually cease. Night traffic on that lonesome road was rare, and I could feel the tension in the house as the hum mounted to a roar.

Suddenly there was a screeching of brakes, the whistling of tires in loose gravel, and a beam of light moved across the drawn blinds as the speeding car skidded into the driveway.

Everyone in the house had the same thought—police.

"Douse the lights," came a raucous whisper from the kitchen, and like magic the house was plunged in darkness.

Chairs overturned as men leaped to their feet. Tables crashed as they were hurled out of the way.

Mrs. Goetz and I had cleaned the house every day and found only two guns, but in a brief flurry of confusion guns were produced from dozens of hiding places we had not discovered. There were revolvers, sawed off shotguns and machine guns. Some had been concealed under the cushions of the divan, others had been in the cabinet back of the dishes, some were suspended inside suits of clothes in the closet. Every man was armed to the teeth in a trice.

Mr. De Andrea grabbed Mrs. Goetz and me by the elbow and whispered hoarsely: "Get down on the floor," but I jerked loose and started groping through the house in search of my husband.

There was a man at every door and window, armed and waiting in grim silence.

There were no sounds, the car could not be seen, and everyone thought the police were surrounding the house. Eyes filled with death peered through cracks in drawn blinds, and in the moonlight that filtered through the French doors I could see George Goetz, a "tommy" gun gripped in rigid fingers, his lips drawn back from his teeth in a savage snarl.

I continued searching for Gus, but failing to see him in the darkness, finally stood perfectly still.

My nerves had not settled down from my last collapse, and my muscles were so stiff from fright I could not blink my eyes. Minutes passed in absolute silence, then I began to hear a faint but regular thump, thump, thump. I strained my ears to listen, then realized I was hearing the beating of my own heart.

Ten minutes—an eternity—rolled by. I felt that I could stand the strain no longer. If only there was one little sound to break that awful stillness.

It came. It began with a rattle like a man strangling. It was George Goetz.

"Put 'em up, put 'em up, I say!" he was gasping. His voice gained strength, and mounted as he spoke. "I got you covered, I'll blow you to hell. Come out of there, come out I say."

He was gibbering in a hysteria of terror, standing clearly outlined in the half-opened French doors, waiving his machine gun back and forth.

Gus leaped out of the darkness, a pistol in his hand, and took a standing in the moonlight beside Goetz. Then he relaxed against the door frame and I could see shoulders quivering.

He was laughing.

The tension broke, everyone flocked to him. He pointed mutely at the bushes outside the window where a lonesome and very much unconcerned hound dog rustled about the leaves.

Investigation showed that the automobile that frightened them had merely come into the driveway to make a turn.

The lights were turned on and everyone tried to laugh it off, but laughter was shaky, and conversation from then on was subdued, for George Goetz' fear was no joke.

For myself, my nerves had been under such strain I had to go to bed.

One Saturday night a few days later a car stopped a short way from the cottage, and its lights were turned off. The lookout gave the alarm, and two of the boys armed themselves and investigated. Seeing only a couple of spooners, they represented themselves as police officers and sent them on back to St. Joseph.

It was plain to see the boys had about as much strain as they could stand. The next day, Sunday, Gus started to drive me to a doctor in the city, but near the city limits he saw an empty police car parked at a gas station.

"Oh, oh," said Gus, bringing the car to a halt. "The cops are asking the way to the cottage." He wheeled the car about and at breakneck speed we returned to the cottage. One man was put on watch while the others packed preparatory to making a quick getaway. While everyone was busy the police car came by. The man in it proved to be a vacationing officer from Chicago.

But the boys had had enough of it. They decided to split up and vacate the cottage. Gus and I went to Gary, Indiana, and Bob Carey to Hammond.

16

ON THE RUN

We had been in Gary only one day when Gus came in and said he had seen Fred Burke in a Calumet City saloon.

The newspapers and police branded Burke "The Killer," as the result of the St. Valentine's Day Massacre, which they believed he had engineered. So Gus and Burke were dodging retribution for the same crime.

Gus explained that Burke was living in Hammond under an assumed name with some girl, and I was not surprised, because every time we met Burke after any considerable absence he had a different girl, some of which he married under different names.

Gus said Burke had a camp at Grand Rapids, Minnesota, which he intended to occupy, and has asked us to go along. He was leaving that night.

The camp sounded like a safer retreat than Gary, so I agreed to go and started packing immediately.

In the meantime Bob Carey was drinking heavily, much to the disapproval of Al Capone, and to save him further trouble Gus hunted him up to take him along.

This was just another act of loyalty on Gus' part—the same loyalty he accorded all his underworld associates, and which was not always appreciated.

Gus brought Carey from a saloon "blind" drunk, and we arrived at the Grand Rapids resort the next day.

Gus and Fred had a great time, for they had not seen each other for months, in spite of newspaper reports that linked them in almost every crime.

However, I did not care much for Burke's new girl, Viola, and she must have known it for she told the police as much when she was taken into custody a short time later while Burke was being sought.

Carey tried to stay drunk on the Minnesota "mule" manufactured in the neighborhood, known locally as "fire-water," but it didn't agree with him, so all three men spent their days playing golf on a nearby links.

But Fred's conduct during the day didn't last through the evening, for he usually succeeded in getting on a fine "jag."

I employed a guide to show me the best fishing holes, and for the first time in several years the weight of worry slipped from my shoulders and my nerves settled. I usually went to bed before sunset, dropping off in the heavy sleep of exhaustion, since there was no immediate fear of Gus' capture.

Our situation would have been entirely satisfactory if Gus and Bob Carey had received their pay from Phil De Andrea. At first they thought nothing of it but when a month had passed with no word from him, they talked it over at our cottage. Burke's girl was never allowed to take part in these "business" conferences since Gus and Bob shared my dislike for her.

At the same time I felt sorry for her, for she had a young daughter, and it was evident she had not had much experience with men of Burke's character.

I tried as discreetly as possible to show her what she was letting herself in for. I told her something of my own life, my continual state of fear, midnight flights, worry and nerves. Without accusing Burke of being a philanderer I tried to show her how his other affairs had ended, but of course she quickly assumed I was meddling in her business. One day Burke invited me to go to town with him and his girl, whose name was Viola [Brenneman], and although I could tell he had been drinking, I accepted the invitation since I had to make some purchases.

Burke got into a drug store where he and the clerk spent the afternoon mixing fancy drinks, and when he got ready to drive home he was completely soused.

I asked him to allow me to drive, but like most drunks, he insisted he was all right. Viola agreed with him. His driving would have frightened an iron man, and my fears were realized when we had driven only a few miles and the car ran off the road and turned over on its side in a field. Fortunately some people from the camp drove by, and recognizing us righted the car. Burke rode back with them, and one of them drove his car.

Not having heard from Phil De Andrea about the money, Gus decided to take me and drive to Hammond to investigate.

When we were ready to leave Burke's girl decided to go along. We left Grand Rapids at 4 A M and arrived in Hammond at 1 P M after leaving Viola at Maywood, Illinois. Gus claimed that it was a record for the trip in spite of the fact that he was stopped by a speed cop who decided his speedometer must be wrong when he was a tendered a $20 bill.

The following morning Gus located De Andrea by telephone. Gus could have done his telephoning as easily from Grand Rapids, but did not want to take the chance of having the call traced, since it would have gone into the toll call register.

De Andrea was frightened, because he had disposed of the money. In an honest business he would have been an embezzler.

He said he had taken the first pay and played it on the races—and had lost. He sent the second pay to the tracks in an effort to recoup—and lost again. He owed Gus and Carey $1,600 each. He begged Gus not to tell Capone, promising to make it up.

Gus took the promise at its face value—thereby losing $1,600.

Funds were short to stay in Minnesota, so the boys returned. Bob Carey located in Hammond, Gus and I took a hotel apartment in Gary, while Burke and his girl took a cottage near St. Joseph, Michigan. We understood Mr. and Mrs. Goetz were living near there.

Gus again became interested in aviation, studied much on the subject, and that winter learned to fly an airplane.

17

"KILLER" BURKE AND THE POLICEMAN'S MURDER

During the winter I heard Gus mention some friends he and Bob Carey had met in a Calumet City saloon.

He called them Harvey Bailey, Bob "Slim" Morris, a man I heard him call nothing but "Jack," and several others I can't recall. Bailey is now in Alcatraz Prison for the Urschel kidnapping. Morris is dead. Although I didn't know it, some of the gang were escaped convicts.

On the surface things were moving easily until Bob Carey started making frequent visits to our home for conferences with Gus. I heard considerable conversation concerning some bonds.

On one occasion I heard Gus say: "Don't be a fool, Bob, you'll only get in Dutch with Capone and the police. Lay off that stuff."

Carey replied: "Bailey and his boys are smart enough to know what they are doing."

Then I heard Carey ask Gus to take him to Burke's place near St. Joseph, Michigan. He said he wanted Fred to keep some bonds, which he apparently had taken over from Bailey, until some dealers came from St. Paul, Minnesota, to buy them.

Gus agreed, for the next morning, December 15, 1929, Carey came over with a grip, and they left in our car after Gus promised to be back by six o'clock in the evening.

When Gus got back he said they found Burke drunk, and still drinking when they left. He said on the way back Carey regretted leaving the bonds in Burke's care, and might go back after them after talking it over with Bailey.

Gus told me the bonds were taken by Bailey and his boys in a hold up of the Farmers and Merchants Bank at Jefferson, Wisconsin, on November 7, 1929.

Bob Carey and his girl friend visited us the next day, and the four of us had just settled down to a game of bridge when the telephone rang and someone asked to speak to Gus. After listening a moment he turned pale and ejaculated, "What," then listened for a moment longer with a peculiar look on his face. "Well I'll be damned," he said finally. "Okay, I'll do it right away."

When he left the phone he beckoned to Carey and me to follow him into the kitchen.

"Bob," he said with the odd look still on his face, "that call came from the syndicate office, and we've both got to go to Michigan right away. Someone is in trouble. I expect it's George and Irene [Goetz] so we better make it snappy."

They left immediately and I tried to entertain Bob's girl, but I had a strange feeling that something was wrong, and I couldn't free my mind of the worry. My nerves were on edge, although I knew Gus had been in no recent trouble.

A newsboy's cry of "extra" gave me a start, for it carried me back over a year when every newspaper on the street was a new source of worry. I called the hotel clerk to send me a paper just as the telephone rang. It was Gus.

"Pack everything, and hurry if you ever did in your life," he directed. "Someone will be after you in a minute."

"What about Carey's girl?" I asked as my knees started to tremble.

"Send her home to pack and Bob'll take her along," he said.

I explained to Bob's girl that the boys were going out of town and wanted to take us along. I tried to keep from frightening her, but I don't see how she could have overlooked my pale face.

I had a Christmas present for her, and not knowing if I would get a better opportunity to present it, gave it to her then. It was a musical instrument known as a "tipple," resembling a small guitar. I had one of my own she admired very much. It was in a black case.

I mention this fact because later, when the police investigated our disappearance, they learned she had left the house with the case, and announced that it had contained guns, destined to reach the hands of gangsters.

She left in a cab and I looked at the papers. The necessity for haste became clear. The headlines said: "Killer Burke Kills Policeman."

Burke had shot Policeman Charles Skelley in cold blood at St. Joseph, Michigan, December 15, in an argument over an auto accident. Burke had been intoxicated and was the most hunted man in the country. They had arrested Burke's girl, and since she knew where most of the boys lived, and was likely to tell it, the entire gang had to make a quick getaway. [Skelley is the spelling on the police memorial, although newspapers all spelled it Skelly, and on his tombstone it is Skalay, the original family name.]

In a few minutes one of the boys came for me and together we started packing. We were frantic in our haste, grabbing at the same thing, hurling drawers on the floor, and dropping garments from fumbling fingers. We emptied the contents of drawers into four grips and two trunks, and after we were packed I discovered that all my clothes were locked in the bags, leaving me in red lounging pajamas and house slippers.

There was not time to change. We did not want to be seen leaving, and tried to leave by the back exit.

The night man gave us an argument and we lost valuable minutes in the dark rear hallway, but $25 finally induced him to let us out.

I was right in my conjecture about Burke's girl, for the police arrived ten minutes after we left.

We drove first to Carey's home and got his girl, then to another address where we picked up Lefty Louie Campagna, Frankie Reo, and another of the boys from the syndicate office, all of whom were equally disgusted with Burke. They did not hesitate at killing, but resorted to it only in line with their business. They did not approve of taking unnecessary risks when there was nothing to be gained.

Lefty and Reo instructed me to go to St. Louis on the morning train, and wait there for word from Gus. My visit was a trial, for my sister was ill and I was worried because I did not hear from Gus. By Christmas Day I was nearly frantic, until a friend of Gus' came to the house and said my husband sent for me.

He took me to East St. Louis to catch the midnight train for Chicago. It was bitter cold. With the new clues in their hands the police were determined to catch the long sought Winkeler, and the net was almost nationwide, so Gus' friend would not allow me to go into the station for fear of being recognized. I stood outside the station, seeking shelter from the wind, and nearly froze before the train came.

I had been instructed to register at the Congress Hotel in Chicago and to wait until someone called for me. After what seemed hours of waiting at the Congress there was a knock at the door and a man I had never seen before inquired, "Georgette?"

He told me to pack and when I had checked out he took me to the home of a Harvey Bailey gangster I know only as "Big Homer" where Gus was waiting. I learned that the man who called for me was named John, and also met his wife whose name was Console, and who led about the same kind of life I did.

Gus took me to a place he had rented on the South Side.

When we had moved into our new quarters I asked Gus about everything that had taken place in my absence and he said he was having trouble with Bob Carey. Carey had made the acquaintance of a girl he called "Babe" who kept him drunk a great part of the time, much to Al Capone's disgust.

"He's not the same old Bob," Gus said. "He's changed."

My health was not very good, so a few days later we packed again and went to Texas, until March, when we returned and located on Clarence Avenue in Berwyn, Illinois. [Texas seems to have been a convenient state for Chicago's and other gangsters to visit, possibly for R-and-R in the so-called Republic of Galveston, which years earlier had exempted itself from both state and national laws. That lasted until the 1950s, when Texas Rangers were ordered to blockade the causeway leading to that island city's unrestricted gambling, prostitution, and booze, greatly reducing its attractiveness for Texans and out-of-state mobsters alike.]

A few days after our arrival Gus told me Carey had broken with Capone, having found a racket he believed paid more money. Apparently the racket was Babe's for she would lure men to her room where Carey would take photographs from a place of concealment. Later they would use these photographs for blackmail. This scheme, it seems, worked successfully for a time until they trapped a friend of Capone's much the same as Gus had done when he engineered the kidnap racket.

When Bob tried to extract $25,000 from his victim he and the girl were called to Capone's office, given some money, and ordered to get out of Chicago and stay out.

Gus saw Carey before he left the city, and expressed surprise that Bob would sink to blackmail and cross Capone.

"Watch me," Gus said Carey told him. "I'll pull a job that will set the world by the ears." We never saw them again.

They were found slain in their New York apartment. [Police wrote this off as a murder and suicide, although author Rose Keefe, then unfamiliar with the name Carey, learned from a one-time Moran truck driver that "Bugs" told him that he'd just returned from the Coast, where he'd "taken care of Bob Carey."]

I have often wondered if the "job" Carey referred to was the Lindbergh baby kidnapping.

Fred Burke Goes into Hiding

Thanks probably to Fred Burke's high profile as a killer and to an after-the-fact witness who spotted a speeding detective car driven by a man with teeth missing, he was declared the leader of the St. Valentine's Day Massacre—and thanks to the cops who otherwise were rounding up such "usual suspects" as Jack McGurn, who was not labeled "Machine Gun" Jack McGurn until after the Massacre, which they believed he had masterminded.

Burke quickly had gone into deep hiding while Gus Winkeler, his wife Georgette, Fred Goetz, and others laid low at a comfortable house in St. Joseph, Michigan, that was owned by Phil D'Andrea and had long served as a hideout for mobsters on the run. St. Joseph was a popular tourist town on Lake Michigan sometimes visited by Al Capone himself, who went for its springs and usually rented the entire floor of a local hotel.

While Gus was staying out of sight in Michigan (possibly using the name James Ray) he encountered Burke at a Calumet City tavern operated by a mutual friend from St. Louis, Willie Harrison, and he and Georgette decided to join Burke at his place near Grand Rapids, Minnesota. They summered in Minnesota, playing golf and drinking—often to excess—and moved back to the Chicago area only when their money supply was cut off by D'Andrea, Capone's paymaster. Those difficulties are described by Georgette.

She and Gus then holed up at a hotel in Gary, while Burke and a new girlfriend, Viola Brenneman, moved into a cottage near Stevensville, just outside St. Joseph, Michigan, as Mr. and Mrs. Frederick Dane. Once Gus

EXTRA   THE HERALD-PRESS   EXTRA

"REACHES THE HOMES IN BERRIEN COUNTY"

ST. JOSEPH, MICH., MONDAY, DECEMBER 16, 1929   PRICE THREE CENTS

POLICEMAN'S MURDER BARES $320,000 LOOT

Charles Skelly, St. Joseph Officer, Shot To Death By Desperado Who Makes Escape

$10,000 Is Price Put On Head Of Killer Who Slew Officer Skelly

Veritable Arsenal Found In Lake Shore Drive Home Of Slayer, Who Eludes Pursuing Deputies And Today Is Object Of Nation-Wide Hunt—Slaying Occurs Almost At Door Of St. Joseph City Hall And In View Of Scores of Persons

Slain Officer And His Comrades

St. Joseph, Chamber Commerce, Insurance Co., Put Forth Offer

'They Call Women Dumb, And I Guess They Are!' Murderer's Wife Sobs

overcame the obstacles to making the payments, the "Danes" furnished their place with the elegant if somewhat gaudy furniture of the day and might have lived there indefinitely but for Burke's continuing love affair with crime and alcohol.

Burke already was one of the country's most wanted criminals. As early as 1927 his picture had appeared on the cover of *The Detective,* a Chicago-based professional law-enforcement journal published by Al Dunlap, who, incidentally, also was the local Auto-Ordnance representative selling Thompson guns. He had close enough ties to the criminal community that he was questioned by the coroner's jury investigating the Massacre, just as he had been questioned three years earlier following the murder of Assistant State's Attorney William McSwiggin, who had the bad luck to be with some bootlegger friends when they were machine-gunned by the Capone mob outside a Cicero tavern.

Burke's victim, Officer Skelly.

Fred Burke, as depicted in a periodical
shortly after his capture.

Despite plenty of evidence pointing to Burke, Winkeler, and other
hoods from St. Louis, the police had gotten nowhere in their efforts to
"solve" the Massacre. This possibly was because Chicago's Chief of Detectives John Stege did not want them turning over rocks that would
have uncovered two Chicago politicians who had been at a lodge in
Wisconsin when the killing of Northsider Bugs Moran was discussed.
(This was a claim made by Massacre lookout Byron Bolton after he was
arrested in 1935.)

In any case, Burke had remained in close touch with some of the
country's top bank robbers, particularly Harvey Bailey, and was dabbling
in stolen bonds when Burke's drinking led to the murder charge in St.
Joseph on December 14, 1929.

18

NEW FACE AND NEW FINGERPRINTS

Shortly after we moved to Berwyn, Ray Nugent undertook to open a Miami, Florida, saloon. He had been on Capone's payroll and naturally was expected to buy his "merchandise" from Capone.

Trouble developed when he failed to do so. Ray Nugent disappeared and has never been heard of. The last I heard of Mrs. Nugent she was employed in a Toledo, Ohio, hotel trying to care for her children.

This meant only one thing—the syndicate had "disposed" of her husband in their own way. Otherwise, his salary would have been paid to his wife.

We had not been in Berwyn long when I was called to St. Louis on account of the illness of a sister. I was there for two weeks.

When I returned to our flat I was met at the door by our colored maid. She was giggling as she opened the door, and her smiled was so broad she could not answer my greeting.

The first thing I thought of was that Gus was prepared to play some prank on me, and I looked all around the sitting room for some evidence.

Seeing nothing suspicious I turned to her and asked where Gus was hiding.

"In da kitchen," she replied, quivering with laughter, then raising her voice, "Mist' Gus, Miz Gawge [Georgette] done come home."

When Gus entered the room my eyes bulged and my mouth dropped opened, for the man who stood before me certainly did not look familiar.

Gus leaned against the wall and laughed until the tears ran down his face.

"How do you like it?" he asked finally, pointing at his nose. "Pretty doggie, eh?"

It was indeed. It actually resembled a bulldog's.

"My God, Gus," I finally managed to say, "what on earth has happened to your face?"

"Plastic surgery, Honey," he said, as if he had done something to be proud of. "I admit my nose looks as if I smelled something rotten in Denmark, but it sure does change me."

He was right in that respect. His once Roman nose was now badly "pugged," which certainly did not contribute to his good looks.

The humor of the situation finally struck me and I laughed, although I must have sounded a bit hysterical. To find a new face on an old husband would be a shock to almost anyone.

"Hell, Honey, if you think I look funny you ought to see Fred Burke. The sawbones did him up in great style.

"He looks like a Boston terrier, and has a peach of a hair-lip. He looks like the very devil, but even you wouldn't recognize him."

As I looked at Gus ruefully he waxed enthusiastic, apparently trying to defend himself.

"That doc knew his groceries, look at these hands," he continued, holding his palms in front of my face.

"See. These lines are completely changed. The next time they take my fingerprints I might just as well be Andy Gump for all the luck they'll have classifying them. So far as they are concerned, Gus Winkeler is now off the records."

"Maybe you know what you're doing but it looks like foolishness to me," I told him. "You certainly have succeeded in spoiling your looks. Besides that you don't look well. Have you been sick?"

"Deed he has, Miz Gawge," chimed in the maid. "He look pow'ful sick when I seen him after he been to doctor's office."

She said Gus and Burke had gone out in the morning and had been at the doctor's office all day. She was out when Gus came home that night, and in stumbling around in the dark looking for the light switch he bumped his nose on the door, tearing the stitches. Gus rushed back to the doctor before the maid came home.

The maid said that when she came in and turned on the lights she was "most scared white." There was blood on the bathroom floor, bloody towels on the racks, splotches of blood on the sheets and around the bed, and worst of all, a bloody handprint on the wall.

"Somebody done been killed heah," the maid said, continuing her recital. "Mist' Gus in plenty trouble now."

So the loyal maid started to mop up the blood, and to burn the sheets and towels in her efforts to rid the place of the evidence. Gus saved her this trouble by returning, and explaining what had happened.

Gus explained that Burke was afraid to travel since killing the policeman, and that he came into Chicago to get Gus to find someone to alter his features.

"It struck me as a good idea for me too," Gus said.

But Gus really was not feeling well. By July he could not keep food on his stomach. He grew weaker and weaker and eventually began to run a high fever and talk out of his head.

His babblings were terrible. He chattered disconnectedly of murder, "jobs," robberies, and his companions in crime. Some of the syndicate men were at the house on one occasion when Gus launched into one of his feverish monologues.

They were in turmoil for fear he would be overheard.

They insisted on calling a physician at once, and got Dr. David Omens, M.D., from his office at 1211 Independence Blvd. Dr. Omens examined Gus but could not diagnose his ailment. However, since Gus continued to babble, he decided to try to treat him at home.

But when Gus got out of bed on a morning and collapsed in the hall, Dr. Omens made arrangements to take him to the hospital.

This was dangerous, for Gus was still sought for crimes dating back to the Portland Bank robbery in Louisville. Dr. Omens made arrangements to take Gus to the Jefferson Park Hospital under an assumed name, where he also made arrangements for confidential attention. Fearing to call an ambulance, he took him in his automobile.

He was registered under the name of either M. J. Rand, or M. J. Reed. I cannot recall which for he often used either. He was assigned to room 201, and Dr. Omens procured the services of a Mrs. Roberts, a registered nurse, to watch over Gus constantly to prevent him from babbling the secrets of the syndicate. I later understood that she often threatened to plaster adhesive tape over his mouth to keep him from talking when anyone else was within hearing.

Gus failed to improve and the syndicate told Dr. Omens that, unless he found out what was the matter with him, they would call in another doctor. Apparently Omens felt that if another doctor was called in it might be discovered that he had taken unethical steps in the case, so he started to treat Gus for intestinal influenza.

My husband responded to this treatment, and soon regained his health. I do not believe the hospital attaches ever learned his true identity, so closely was it guarded.

BEFORE

Gus Winkeler's left ring finger before and after its characteristic formations were changed by skilled surgery, throwing classification entirely out of line

AFTER

19

"KILLER" BURKE ON THE LAM

A rap on the door late one night broke the peace and quiet that had reigned in our home for weeks.

When I opened the door I was startled. The man before me was a stranger. He had a turned up nose, and a bristling mustache that poorly concealed a hair-lip.

It was the last item that helped bring recognition when he said, "Georgette, invite me in."

It was Fred Burke's voice, and although I stood aside and mutely motioned for him to enter, he was the last man in the world I wanted to see.

For Killer Burke was the most sought man in the country, and in spite of his old friendship with us, I could not help but feel that he did us an injustice by coming to our home and exposing us to possible apprehension.

Burke made himself at home, and as he lounged in an easy chair I marveled at his changed appearance. The only two words I could think of to describe his appearance were "imbecilic" and "insipid."

In physique too he was changed. He was paler, he drooped and lacked his old vitality, and there was something cringing about him—reminding me of a dog that expects to be struck.

When I saw him shiver occasionally it came to me he was a victim of shattered nerves, and as he told of his wanderings to evade capture I realized that the desperate, swaggering "Killer" was just an ordinary man after all who was being swept under in the backwash of his own foolhardiness.

He said he had been in hiding near Green City, Missouri, at the home of Harvey Bailey's relatives.

When Gus came home he was only momentarily joyful at meeting an old friend, then angered that Burke had taken advantage of us. After telling Burke off, he asked him what he wanted.

Burke explained that he had to have an automobile, but was afraid to undertake to make a deal for one.

The next day Gus told the syndicate men of Burke's unexpected reappearance, and since everyone knew that Burke's presence was dangerous to them all, they were not hard to convince that the easiest way out was to buy Burke a new car and send him on his way.

But Burke showed not the slightest intention of leaving. It was evident that the presence of friends gave him a certain feeling of security that comes to nearly all people in circumstances when they feel that strength comes from shoulders to lean on.

Fred Burke probably felt secure for the first time in many days, for he knew he did not risk exposure while with us, and he was acquainted with Murphy's wife, who was our maid.

Behind the drawn blinds of the apartment he appeared to have settled down for an indefinite stay.

He tried to bolster up his faltering courage by drinking copious quantities of whisky. His drinking began on rising in the morning and continued into the night.

His drinks were so frequent he gave up bothering to mix them one at a time. He would empty a pint of liquor in a pitcher, throw in the chipped ice, fill the pitcher with ginger ale, and pour highballs until the pitcher was empty. Then he would prepare another.

Part of the time he spent in front of the radio, his pitcher at his elbow. Then seemingly overcome with nervousness, he would pace the floor, carrying his glass in his hand.

Many of his trips took him to the windows where he would stand for minutes peeping through a crack in the blinds.

Although "Killer" Burke had become almost a stranger to me, I could see his old tendencies crop out whenever a woman passed the house. His eyes would narrow, he would draw one end of his mustache between his teeth, and chew at it until the woman was out of sight. Then he would heave a deep sigh, take a swig of his highball, and move back to the radio.

Burke's presence frightened me, and his actions drove me to distraction. He complained querulously about everything.

Repeatedly I asked Gus to make him leave, but although Gus was as anxious to get rid of him as I was, he was as loyal to him as he was to his other friends.

There is no way of knowing how long Burke would have lingered out of fancied security if he had not received a scare one night that started him longing for a new hiding place.

Gus was at the syndicate office and it was long past his usual time of return. Burke was nervous and paced the floor, occasionally moving over to the window to peer into the street.

I saw him suddenly stiffen and whisper "Cops" in a low voice. I ran to the window and looked out. A police car was driving slowly down the street, an officer leaning out of the door, apparently looking at house numbers.

"They've found me," Burke said hoarsely. "They've probably got Gus and found an address on him. Sure, that's the reason he isn't home yet. I got to get out of here quick."

Burke was so drunk he could not reason logically. He was frantic with fear. He jerked off his house slippers and started yelling frantically for his shoes. He twisted and turned in the middle of the floor, almost screaming.

"I won't get you killed, Georgette, I'll get out right now. Where the hell is my coat, where's my hat? They'll shoot us both, we haven't got a Chinaman's chance. Oh God, Georgette, get my hat, can't you hurry?"

Then he would start beseeching me to hurry all over again.

In a minute he had me as frightened as he was and I couldn't supply a one of his demands.

Finally, he grabbed his gun in one hand, his house slippers in the other, and started for the back door. He said later he thought he was carrying his gun and his hat.

As he started out the door Gus appeared on the landing and with one push sent Burke back into the room saying, "Get inside you crazy fool, what in hell is the matter with you."

Burke was livid with terror, and I was standing in the middle of the floor wringing my hands. Burke tried to explain, and all the sympathy he got from Gus was laughter.

But Burke had had enough. The next day he left.

His presence had been such a strain on my nerves that I became seriously ill. I vomited blood, and what first appeared to be a stomach ailment, finally was diagnosed as severe nervous disorder. I spent two days in the hospital.

Shortly after I recovered Lefty Louie Campagna, the Paul Revere of gangland, warned us that the house was under suspicion. We moved to an Italian neighborhood in Cicero, then learned that like most of Lefty's warnings, that one too was false.

The Capture of Fred Burke

After the murder of Officer Skelly in St. Joseph, Michigan, which led to the discovery of the Massacre machine guns, Fred Burke wrecked his car and tricked or forced three motorists into helping him escape. Philip D'Andrea, Louis Campagna, and Harvey Bailey all lived in the same area and he might have found a hiding place with one or another, but he apparently hooked up with his bank-robbing friend Bailey, for he went into hiding at a farm owned by Bailey's relatives outside Green City, Missouri. This left his unofficial wife, Viola Brenneman, to take the heat in Michigan.

While lying low in Missouri he posed as Richard F. White, a prosperous oil and real estate man, and was driving an expensive Hudson straight-eight coupe that must have been the closest thing to a tourist attraction in Sullivan County, where Model T Fords were outnumbered by horses and the Model A was practically a luxury car. So it was that the newcomer, Burke, alias White, and his fine machine aroused the suspicions of handyman, odd-jobber, and would-be sleuth Joe Hunsaker Jr. Hunsaker also was Green City's main customer for *True Detective Mysteries* and in time would become Burke's undoing.

Meanwhile, Burke had begun wooing the daughter of a farmer in nearby Milan. After a whirlwind courtship, he married twenty-year-old Bonnie Porter, a student nurse, in nearby Centerville, Iowa, on June 17, 1930, and as Mr. and Mrs. White they took up residence at a run-down house on his father-in-law's farm.

Scarce as gangsters might have been in a land of gravel and graded-dirt roads that frequently turned to mud, Green City's aspiring sleuth

Burke's house in Missouri, where he was captured.

Burke in custody, with the arsenal recovered at his house in Stevensville, Michigan, a small community adjoining St. Joseph.

noticed that Burke always stayed behind the wheel of his car while his new wife bought groceries and any Chicago newspapers. He was convinced that White resembled Burke and began nagging local police to take action, but they considered him a town "character" and agreeably ignored him.

Sometime around then Burke traveled back to the Chicago area and also rented a cottage at Hess Lake, some thirty-seven miles northeast of Grand Rapids, Michigan. A ne'er-do-well Chicago racketeer named Thomas Bonner somehow got wind of this and tipped off Chicago police, hoping to collect the $100,000 reward then being offered for Burke. Burke got wind of that and presumably killed Bonner the following July. With a license-plate number obtained from Bonner's wife, Chicago police headed to Michigan, secured backup from officers in Grand Rapids, and raided the Hess Lake cottage on July 14, only to find Burke again had vanished. Burke picked up another car at Joe Bergl's Auto Sales, next door to Ralph Capone's notorious Cotton Club in Cicero, and motored back to Missouri.

Hunsaker managed to keep an eye on Burke and reported this to the sheriff, the police chief, a railway agent, a local attorney, and probably

others who had any small-town clout. In fact, the effort he put into tracking Burke's comings and goings aroused so much curiosity among other
Green City residents that it's surprising Burke himself didn't become
suspicious, especially when Hunsaker switched from work clothes to a
business suit, making himself even more conspicuous.

During Burke's absence Hunsaker had feared that his quarry had
flown the coop until he overheard Bonnie's father, Barney Porter, remark that his son-in-law "Dick" would soon be returning from Chicago.
Hunsaker was practically a nervous wreck by the time Burke did come
back, driving a new Studebaker President coupe purchased from Joe
Bergl.

By now enough local lawmen had been pestered into believing that
Hunsaker might be right that they requested backup from some out-of-
town cops and raided Burke's house at 6 AM on March 26, 1931. Burke,
still in bed and seeing he was covered by pistols and a submachine gun,
did not even reach for his .38 revolver.

Burke was taken to the most secure jail in the area, ironically in St.
Joseph, Missouri, a town with the same name as the one in Michigan
where he had killed Officer Skelly. Police and officials from several states
established his identity and sought his extradition. Despite his presumed
involvement in the "gangland crime of the century," the Massacre was
not one of Burke's greatest concerns. When called to the jail telephone
to talk to Chicago's new chief of detectives, John Norton, Burke brushed
him off with a remark that he could beat any rap the city would try to
hang on him. Chicago's paperwork may have been mostly a formality,
or there may have been some municipal meddling out of fear that an
unfixed trial before a reform-minded judge would put some politicians
too close to the St. Valentine's Day action.

In any event, after an exchange of calls among governors and prosecutors, Illinois (and several other states) deferred to Michigan because
of its airtight case against Burke, and Michigan was determined not to
let its Skelly-killer go anywhere else.

On Saturday, March 28, after a fifteen-minute hearing, Missouri
Governor Henry Caufield approved Burke's extradition to Michigan.
Using an armored car outfitted with mountings for machine guns and
accompanied by an army of guards, Burke's trip from St. Joseph, Mis-

souri, to St. Joseph, Michigan, began Sunday at 4 AM. The caravan was led by detectives from St. Joseph, Missouri, and following behind were Berrien County Sheriff Fred J. Cutler, Undersheriff Bryan Wise, and prosecuting attorney Wilbur W. Cunningham. In another vehicle were Michigan state troopers B. F. Watterman and Lyle Hutson, St. Joseph City Police Chief Ben Phairas, and Berrien County Deputy Fred Taylor.

By late afternoon a large crowd began filling the streets surrounding the Berrien County Sheriff's Department. Disregarding the cold winds and early darkness, onlookers continued waiting until the caravan arrived about 8 PM. After clearing a path with their sirens, officers led Burke to the Berrien County Jail. Few people got more than a fleeting glimpse of him.

He was taken to an office where deputies booked him at 8:26 PM. During the booking, deputies remarked to Burke that he looked scared as he entered the jail. He replied, "No, I wasn't scared, but that crowd outside made me kind of nervous. You know, you never can tell when someone might lose his head."

Refusing to talk to reporters, Burke was locked in his cell, the third from the front on the east side lower level. He requested a "big thick beefsteak," which soon arrived along with French-fried potatoes, sliced tomatoes, bread, butter, and coffee. Extra guards were posted both inside and outside the jail twenty-four hours a day.

Chicago authorities questioned Burke but only were told how much he liked their city. When questioned by New York authorities, Burke even parried questions about his religion, saying he was a Hindu. Asked what he'd done with his turban, he said he had put it over a photographer's camera.

Burke was charged with Skelly's murder by the Berrien County prosecutor, pled guilty before Circuit Judge Charles E. White in a Benton Harbor courtroom, and was sentenced to life in Michigan's state prison at Marquette.

Sheriff Cutler and Burke began the long six-hundred-mile trip to Marquette on April 28, 1931, and Burke softened a little. He told Sheriff Cutler, "I'm glad it's all over. I'm terribly sorry for everything—not because I have to serve my time, I don't mean that. But I'm sorry that I killed that boy."

The following February, Sheriff Cutler died unexpectedly and his wife, Jane Irene Cutler, assumed his duties. Near the end of 1932 she received a Christmas card from Burke with a note that read, "If every boy had a chance to come in contact with a man like Fred Cutler, life would be different."

The sentence imposed on Fred "Killer" Burke would amount to only nine years. On July 10, 1940, he suffered a heart attack and died in his sleep, evidently without ever discussing the Massacre or his jam-packed life of crime.*

---

* Much of this account comes from *True Detective* and newspapers, but especially from St. Joseph's Chriss Lyon, a genealogist and historian working with the Berrien County Sheriff's Department. From Michigan's state prison she learned that Burke had been a model prisoner who raised canaries in his cell.

20

THE CAR CRASH

Gus Winkeler was earning a high place in Al Capone's esteem. He spent much time at the syndicate office, and had won the gang leader's confidence.

His name was beginning to assume a prominent place in that roster of names identified with the operations of the vast underworld empire fostered by Public Enemy Number One.

His rise had been rapid, for his recommendations had been written in the records of a dozen crimes in the Midwest.

Naturally, those who had been in Capone's employ longer than Gus resented his eminence. This was particularly true of the Italian element, termed "Dagoes" by my husband. The Dagoes rarely ever participated in the "dirty" work of the syndicate, although most of them qualified as expert planners. They felt they were entitled to more consideration than Gus, possibly due to the tie of blood between them and their leader.

However, Gus worked hard for his advancement. He watched his grammar, tried to correct his manners, improved his garb, and in all respects tried to appear as genteel as any man in legitimate business. He must have succeeded, for the papers in Chicago described him as bearing the appearance of a prosperous State Street broker. In all his self education he was striving for one thing—the time when he would have some business of his own that would enable him to meet and mingle with the people he had always envied.

When Gus told me in August that he was going up near St. Joseph, Michigan, to meet some friends living there and have a few games of golf,

I was not in the least surprised, for he would often make trips that would bring him in contact with those who might help him later in business.

He promised to return in time to help me celebrate my birthday August 10.

Somehow, when the time arrived for him to leave I did not say good-bye as casually as I usually did. I had an inexplicable feeling that something was wrong, and when he had driven away I returned to my room in tears. During the week I had no appetite, no desire to go out or have visitors, and although the maid tempted me with my favorite dishes, I remained in that state until I was nearly ill. I even declined to read the papers.

On Friday, August 7, 1931, about four o'clock in the morning, a Doberman Pincher which I still own, started running from one end of the house to the other, sniffing and whining. I thought the dog was sick, and in spite of the earliness of the hour, took her out for a walk. But she was hard to handle, and kept cringing against my knee.

My week long apprehensions were verified in the black headline:

WINKELER DYING, DOCTORS SAY

The coffee cup dropped to the table and spilled into my lap as I screamed: "Oh, My God, he can't die."

Neighbors upstairs heard my screams and ran down to investigate. They asked if there was anything they could do, but I was so dazed by shock I could think of nothing but to go to Lefty Louie Campagna. The neighbors took me.

When I ran into his house Lefty look at me calmly saying: "What are you crying about? Just find out about Gus? Hell, we knew that last Wednesday."

"But no one told me," I sobbed.

"What was the use," was the callous reply, "you can't see him."

Anger stilled by sobs. "The Hell I can't," I said closing my teeth. "I'd like to see the man who can keep me away from my husband."

"Calm yourself," he answered, "we've got orders to keep you away from that hospital."

I looked at him a moment in stony silence, then wheeled and walked out of the house, where my friends were in their car.

I requested that they take me to Joe Bergl's garage at 3348 Cermak Road. I knew that Bergl was a personal friend of Gus' and that if anyone would help me he would. I wanted to go to St. Joseph where Gus was, critically injured in an auto accident.

Bergl agreed to take me, but before leaving I attempted to telephone Al Capone. Frankie Reo answered and repeated what Lefty Louie already had said: "If you go up there you'll go to jail," he added.

"But if you do go, see Attorney Charles W. Gore at St. Joseph before you try to get into the hospital," Reo advised.

En route we stopped in Hammond, Indiana, where I hoped to find out more from friends of Gus'. To my surprise Harvey Bailey, Big Homer, and the other Bailey gangster I knew as Jack were there.

All tried to dissuade me.

"He's dying," Bailey said, "and if he don't the law will hang so many raps on him he'll never get out."

I wondered where everyone got their information, and more determined than ever, drove on into St. Joseph. We went directly to Attorney Gore as Reo had ordered.

"He's doing fine, and they think he'll pull out of it," Gore said. "I wouldn't go in and bother him. They'll jail you sure, and that would just be something else for Gus to worry about."

Bergl agreed with Gore and I consented to return to Chicago. We arrived at three o'clock in the morning.

The first thing I did was buy a paper, and what the news story contained was exactly opposite from what I had been told. Gus was not expected to live. So back to St. Joseph I went, and I kept going back for a week, and each time I was persuaded that Gus was recovering.

Since they had advised me against risking arrest, I finally prevailed on Gus' brother to come up from St. Louis and go in to see him. I wanted the truth.

"He's better," he reported, "but his head is so swollen I wouldn't have recognized him. They can't save his left eye."

His brother told me Gus was closely guarded by police and that a veritable treadmill of convicting witnesses was working at his bedside.

In spite of his bandaged and lacerated face, which defied recognition by his own brother, witnesses identified him as a participant in the holdup of the National Bank and Trust Company of Lincoln, Nebraska, September 17, 1930, in which $2,800,000 worth of bonds were stolen; the $5,000 Plano, Illinois, State Bank robbery on December 17, 1930; and a robbery in Jefferson, Wisconsin. I was ill with worry and confined to the house one night when Joe Bergl came over to see if there was anything he could do. While he was there the Bailey gangster I knew as Jack came in. [By now Gus was one of Capone's "American boys" and out of the armed-robbery business, but he still was a handy "suspect" on the basis of his earlier record.]

He seemed worried.

"I'm taking a big chance, but you ought to know this," he said. "Bailey, Big Homer, and the other boys are going up to St. Joseph tonight and try to kidnap Gus out of the hospital. If they can't get him alive they'll kill him in his bed. The idea is to get him away from the police, one way or another."

I was horror struck.

"Why, why, oh why are they going to do a thing like that," I pleaded.

"Well, he's been identified in those bank jobs, so draw your own conclusions," was Jack's answer.

That was not hard to do. Gus had no part in those holdups. If he lived and stood trial he would prove his innocence and the investigation might lead to arrest of the actual bandits. If he died the investigation would die with him. It did not require any deep thought to see that those seeking his death would benefit most by it.

"The boys say Gus hasn't been right since the auto accident, and is losing his mind," Jack continued. "They say he's been talking to the police."

But already I had made up my mind that other motives prompted the scheme.

The thought of those grim men walking into the hospital where my husband was recovering from an almost fatal accident, and taking his life when he was about to live, left me determined to prevent it at any cost.

"Don't go," I begged, "please don't go. I'll go up myself, I'll take care of everything, only don't go."

"You're not going," Jack said with finality. "You're not going because we say you're not." Then he went out.

Bergl volunteered to take me to St. Joseph. As we were ready to leave Jack came back, and I begged him to tell me how he was so sure Gus was losing his mind.

In a flash of desperation I told him that unless he at least gave me time to talk to Al Capone and have him investigate, I would call the police.

He reluctantly agreed to wait a day.

I tried to get Capone on the phone, but every time I called someone in the office would say he was out. Bergl got in touch with Johnny Moore [a.k.a. Claude Maddox], a Capone employee, and Moore passed the story on to Capone. Before morning the order was issued that if Harvey Bailey or any of his gang molested Gus he would wipe them out.

In the underworld a Capone order was law. Jack came back to the house and ingratiatingly tried to make me believe the kidnap plan merely was to prevent Gus from taking a rap.

Gus Winkeler's Car Wreck

If Winkeler was heading to Michigan to win friends and influence people by way of golf, he probably didn't need the gun that caught the eye of State Trooper Myron Gillette. When Gus and a friend left a coffee shop at New Buffalo on August 5, 1931, and began heading north on US 12, Gillette and his friend, Deputy Sheriff John Hovan, hurried outside to their own cars and gave chase. Had Gus been driving he might have managed to dodge in and out of traffic and escape, as he was noted for his getaway skills, but the man at the wheel was less talented. He sideswiped an oncoming car and lost control, and their Ford rolled several times before hitting a tree.

Gillette and the deputy approached the car cautiously only to find both the driver and his passenger too badly injured to run or fight. They also found ammunition, several bottles of whiskey, and $700. Other police arrived, and after the crash victims were taken to a nearby doctor's office both found themselves under guard in the Mercy Hospital at Benton Harbor. The driver was quickly identified as John Moran, and his condition was listed as critical with a broken shoulder, a wired-shut jaw, and a serious concussion that resulted in recurring comas.

Moran was quickly linked to several robberies. His passenger, who had been going by the alias of Jerry Kral, was soon identified as Gus Winkeler, who not only worked for Al Capone but was a known associate of Fred "Killer" Burke, the main suspect in the St. Valentine's Day Massacre, who was now in prison for a police officer's murder in nearby St. Joseph.

While in the hospital, Winkeler found himself accused of crimes in four states, but especially in Nebraska, where he was declared a suspect in the September 17, 1930, robbery of the Lincoln National Bank. Trooper Gillette's daughter, Donna, recalls that the Michigan State Police, who had the battered Winkeler under heavy guard, deemed it wise to send officer Gillette into hiding for a month and then transferred him to a post in northern Michigan.

When Georgette did not even learn of the wreck for several days and then got only bad news from several mobsters who tried to keep her from seeing Capone, she turned to Joe Bergl, the Cicero car dealer, who probably risked his neck by getting her to the hospital and thence to the Berrien County lockup, where Gus was later moved. Bergl would prove to be her most reliable friend. His dealership adjoined Ralph Capone's Cotton Club, and Gus Winkeler was something more than a trusted partner.

Compared to John Moran, who was antagonistic from the time of the wreck through his medical treatment, Winkeler went out of his way to cooperate with both the hospital staff and his captors. When he was later released from the hospital and taken to the Berrien County jail, Moran, although still weak from his ordeal, changed his tune and told reporters he'd been treated well. There he awaited extradition to Illinois, where he was wanted as a bank-robbery suspect.

Gus had lost an eye in the wreck and was otherwise up against it. Several states wanted him for bank robberies, mainly because of his association with Fred Burke and Harvey Bailey, and Nebraska authorities wanted him the most. They were still looking for suspects in the robbery of the Lincoln National Bank on September 17, 1930, and jailing nearly anyone in the bandit business. Several bank employees and witnesses were taken to St. Joseph, where they obediently identified Winkeler, even in the hospital with his blackened eyes, bandaged head, and badly swollen face.

Transferred to the jail on August 31, Winkeler was still weak but now shaven and nattily dressed, and he managed to make it through the booking procedure without much help. He had asked if he could be held in a hotel room where he could order food, but the sheriff refused, probably because a hotel might not care to have its guests running a gauntlet of cops with shotguns. They did make him comfortable, however, and allowed him to order meals and to bring over fans and a radio that refused to work inside the cell.

Meanwhile, he awaited the Michigan governor's decision on whether to accept extradition papers filed by Illinois, Wisconsin, or Nebraska, with Ohio and Indiana on the waiting list.

Nebraska got the nod, and Winkeler, represented by the same lawyer previously retained by Burke after the killing of Officer Skelly, grumbled that he would always regret that his picture had been taken with Burke some six years earlier. Meanwhile, he had gotten along well with Berrien County Sheriff Fred Cutler. He also told deputies not to bother searching for his golf clubs, as he figured he wouldn't do much playing with only one eye.

On September 15 Winkeler was put in leg irons and began the trip to Lincoln, Nebraska, in police cars loaded to the brim with six officers, prosecutors, and a witness who had to be at his Michigan hearing.

21

CAPONE TO THE RESCUE

Up to this time I had not been able to see Gus, neither could I get in touch with Capone. Each time I called, Lefty Louie Campagna, Frankie Reo or some other syndicate hireling would tell me Al was not in. I knew they were giving me the runaround.

One morning I called, and the voice was giving me the customary song and dance about Capone being out, when Al himself apparently picked up an extension phone in response to the call.

"The hell I'm not in," he snapped. "Hello, hello Georgette, don't hang up, it's Al. Come right down here, and come right up to the office, and don't let any of these fellows talk you out of it." [After the Massacre, the "national gangster convention" in Atlantic City, followed by his ten months in a Pennsylvania prison, his picture on the cover of *Time* magazine, his No. 1 position on the Chicago Crime Commission's new "Public Enemy" list, and his current tax problems, Capone acquired such notoriety as the country's "most famous gangster" that it had the undesirable effect of diminishing his ability to conduct the Syndicate's business affairs.]

I wasted no time getting to his office in the Lexington Hotel.

"They've moved Gus from the hospital to the St. Joseph jail," he said kindly after I was seated. "I am going to fix it for you to get in and see him. The boys all tell me Gus is losing his mind and talking his head off to the police. They said Gus has refused my help, and if that's true I don't know what to think about it. On the strength of these reports I haven't done a thing for him. But what I want is some straight dope. You get it, because I can trust you. I think a lot of Gus, and if the boys are wrong I'll do what I can to help him."

I knew why he wanted my report. He felt as I did—that the reports already made were tinged with jealousy.

He told me to come back in a little while and he would have Phil De Andrea take me to St. Joseph. I came back at one in the afternoon and met Phil, who tried to get me to put off the trip, saying his car was broken and being repaired. When he saw I was determined to go he said to go ahead and he would meet me in St. Joseph and bring me back. So I made the trip by interurban and taxicab.

I almost cried when I saw Gus, but after we had greeted each other I told him what Capone had said, and about Harvey Bailey's kidnap plot. He only narrowed his remaining good eye and nodded his head slowly as I told him.

When I had finished I said: "Did the Bailey gang rob the Lincoln Bank?"

"Yes," he replied, "but what can I do about it roosting in this cooler."

"Leave that to me," I said, "until you do get out."

Gus was being double crossed, for he told me that Phil De Andrea had been in several times and told him Capone was doing everything in his power to "spring" him.

When I left the jail I went to the St. Joseph Hotel to wait for Phil, but although considerable time had elapsed, he did not come. Just as I was completing arrangements to rent a car, the hotel clerk said I had a telephone call.

It was Phil De Andrea. "Don't go to see Al when you get back," he requested. "Come straight to the Congress Hotel and meet me."

When I arrived at the Congress at one o'clock in the morning I did not go directly to his room, as he had asked, but had the clerk call the room and announce me. I wanted evidence of my presence, for I did not know what De Andrea wanted and I had every reason to distrust him.

When I entered the room I saw Phil's "broken car," a beautiful girl about twenty years old.

He begged me not to tell Al he had not taken me to St. Joseph, and asked me to wait until morning to see him, then say I had just arrived in Chicago. He was frightened because he had disobeyed orders.

Without making any promises I said coldly: "Phil, who told you Gus is losing his mind and is talking to the police?"

"Why—why, Gore, that lawyer we got for him," he stuttered.

"Gus is perfectly sane," I continued, "and even if he wasn't he still would have more sense than any of you greasy Dagoes," on which I turned and left the room.

The next morning I reported to Capone what I had learned at St. Joseph, and although I owed Phil De Andrea nothing, I did not mention that he had disobeyed orders.

"Georgette, I'm going to leave it up to you," Capone said when I was finished. "You're honest, and you can work out the details to suit yourself. I'll give you all the money you need."

He handed me a big roll of bills and I left the room. As I went through the office Frankie Reo stopped me and inquired how much money had been turned over to me. I told him the exact amount.

I later learned from Gus that the same amount was deducted from his pay without Capone's knowledge, and that Reo apparently had pocketed it. But Gus never reported Reo.

In the meantime, the syndicate boys continued to circulate the story that Gus was crazy. A few days later I saw Capone and told him that I intended to discover the source.

"I'd like to know myself, and I'd like to know why it's being done," he said.

I went to St. Joseph in search of Phil De Andrea, and failing to find him got in touch with attorney Gore and told him I wished to contact Phil at once. He consented to take me to a place where he could be found.

It proved to be a beer joint a few yards from the ninth hole at the Municipal Golf Course. Sure enough, Phil was in the place drinking beer with another pretty girl I had never seen before.

He started with surprise when we walked in, sent the girl out immediately and came over to our table.

"Well, well, this is a surprise, Georgette," he said with assumed affability. "What'll you have to drink?"

"I'm not drinking," I said curtly, and his eyes narrowed, for he could tell I had something on my mind.

But he ordered three beers, which remained untouched while I began. I turned to Gore with, "What's the idea telling Phil all those lies about my husband's mental condition?"

"I don't know what you're talking about," said the attorney springing to his feet. "Whoever said I told anything like that is a liar."

Phil De Andrea's face flushed as I continued: "Nevertheless, it is being told, and it's got back to Capone that Gus is giving information to the police. I want to know who started it."

By this time we were all standing, and creating something of a scene.

"We've got to get out of here," Phil whispered hurriedly. "I've got to get back to town." He grabbed my arm and started to lead me out, but Gore grabbed the other and detained me. For a few seconds they tugged and hauled at my elbows, each apparently afraid I would go with the other and get a one-sided story.

But I had made my point. Phil De Andrea was the double-crosser. I winked at Gore and went out with Phil. We drove to the hotel, and although Phil tried to place the blame on Gore, I now knew the truth and paid no heed.

22

THE GREATEST BANK ROBBERY

Later Gus was moved from the St. Joseph jail to Lincoln, Nebraska, to face trial on the bank robbery charges. Before he was moved he instructed me not to come to Lincoln, but a few days after he arrived there I received a telegram from a Lincoln attorney saying that Gus wanted to see me at once.

I left post haste, and found that Gus was not being held in jail but in the penitentiary. Tom O'Connor, his old St. Louis friend, Harold "Pop" Lee, and Jack Britt, who had been arrested previously as suspects in the robbery, also were in the penitentiary.

All were confined in the almost inaccessible "death row." The authorities evidently feared that some concerted effort would be made by the underworld to free them. Each was held for $100,000 bond.

Up to this time Gus had been comparatively optimistic about his chances to beat the case against him, but now he was downcast.

"They're working up an airtight case with a bunch of phony evidence," he said. "If I could get out of here I could find the fellows who have those stolen bonds and get them back."

As a sample of the kind of evidence to be used against him Gus explained that at his arraignment, when the woman bank employee who identified him as one of the bandits while he was in St. Joseph, undertook to identify him for the Judge, she made a serious error.

"Attorney Mann was with me in the courtroom," Gus said. "They led this woman in and asked her to identify the bandit. She looked around for a minute then pointed at my attorney. 'That's the man. That's Gus Winkeler,' she said."

Gus said everyone laughed, much to Attorney Mann's embarrassment. Mann is short and heavyset, while Gus was slender and over six feet tall.

I was nearly certain I knew who had the bonds and I felt sure that if Gus was out long enough he could get them and the charges would be dropped.

So, back to Chicago, and directly to Al Capone to whom I explained the whole situation.

"If you can get a good line on those bonds, I'll furnish the bail for Gus to get out and get them back," Capone promised.

I sent for the Bailey gangster I knew as "Jack."

"Jack," I said, putting the case directly to him, "I've got to get a line on these Lincoln bank bonds to get my husband out of jail. You've always claimed to be a friend of his, and now's your chance to prove it. Can you, and will you, help me?"

"Well," he said, thinking it over, "it'll be a tough proposition, but I'll tell you all I know about the job, then maybe you can see daylight."

And he did.

A gangster known as "Old Chuck," because he was nearly sixty, accompanied by his wife, moved to Lincoln, and located less than four blocks from the bank.

Chuck "cased" the institution for weeks, until he was thoroughly familiar with the hours, coming and going of employees, peak of the business day, volume of passing traffic during different banking hours, and all other details.

One at a time the rest of the gang drifted into town, locating in different neighborhoods to avoid suspicion. The late comers planned the escape, known in gangland argot as the "gits." They traveled every highway and byway in the region surrounding Lincoln. They surveyed the most remote country lanes to avoid the customary police blockades on main traveled roads.

They selected the most likely places to park other machines, so they could abandon their escape cars in case their original plan went wrong.

The original plan called for chartering a large enclosed moving van. The car used in the holdup was to be driven into the van, and the auto, bandits, and loot were to be run through the police blockade.

This plan, Jack told me, worked without a hitch, and the gang made a clean getaway, without having to utilize the elaborate plans they had laid in case of emergency. Nebraska authorities have long been mystified about this escape.

When he had told this story Jack asked me if I had ever met Bob Maros, known also as "Slim" Morris. I told him I had met Slim a couple of times while I was out with Gus.

"Slim was killed the other day up in Red Wing, Minnesota," Jack continued, "and his wife knows we have the bonds. She wants her money, so what can I do? If we turn these bonds over to Gus and don't give her some dough she'll squeal to the Gee [government]."

I asked Jack where she could be found and he told me she had just left a place on 22nd Street.

I had met Mrs. Maros once before and I knew I would recognize her, so I went directly to the address Jack had given me. It was a saloon, and I felt foolish walking in alone, but was comforted at the sight of the owner's wife tending bar. She greeted me, remembering that Gus and I had stopped there on several occasions.

Slim's wife asked at once about Gus.

Then I went into my act. As pitifully as I could I told her he was being held in the Nebraska penitentiary death row.

"Gee, kid, I feel sorry for you, you must be awful lonely," she said.

"I sure am," I said, seeing an opening. "I wish you'd come up and have dinner with me tonight."

She said she would be glad to go, and if I would wait until she met some people coming in, she would go right home with me. I was glad to wait, and fortunately I did, for the fates were with me.

The "people" were none other than Harvey Bailey, and Big Homer, and I took advantage of the opportunity to get better acquainted with them.

When they left, Mrs. Maros accompanied me home, and immediately I started serving highballs. I was not sparing of the liquor in her drinks, but drank only a weak concoction myself.

When she waxed talkative I brought up the subject of the bank robbery, and said Gus was going to try to raise money to buy back the $2,800,000 worth of stolen bonds.

She was in a mellow mood and out came the welcome words: "He can have my share so far as I'm concerned if it will do Gus any good." For some reason she seemed angry at Jack and the others.

The next day Jack brought "Old Chuck" to the house, and after we had talked for a while, went out and brought back a man he introduced as Verne Miller, later to be known as one of the most notorious criminals in the country.

They gave me to understand if I could get Gus out they would help him recover the bonds, but made it plain "the people who have them will want plenty of sugar."

At no time did any of them admit they had possession of the bonds.

I went to Capone and reported the progress I had made and on the basis of what I had learned he said he would arrange to pay Gus's $100,000 bail.

"Help me get him free and he'll prove he isn't guilty of that job," I told him.

"I don't believe you'd lie to me, and I'll get the bail," was the reply.

So I returned to Lincoln and explained developments to Gus.

In the meantime Capone sent Phil De Andrea to Lincoln to negotiate Gus' release, and at the same time chartered a plane to bring securities from New York to Chicago, to be deposited as surety on Gus' bond in Lincoln.

The arrangement was finally accepted by the court, and Gus was again a free man.

23

CHICAGO'S "SECRET SIX"

Since Gus knew from what I had told them that he would have to "pay through the nose" to get back the bonds, he naturally expected some security in return.

So he went directly to the Secret Six, that citizens' commission organized in Chicago to stamp out crime, and told them he believed he could recover the bonds, and with their assistance clear himself of the charges.

I am not sure of the nature of the agreement Gus made with the anti-crime organization, but I am sure it was satisfactory to both, for Gus started conferences with Secret Six operatives immediately, all aimed at procuring the bonds and disposing of the charges.

When Gus explained to Alexander Jamie, chief director of the Secret Six, that the bonds were available for a price, and he believed he could locate them, Jamie replied: "That's why you got the rap. We did not feel you were guilty, but with your connections we were confident you could help us recover the bonds."

So, after a fashion, the charges against my husband were a blackmail.

Gus' bank account was far short of the sum needed to buy the bonds from those holding them, for knowing Gus' predicament, most of the gang held out for high prices. So again Al Capone came to the rescue, providing money as fast as Gus made the proper contacts.

At the same time, however, the chief expected Gus to clear himself, which meant that his services with the syndicate could be resumed as soon as possible.

Capone knew that Gus was in Buffalo, New York, at the time the Lincoln bank robbery occurred, since he himself had sent him there on business, but naturally Capone was in no position to go court and testify in Gus' behalf.

So through the Secret Six Gus asked the Lincoln authorities to accompany him to Buffalo to establish his alibi that he was in that city September 17, 1930, when the Nebraska holdup was staged.

Max Towle, special Nebraska prosecutor assigned to the case, was sent to Chicago, and accompanied Gus and members of the Secret Six to Buffalo.

Arriving in Buffalo, Gus' alibi received a setback—for he could not remember under what name he had registered at the hotel.

Fortunately for him, the memories of the bellboys and the room clerk had been sharpened by generous tips while Gus was there. But Mr. Towle expected concrete evidence, and it was up to Gus to produce it.

Alexander Jamie.

So Gus and the rest of the investigating party undertook a subterfuge, and I understand it was accomplished without the Nebraska prosecutor's knowledge.

They got a registry card from the files of the date of September 17, and by the use of ink remover, obliterated the signature it bore, after which Gus signed the card with an alias.

"That favor cost me plenty," Gus told me later.

However, the money was thrown away, for on the way home those "in" on the card change got cold feet, and rather than risk detection if someone analyzed the card, destroyed it.

Those who made the trip to Buffalo told the Nebraska authorities that although the card had disappeared, they had seen it, and it was this testimony that led to the dismissal of the indictment.

But many officials believed the card testimony was a fake, influenced by the bank's anxiety to recover the bonds at the expense of Gus Winkeler and Justice.

These included Governor Charles Bryan of Nebraska, who termed the dismissal: "The darkest page in the state's history."

In the meantime Gus was making final arrangements with the Bailey gang, and the bonds were retrieved and paid for. When the deal with the gang was finally completed, Bailey and some of the boys brought the bonds to our house in a brown suit case.

Incidentally, concerning the recovery of the loot by my husband, the Chicago *Herald-Examiner* said: "Explanation of how Winkeler got possession of the loot was offered in the fact that Winkeler was held in high esteem by Harvey Bailey, who preferred to give him the loot rather than see him go to the penitentiary."

The bonds were at the house all night, and I saw Gus in a light-hearted mood for the first time in many days. I even feared that someone of the gang might take it upon himself to organize some of the underworld and come after them—for they represented a large fortune.

Gus made light of my fears and opened the grip and emptied the contents on the floor in front of me, then picked up a package and tossed it in my lap. I thought of the danger of leaving fingerprints and refused to touch them.

"Go ahead and take a look, Honey," Gus laughed, "for you'll never see so much money again at one time if you live to be a hundred."

"I can't get interested in this stuff now," I replied soberly, nodding at the heaps of gilt-edged securities. "They almost cost you twenty five years of your life, and they did cost you every cent we had, not including what Al Capone gave you. All the money they cost you doesn't include your grief and my worry."

The next morning Gus set out alone with his suitcase to meet Lincoln bank officials and the Secret Six at an office in a Loop building.

Gus said later that after they had a few drinks he opened the suit case and bonds were examined by the bankers. The bonds were negotiable, and had a value of over a half-million dollars. He said he gave them affidavits that the registered bonds, amounting to over $2,000,000, had

How the "Secret Six" Coaxed $3,000,000 Loot Home in a Suitcase

"Crash!" Went the Gangsters' Car Into a Truck, and Then Came This Unparalleled Finale to the Biggest Bank Robbery on Record

been destroyed. This was true, for they were of no use to the unregistered bearer.

"They were satisfied," Gus said, "and why not. They got their bonds back and I paid for them. That wouldn't hurt so much if they really thought me guilty, but having to buy them, even though I had nothing to do with the robbery, is what burns me up."

The method of recovery of the bonds as released to the newspapers was entirely different from the above story. The reporters were informed that a voice on the telephone had arranged a designated spot where the bonds would be found under a lamp post at a certain hour. Those releasing the story said they agreed to the arrangement and found the bonds as promised.

Just that simple.

Gus was disappointed in the final disposition of the case, however. His old friend Tom O'Connor and Howard "Pop" Lee were tried first in the robbery case and sentenced to twenty five years in the Nebraska penitentiary. Gus' recovery of the bonds and the deal with authorities exploded the case, and as a consequence, Jack Britt, who was tried last, was found not guilty.

Up to the time of his death Gus had hopes of getting their sentences set aside. He had information that their release could be obtained for $10,000 each, and was planning to raise the money to free them when he was killed.

Gus knew how to sympathize with them, for although he participated in many crimes in which he was not arrested, time without number he had been unjustly accused.

O'Connor and Lee still are serving their sentences.

In the meantime Capone had been sentenced for income tax evasion, since no amount of investigation could reveal his connection with the underworld and the law was helpless on that score. But it was generally understood, and largely true, that he continued to rule the underworld during all the time he was held in the Chicago jail before being moved to the Federal prison.

Gus was left without Capone's aid in proving his innocence in the $5,000 Plano, Illinois, bank robbery in which he also had been identified by both Charles M. Jones, cashier, and Melvin Henrickson, assistant cashier.

The identification was made chiefly by Jones who viewed Gus as he lay in the St. Joseph hospital, practically disfigured. State Highway Policeman Buck Kempster, a friend of Gus' had warned him that "someone in Plano" was going to "take" him for some money.

Gus told me later that Buck was right—that it cost him $5,000 to prevent identification in the courts. He also learned another interesting sidelight of his identification. A newspaper photographer, present to take pictures when the holdup victims came to look at Gus in the hospital, said he overheard a police officer instruct the witnesses before they entered the ward just which man to point out.

When the case came up January 3, 1933, in the Kendall County Circuit Court in Yorkville, Illinois, Judge John K. Newhall was forced to throw it out because Cashier Jones had undergone a "change of heart" and would not identify Gus. Furthermore, Jones, who claimed Gus hit him with a gun during the holdup, and had filed a $50,000 personal injury suit, dropped it when Gus made a settlement out of court.

So Gus was cleared of the charges, although only at considerable expenditure.

The Chicago Crime Commission and Its Secret Six

The "Secret Six" was the extralegal action arm of the Chicago Crime Commission, whose charter gave it no police powers—a handicap temporarily remedied by *Chicago Tribune* publisher Robert Isham Randolph. He prevailed upon several prominent but anonymous Chicagoans to hire the services of Alexander Jamie, the brother-in-law of Prohibition czar Eliot Ness of "Untouchables" fame. Jamie in turn recruited an also-secret assortment of off-duty cops, private detectives, and Prohibition agents who closely resembled vigilantes.

The Secret Six collaborated with Gus Winkeler and Nebraska officials in returning the loot that robbers had hauled out of the Lincoln National Bank on September 17, 1930. Georgette makes the interesting point that the suitcase full of negotiable bonds and other booty was not picked up cloak-and-dagger style on a nighttime street corner, as the Secret Six reported to the newspapers. She says that Gus simply went to their office the following day and plopped it on a table.

The Chicago Crime Commission itself was the country's first such organization, established in 1919 by the Chicago Association of Commerce. It was set up largely in response to the city's first major daylight robbery, at a factory two years earlier in which two Brink's Express payroll guards were killed. "Ammunition Eddie" Wheed and his accomplices stood off police during a two-hour gun battle that finally led to Wheed's capture and later his hanging.

As a privately funded but powerless organization, the CCC had mainly harped about police and political corruption and the rising crime rate following the world war. It started keeping a body count of gangland-style murders but did not find much citizen support until the Chicago Beer Wars became too bloody and too public after 1925.

By then other states were falling into line, and a National Crime Commission was organized with headquarters in New York. After the machine-gun murder of Chicago's Assistant State's Attorney William McSwiggin in 1926 (he just happened to be a buddy of some bootleggers encroaching on Capone's turf), the Chicago Crime Commission found itself compelled to support some kind of action. Several grand juries were called, but they could find nothing definite to pin on Capone.

In 1928, after the city's "Pineapple Primary" of bombings and shootings that were making Chicago a national spectacle, CCC director Frank Loesch arranged a secret meeting at the Lexington Hotel with his nemesis, Al Capone. He asked Capone to please put a lid on the gangland violence prior to November's national elections, and Capone, obviously flattered, agreed.

Papers picked up on the meeting later and by some accounts Capone said, "All right. I can take care of the Dagoes, and I'll have the cops send out squads the night before to jug all the other hoodlums and keep them in the cooler until the polls close." Such was Capone's police and political clout. He earlier had warned city officials that any closing down of his bootlegging operations would only put the criminals he now employed out of work and out of his control, setting them loose on a citizenry that felt personally safe in spite of Chicago's reputation as the country's "crime capital." In an editorial the *Chicago Tribune* sarcastically joked that people in other lands would automatically assume that all Chicagoans were armed to the teeth and must have a special hardihood to live in a city whose streets were routinely swept by machine-gun fire.

After the St. Valentine's Day Massacre, Loesch took an idea from another commission member and cooked up the first "Public Enemy" list in 1930, naming Capone as No. 1 (which he did not consider flattering). Several other cities and states followed Chicago's lead, and Loesch proposed that the U.S. Justice Department adopt a national list, only to have J. Edgar Hoover reject the idea on the disingenuous grounds that it would invite criminals to compete for its top position.

But the press loved the "Public Enemy" idea so much that it began applying it to any headline criminals of the day and to anyone the FBI declared to be their most-wanted outlaw, sometimes getting their "public enemies" tangled up in the process. (To this day the FBI is credited with inventing that phrase, which Hoover was always careful to avoid using, although he later was forced to create a "Ten Most Wanted" list.)

When Alexander Jamie's Secret Six operations started making news, most Chicagoans applauded their gun-toting activities and were only disappointed when members of its staff were accused of corruption, thievery, and extortion. Indictments forced the CCC to disband the Secret Six and its merry tricksters on April 19, 1933.

24

ENTER FATHER DWYER

Gus emerged from these court tangles a stronger man than ever. Already he was recognized as one of the truly "big" men in the Chicago underworld, and his influence in city politics was being felt.

Although the Italian element of the Capone syndicate was jealous of Gus and his position, at the same time they realized his ability as an executive and his importance to the machine.

And at this time every valuable man was needed. Capone was behind bars, and although he had much to say concerning operations of his business, it suffered from lack of his personal supervision. Then too, the Depression had arrived, which was a serious blow to the alcohol business, the mainstay of the syndicate.

As a matter of fact, the vast underworld empire of Al Capone was beginning to crumble.

Profits were large, but not large on the scale they had been two years before.

Literally Gus had "met the enemy and they were his." He had been in court, charged with the biggest robbery in crime history, and had emerged triumphant. He could hold up his head in the presence of the law—a fact to be reckoned with in the underworld.

And this fact made him a valuable "front" man.

Gus Winkeler tried to look the part. His clothes were conservative in cut and came from the best tailors. He kept himself carefully groomed, and to tell the truth he was rather vain of his appearance.

He was extremely sensitive of the loss of his eye in the St. Joseph auto accident, and tried his best to conceal it. He assumed nose glasses, which added greatly to the gentility of his appearance, and incidentally gave birth to a number of amusing stories in the newspapers.

Murphy, the negro who stood by him in the Toledo investigation, was his chauffeur, and as chauffeur drove only the finest cars.

Gus had a very kindly feeling toward the colored man, and although he always referred to him as "Murph," it afforded him a great deal of amusement to call him "James" when anyone was within earshot. This too amused the reporters.

My husband was beginning to be known both to friend and foe as "Big Mike." Practically every underworld figure had a nickname, most of them far-fetched, but I believed Gus got his from the fact that he had used the name of Michaels so often it had become synonymous with his real name.

To be truthful, Gus' real name was so seldom used that no newspaper ever spelled it properly. The first "e" was always dropped.

Although Gus took pride in his new influence, it was gained at the expense of my health. Nearly ten years of fleeing from the police, hiding, worrying, and living in terror from hour to hour, hairbreadth escapes from the law, all topped with those days when I believed he was to be sent to prison, had taken their toll on my nerves.

At no time could I see the end of my worries, although with his improved station I believed there was less danger.

So I was glad when a large Canadian distillery approached him after his release in the Nebraska case, and offered him $1,000 a month for the use of his name.

This, I might explain, was for the purpose of selling legitimate whisky manufactured in Canada, to illegitimate retailers in Chicago, for prohibition had not yet been repealed. Actually Gus had nothing to do with the business. Agents of the distillery made the calls, merely using my husband's name as an endorsement.

It is quite likely the use of his name was sometimes prostituted, for I have no doubt that more than once it was used in the nature of a threat.

I thought that $12,000 a year would be sufficient for our needs, but our latest experience with the law had made me wonder how long this new security might last. Every crime I read of in the papers gave me a new fear that Gus might again be accused.

Living in such a constant state of mental turmoil one might ask: "Why did she stick?"

To me it was simple. I loved my husband. So far as was possible under the circumstances, Gus was always kind and considerate. When he was able he supplied my every comfort.

Then too, I was sincere in my marriage vow. We had first been married by a Protestant minister in St. Louis, but it was a dying request of Gus' mother that we be remarried in the Catholic Church. This we agreed to do, and after her death returned to Chicago and were united by the late Reverend Father Dwyer, one of the finest men I ever knew.

Gus had the utmost confidence in Father Dwyer, advised with him frequently, and always told me that I could go to him for help at any time.

It was about this time that the most colossal crime in American history occurred—the kidnapping of the little son of Colonel Charles Lindbergh.

When we read the first accounts in the morning papers Gus was highly incensed, first because the victim was a baby, and secondly because the father was an aviator and a St. Louisan. Gus always felt a kindred spirit with pilots.

"I'd like to get my hands on the rat who would do a stunt like that," he said bitterly.

"If you aren't called in on it I miss my guess," I replied.

I was right. The authorities asked him to report at headquarters and he did. Of course no trouble developed and he came home immediately.

Everyone will remember that it was intimated that Al Capone had ordered the kidnapping in order to use the child as a club over the head of the Government to gain his release.

Anyone acquainted with Capone knew this intimation was ridiculous, for although the Public Enemy Number One had ordered many crimes, under no circumstances would he have harmed a woman or a child.

However, the theory gained some weight when Capone offered to aid in the search, either at liberty or from behind the walls of his prison.

In fact, he sent word to Gus to utilize every resource in the underworld to ferret out the kidnappers. Gus was glad to undertake this assignment. My husband exercised every gangland connection he knew of. Grapevine telegraph, pipelines, stool pigeons and every other known source of information was tapped, but there was not the remotest clue.

This much I can guarantee. The Lindbergh kidnapping was not an act of the underworld. [This kidnapping took place while Capone was still in Leavenworth, and he went so far as to offer his brother Ralph as a prison "replacement" to guarantee of his own return.]

25

THE SHOOTING OF FRANK NITTI

Recognizing the fact that the Capone syndicate was disintegrating as a result of economic conditions and Capone's imprisonment, other officials of the organization began desperately to cast about for ways and means to salvage the remnants of the crumbling empire.

They realized that with the vast number of unemployed throughout the city it was next to impossible to expect the same returns from the Far South Side and other sections of the city where the laboring people made their homes.

So they turned their attention to the great North Side, the "gold-mine" of gangland.

And in doing so the operations of Ted Newberry [formerly with Bugs Moran], youthful North Side boss, came under their scrutiny.

Before going any further it would be well to outline briefly and generally the method of operating syndicate business in Chicago.

By its geography the city was, and is, divided into sections. In each of these sections a "boss" is generally recognized by all syndicates, large or small. A boss is the man who has risen to a dominant position, either by force or by political influence or because he was put there by a powerful organization. His word is law to all those minor satellites who make their living by illegitimate business—mostly alcohol dealers, speakeasy proprietors, and gambling and nightclub operators.

Usually even legitimate businesses recognize these bosses, partly through the doubtful "protective" associations that guard them [usually from the same protective associations], and exact a regular toll for the service, and partly because they have money and influence.

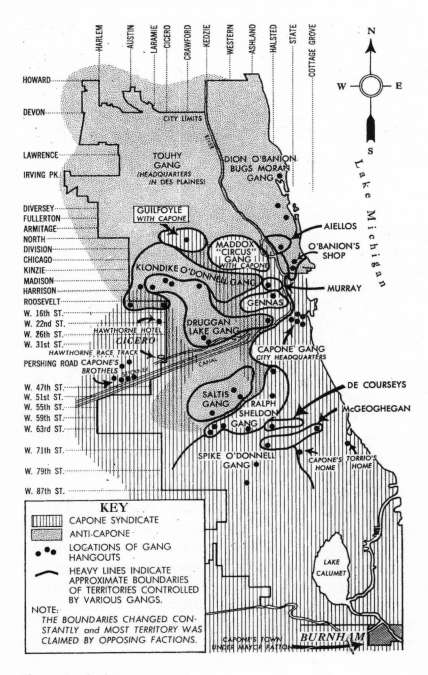

Chicago Gangland Territories, 1926.

Anyone expecting to sell alcohol in a territory, or operate a gambling establishment, must deal with the boss. This chieftain may even have clubs and properties of his own. [In Chicago, district police captains usually owed their jobs to precinct politicians who knew what kinds of vice their constituents found acceptable.]

Newberry's connections with the syndicate had been satisfactory, but now the members believed he was not making the most of the possibilities of the North Side, and since the wealthier people of Chicago lived there, believed there was no excuse for the dwindling profits.

Newberry for some time had been a personal friend of my husband, and I knew from Gus' remarks that his business was in a bad way. Newberry did not know how to meet conditions, he was worried, and like many men had resorted to drinking to relieve his mind. He was deeply indebted to the syndicate for alcohol purchased and never paid for, and while the syndicate saw no way of collecting its money, Newberry was equally mystified how to pay it.

The syndicate began to negotiate with Newberry for the privilege of putting one of their own men in the North Side as his business partner and adviser. It is quite possible they might have killed him outright, if it had not been for the fact that Newberry himself operated a number of properties.

Newberry agreed to the appointment of a partner, since he saw no other way out of his difficulties.

There was only one man in the syndicate qualified to act as the "front" on the North Side. It was Gus Winkeler—so they appointed him. This was highly pleasing to Newberry, who had confidence in Gus and very little in the Italian members of the syndicate.

Gus immediately ordered his name removed from the syndicate payroll. He was not severing his connections but planned to start some enterprises of his own.

When Gus went into the North Side as co-manager, he learned something he did not know before. He learned that in spite of Newberry's consent to the alliance, he did not trust some of the syndicate leaders—chiefly Frank Nitti, who was Al Capone's business manager,

THE BIG PARADE

and now virtual leader of the syndicate, and Lefty Louie Campagna, Capone's lieutenant.

Newberry felt that a large part of his troubles resulted from the activities of these two and their friends. He told Gus he believed that they had been "muscling in" on the North Side at his expense.

Since the present business channels were not productive of much revenue, Gus conceived the idea of opening a place, or a series of places, catering exclusively to those people who still had money and were spending it.

So, in spite of discouraging business conditions, he opened the luxurious Chez Paree night club, which is still flourishing in Chicago and is one of the favorite night spots of the elite. [The Chez Paree was a reincarnation of the Gold Coast club formerly called the Chez Pierre at Ontario Street and Fairbanks Court, where, author Rose Keefe learned, Bugs Moran had been winged in an assassination attempt on January 13, 1929. This was also about the time that surveillance of Moran's North State Street place began and Jack McGurn had gone into hiding, setting the stage for the St. Valentine's Day Massacre a month later when Moran assembled his lieutenants to plan retaliation.]

AMERICA'S SMARTEST THEATRE RESTAURANT

CHEZ PAREE, 610 FAIRBANKS COURT, CHICAGO, ILL.

Although Gus was a heavy stockholder and the club virtually was under his direct management, his name was never linked with it publicly.

He received dividends on both the cabaret on the main floors, and the gambling casino. The managers at that time were the same men who operate the club at present, and they too collected a percentage of the proceeds.

The syndicate received a share only on the casino, but on account of the interest in that concession, insisted on putting syndicate men in the gambling rooms.

This setup convinced Ted Newberry that he was about to be toppled from his North Side throne, since he was not permitted to run his own business interests. He realized that the syndicate now had a foothold and that without doubt he would be forced out.

He brooded on this until he became morbid, and in his own defense plotted the overthrow of the man he believed responsible for his predicament—Frank Nitti.

This he knew could be accomplished only by Nitti's death, and he also knew that if the attempt could be traced back to him the other members of the syndicate would exact retribution.

I do not know the exact mechanics of his plan. Possibly he laid damaging information before personal friends in the police department.

At any rate on December 19, 1932, Detective Sergeant Harry Lang and a raiding squad forced an entry to Nitti's office, and under the guise of confiscating his papers, indulged in gunplay.

Nitti was seriously wounded by several bullets from Lang's gun, and the sergeant suffered a wound in the arm.

Nitti did not die, and was hailed into court. He said Lang smashed his way into the office, drew a gun and started firing. Lang said Nitti fired the first shot in an effort to prevent him from removing some papers from his desk.

Lang was the loser in the court tilt, and was forced to resign from the police department.

Nitti apparently knew what it was all about, for the North Side immediately was plunged into a state of guerilla warfare. There were no killings of major importance, but places were bombed, and several "small fry" got "one way tickets." There was no doubt in Nitti's mind who engineered the plot against him.

It was customary for the syndicate to hold weekly meetings in Berwyn, Illinois, and Gus told me that at the first meeting following the Nitti shooting, he had to exercise all his influence to prevent the syndicate from ordering Newberry's execution without further delay.

"Ted makes his mistakes, but he's a good boy when he's normal," Gus said.

Then, too, Gus could not forget his personal friendship with Newberry.

Both of us remembered the previous New Year party at the Newberry home. As the clocks chimed midnight and the bells and whistles all over the city broke into life, Ted had drawn both Gus and me aside, and had raised his glass in a toast: "God willing we'll all be here at this time next year. Where one is, God grant we may all be."

That toast nearly was fulfilled, for I alone am left of the three.

26

NITTI'S REVENGE

The average maximum age of a man who follows a criminal career is about thirty-five years, excepting of course, those who find safety and security behind prison bars.

Naturally there are many men now living who have spent years in gangland activities, who are older. But this fact is more than offset by the hundreds of boys who fall victim to gangland guns each year.

Racketeers and gangsters themselves realize that they have little reason to expect to reach a "ripe old age."

Ted Newberry was one of these.

I often heard him say he was "living on borrowed time."

So in view of his failure to stamp out Nitti, I am sure he was aware that he was "due for a markdown."

Gus too realized he gradually was losing his fight to save Ted, but the end came much sooner than either Ted or Gus expected.

It was the evening of January 7, 1933, scarcely two weeks from the date on which Nitti was wounded, that Newberry was having dinner at our home on the fifteenth floor of an apartment house at 3300 Lake Shore Drive. It was an exclusive apartment house in an exclusive neighborhood, where we were known under Gus' alias of Michaels. Newberry had an apartment on the thirteenth floor.

Gus failed to come home for dinner, but about seven o'clock telephoned the apartment and talked to Ted. Before leaving the phone Newberry said Gus wanted to talk to me, and when I answered was instructed to go to Joe Bergl's garage in Cicero and get the letters that had been sent to Gus at that address.

After dinner Newberry went down to his apartment and I departed for Cicero. When I returned I went to the Newberry apartment to see if Gus had come there. He was not there, and neither was Ted, but I found Ralph Pierce, a member of the syndicate; Sam Hunt, a Chicago hoodlum; Davie Goldblatt [elsewhere Davie is called Benny], who worked for Gus; "Willie" Weber, a New York theatrical producer [not to be confused with County Commissioner Charles H. Weber, who later joined Winkeler in a legal beer-distributing business]; a young man employed by Gus to pilot his plane; and another of Gus' employees I knew only as "Red."

I thought it was odd that so many of Ted's friends had assembled at the Newberry apartment while Ted was out, presumably alone. All were playing cards. A short time after I sat down to watch, Ted returned, and I showed him the letters, asking if he knew where I could find Gus.

"Oh, he's out with some of the Dagoes," Ted said lightly, "he's okay." Then he turned to his guests. "Listen everybody," he announced. "I'm expecting a call, and if the phone rings no one is to answer it but me."

The phone rang a minute later.

After answering it Newberry said he was going out. As he left the thought again occurred to me that something was wrong. During the last few days Ted had never gone out alone, but here were his friends and employees, permitting him to venture out at night without escort.

I had a peculiar feeling—the same sensation I often had when I realized that my husband was in danger.

I felt so uneasy that I went up to our apartment and rehearsed everything I had seen and heard that day, trying to find a clue to Ted's unusual behavior, Gus' failure to come home, and the negligence of Ted's friends. My complete inability to discover any hint only added to my worry, which I extended to include my husband.

I attempted to sleep, but my mind seethed and I gave up and tried to calm myself by reading. But my mounting worry over Gus' safety caused me to abandon that, and by one o'clock in the morning I was pacing the floor and biting my nails. At five o'clock I was a nervous wreck, but the sound of Gus' key in the door quieted my fears for him.

One look at my husband told me something was wrong. He tried to act casual and asked me why I had not gone to bed, but I countered with the question: "Why didn't you come home?"

Joe Bergl's car dealership, adjoining Ralph Capone's Cotton Club, also provided Al Capone with an office and a safe telephone.

He sat down and I noticed his face was tired and drawn.

"I couldn't," he said simply. "The Dagoes wouldn't let me. They practically held me prisoner and if I had tried to leave somebody would have found me all shot up this morning."

Just as I was going to question him he said: "If Nellie (Newberry's girl) calls and asks you when I came in, tell her I came home early. I want to spare her as long as I can."

A horrible suspicion was aroused in my mind by this request, but before I could ask more questions the phone rang. I answered it. It was Nellie telephoning from Newberry's apartment.

"Is Gus at home?" she asked, and her voice was strained.

"Why yes, he came home early, Nellie," I lied.

"Please Georgette," she pleaded, "get Gus out of bed and send him down here. I'm terribly worried about Ted. He didn't come home all night and I want to talk to Gus right away."

I told her not to worry and I would send Gus down, then turned to him and repeated what she had said.

"I was afraid of that," Gus said soberly. "I tried my best to help him, but maybe it wasn't much use."

"Gus, "I demanded, "tell me right now what has happened to Ted,"

"I wish I knew," Gus replied, shaking his head. "I'm not sure yet myself. Maybe he's just been stepping out on Nellie, I'm not sure. Go down and calm her," he continued. "I'll be down very shortly."

As he spoke he turned toward the windows, and I could see tears gathering in his eyes. He stared out over the heaving grey waters of Lake Michigan, his hands clenched behind him.

Not having had time to learn from Gus the events of the night, I tried to make myself believe that what he had said about Ted stepping out on Nellie might be true, but the horrible conviction was growing within me that something serious had developed or Gus would not have tried so hard to save Nellie's feelings.

When I got to the Newberry apartment Willie Weber was there with a girl he had brought from New York, and in a perplexed voice he told me they had been trying to locate Ted all night without success.

Nellie was angry, for she was convinced I had lied to her about Gus coming home early the night before. She had asked the night clerk several times during the evening if Gus had come in and he had told her he had not, but I finally convinced her Gus probably was not seen when he came in.

Eventually Gus came, and after hearing what Nellie and Weber had to say, started telephoning all the places where he thought Newberry might be found. He failed to locate him but succeeded in arousing some of the North Side employees who came to the apartment.

At about eight o'clock in the morning he told the boys to come along and they would go out and try to locate Ted. I was sick with nervousness, and after they left decided to drive to the doctor's office. For some time I had been under treatment by Dr. David Omens, the same doctor who pulled Gus through his attack of intestinal influenza.

The office was located at Roosevelt Road and Independence Boulevard. I understood from Gus that Dr. Omens was physician for nearly all members of the syndicate.

The doctor was busy for some time, and I waited in the anteroom until everyone was gone.

When I entered his private office I told him all about Ted, for the doctor frequently was a visitor at the Newberry home.

Dr. Omens appeared considerably concerned and said he was mystified.

"I can't understand it," he said, "because there hasn't been any trouble that I know of."

He kept me telephoning the Newberry apartment asking for news.

On my last call when the maid took down the receiver I could plainly hear Nellie screaming and the blood froze in my veins. Apparently Nellie knew I was on the wire, for she rushed to the phone crying: "Georgette, oh Georgette, please hurry home."

I tried to answer. I wanted to find out what had happened and if Gus had returned, but my tongue clove to the roof of my mouth, and I only stood making unintelligible sounds.

I was weak with fear. If something happened to Ted Newberry, then what was to prevent the same thing from happening to my husband, for they were business partners.

I collapsed in my chair, and Dr. Omens must have been alarmed, for he hastened to mix a sedative, and a few minutes later I regained my voice.

"I've got to go home right away," I said, "Nellie wants me."

"She doesn't need you that bad," the doctor said, trying to quiet me. "Sit quiet for a while. You're in no condition to drive a car. Try to collect your nerves."

He left the room and shortly returned with a glass of water which he gave me.

"Brace up," he said. "I just learned that Gus is all right."

"Thank God," I breathed fervently, "but what about Ted?"

"They just found him," he said slowly. "His body was riddled with bullets."

27

"THE INFORMER"

"Are you certain?" I gasped.

"Positively," he answered, and his voice was emphatic.

Without another word I staggered out of his office, and ran to my car. I was ill before I left the office. I had received a terrible shock while there, and how I drove from Independence Boulevard to 3300 Lake Shore Drive without being killed is a miracle. I was in a daze and do not remember one detail of the trip.

Gus was not at home. When I investigated I found the boys had taken Nellie to a place on the South Side, and were hurriedly removing Ted's belongings to an apartment at the Lincoln Park Arms where Gus and Ted maintained an office.

They knew that before long the police would be there to investigate the death of Newberry, and they did not want a shred of his property on the place.

I hurried on down to the eleventh floor of the apartment house where Mr. and Mrs. Edward Sherman live. They were good friends of both Gus and Ted. Eddie Sherman operated the fashionable Sky High Club atop the Lincoln Park Arms for Gus.

Mrs. Sherman arrived at her apartment just as I did. She had been at the beauty parlor and when her maid had telephoned her, she had left the shop before her hair was done, and like myself was nearly hysterical.

Both Mrs. Sherman and myself felt that Newberry's death might be the beginning of the end for both Gus and Eddie. Besides that she thought a great deal of Ted, who visited at the Sherman home often.

We were walking the floor in tears when Gus, Eddie and some of the boys came in.

Seeing my condition Gus took me aside and said encouragingly, "Now snap out of it and don't make yourself sick."

He assured me there was no immediate danger.

"But Gus," I argued, "if they have taken Ted they will take you next."

"Don't worry," he said. "Big Mike can take care of himself and he isn't afraid of any Dago who ever breathed. Stop crying."

I had no further opportunity to talk to him, but later in the evening we drove over to the South Side to the home of a politician who was friendly to Gus and Ted. Nellie had been taken to the politician's house. We did not return home that night, for we knew the police would want to question Gus, but instead spent the night at a hotel.

When we were alone I asked Gus if he couldn't have saved Ted.

"God, Honey," Gus said distractedly, "I did everything I could for him, but this was a showdown. If I had bucked them any further they would have finished me off last night too. They had made up their minds, and there was nothing I could do. They kept me with them all night so I couldn't warn Ted."

In answer to my question Gus said their decision to give Ted "the works" was prompted by his plot to have Nitti killed.

"What I can't understand," I said in bewilderment, "is where they got the straight dope on the plot unless some one double-crossed Ted."

"That's just about what happened," Gus replied after a minute of reflection.

"You remember when Dr. Omens was at Newberry's house a few nights ago. You remember everyone got to talking about the Nitti shooting. Maybe you noticed how interested Dr. Omens was, and how he asked Ted all kinds of questions.

"He kept everybody drinking, especially Ted, and kept dragging him off in the corner and pumping him. Well, finally Ted got pretty tight and he told him about it.

"That was what Omens had come for. He went straight to Nitti with what he had learned. Sober, Ted wouldn't have told a soul about that plot, but signed his death warrant that night with a whisky bottle.

Police Records Reveal Story
of Winkler's Rise in Crime

Gus Winkler's record as an underworld character shows how he started as a gun toting ruffian in St. Louis when he was still in his teens and rose to be the suave leader of the north side remnants of the old Capone syndicate. The police records list many major crimes in which he was accused of taking a leading role.

He was suspected of a dozen killings, extortions and bank robberies in which loot totaling millions of dollars was taken. With his pal, Fred [Killer] Burke, who is now serving a life term in Michigan for killing a policeman, Winkler was questioned concerning the Valentine day massacre in which it was believed he had a hand.

One of the Egan's Rats.

From 1920, when the St. Louis police first learned that the young hoodlum, then only 20 years old, was a member of the notorious "Egan's Rats" of that city, he never passed a year without being in police custody. It was reported that he had been a safeblower and a gangster before then.

He seemed to be almost continually in trouble with St. Louis authorities. He was sentenced to prison for burglary, assault with a deadly weapon, and felonious wounding during the years from 1920 to 1926. In 1923 he was arrested for petty larceny; in 1924 he was locked up as a suspected robber, and in 1925 he was fined $500 for carrying a gun.

A Suspect in Massacre.

In succeeding years he was arrested for gun toting and as a robbery suspect until he left St. Louis, after having become a pal of Burke. He came to attention in Chicago in 1929 as a suspect in the Valentine day massacre on North Clark street.

In September, 1930, six men with machine guns robbed a Lincoln, Neb., bank of $2,800,000 in securities. Winkler was seized for that crime the next August when the automobile in which he was riding crashed into another car in Michigan. After months of litigation Winkler, who had become dapper, calculating, and smooth tongued, won his freedom when he struck a bargain with the authorities, turned over $583,000 worth of negotiable securities taken in the bank robbery, and furnished proof that registered securities worth $2,217,000 had been destroyed by the robbers.

Takes Newberry's Place.

When Ted Newberry, who had been piloting the north side affairs of the Capone syndicate, was slain, Winkler took charge in his place. He not only took Newberry's place in the gang's affairs, but he and his blonde wife moved into the Newberry apartment at 3300 Lake Shore drive. It was there he was arrested two weeks ago in connection with the robbery of federal reserve bank mail in the loop and the killing of Policeman Miles Cunningham.

In recent years Winkler had striven to appear gentlemanly. He donned eyeglasses to give himself a more dignified air and to make less noticeable the glass eye which resulted from his Michigan auto accident. When in custody he was quiet and generally respectful to his captors. However, his outward demeanor did little to sway the police from their knowledge of his true character as a gangster.

"With that information in Dr. Omens' hands, there was nothing more I could do to save Ted. He was ripe for the mark down. From here on out keep a closed tongue in your head when you go to that doctor. He's made some cracks to me and some to other people about me."

About two weeks later I went to Dr. Omens' office again for a treatment.

"Say, is Gus mad at me?" he asked. "I haven't heard from him in a long time."

"Don't be silly," was my laughing reply.

I told Gus what the doctor had said as soon as I got home.

"The next time he says anything about it, you tell him this—," Gus said, and gave me a message for the doctor.

A week later I went to Dr. Omens' for my usual treatment.

"How's Mike?" he asked as soon as I stepped in his office, seeming to be more concerned about Gus' feeling toward him than he was about my condition.

"He's fine," I answered, "and I told him you asked if he was mad."

"What did he say?" said the doctor quickly, flushing to the roots of his hair.

I gave him Gus' message word for word: "Tell him I'm not angry, but remind him that my name is Gus Winkeler and not Ted Newberry, and Winkeler is not so easy to pump."

Thereafter I was always careful to speak respectfully of all members of the syndicate when I was in Dr. Omens' presence.

28

THE BOOM DAYS

While both the Department of Justice and Chicago authorities were investigating Ted Newberry's murder, which had been committed at Chesterton, Indiana, Gus had taken over the reigns of the great North Side and was investigating Newberry's business.

He found his friend's personal affairs in even a worse state than he had anticipated. Gus found on examination of Newberry's records that he was indebted to the Capone syndicate to the tune of about twenty-five thousand dollars, which he realized he would have to pay from the profits of his operations. This he actually did later.

In view of his new affluence, Gus also took steps to improve his social position.

He instructed all the boys to stay away from our home on Lake Shore Drive, in order to remove his home life as far as possible from the stigma of gangland. He informed them that any business they had with him should be conducted through his office in the Lincoln Park Arms.

During the boom days, people had grown to look with tolerant eyes at the suddenly acquired millions of those of the racket world, and had learned to accept the gentleman racketeer as a business and social equal.

So Gus was accepted.

He listed among his friends prominent politicians, high police officials, attorneys, theatrical people, movie stars, and famous entertainers brought to the Chicago clubs and stages. Such people frequented our home.

Gus was happy, for these were the people he had always wanted to cultivate. Quite often his business prevented him from participating in these parties, but the house was always open, whether or not he was able to be present.

It was true that Gus was at home only a small part of his time, for he had discovered that not only had he fallen heir to Ted Newberry's debts, but to his business difficulties as well.

Edgar B. (Eddie) Lebensberger, who fronted for Gus at the 225 Club, at 225 East Superior Street, another of his enterprises, was jealous of Eddie Sherman, who fronted at the Sky High.

This worried Gus for Sherman was an efficient and honest front, and tried to operate a "straight" house, and he did not want to release him just to appease Lebensberger's anger.

Running "straight" games was difficult, for the syndicate had its own men at the wheels, and I understand the games were crooked in spite of both Gus and Sherman.

Lebensberger finally got to the syndicate with the complaint that the Sky High was getting more attention than the 225 Club. As a consequence, Gus was ordered to close the Sky High to keep Lebensberger in a good humor.

With Sherman out of the way Lebensberger transferred his jealousy to the Chez Paree, the finest of the clubs operating in Chicago's Gold Coast neighborhood.

It occurred to Gus that it might satisfy Lebensberger if he had a larger club, so the 225 was closed for a time while remodeling was done at considerable expense. This did not please the syndicate, for the members knew there would be no dividends until the cost of enlarging the place had been liquidated from the proceeds.

Only the fact that Lebensberger was a good front man prompted Gus to tolerate his trouble-making.

Since Lebensberger had no room for further complaint about the appearance of his club, he now turned his attention to other items, namely, the floor shows.

If any other syndicate club in the Gold Coast had an exceptionally good act, Lebensberger insisted on the same act, or one just as good. In the interests of good business Gus usually let him have his way.

Feeling that Lebensberger now could have no objection to the Sky High, Gus reopened it and put Sherman in charge. It began to make money. But it became so popular that in two weeks Lebensberger was complaining again, and the syndicate ordered it closed.

This time Gus made no effort to reopen it. It was evident that both Lebensberger and Sherman could not operate clubs on the North Side at the same time.

Events now transpired that I believe marked the beginning of the end for Gus Winkeler.

Gus had grown farther and farther away from the syndicate since having his name removed from the Capone payroll. This was partly in the interests of amity, for he knew the foreign element in the syndicate resented the American boys.

Gus had hopes of eventually severing all direct connections with the syndicate, and going into business for himself.

Calls for him to attend the regular weekly syndicate business meetings became less and less frequent. It was at one of these meetings to which he was not invited that the syndicate decided to send a man into the North Side as an aide to Gus.

They selected Ralph Pierce, an American, and sent him to Gus with no explanations. When Gus inquired about it, he was told that he needed a bodyguard, and that Pierce was "it."

These tactics on the part of the syndicate were all too familiar to me and I began to worry.

One night while Gus and I were driving to the Chez Paree, I asked him if he trusted Pierce.

"Trust that fellow?" Gus queried, raising an eyebrow in scorn. "Not on your life. Do I look dumb?

"Listen, Honey, they can call that fellow anything they want to, but he was sent to watch me, not to guard me.

"But they aren't getting very far. I don't talk where that fellow can hear anything, and through him I do get a lot of information concerning those syndicate meetings I'm not asked to attend. Pierce is a double-crossing stool pigeon, both ways."

Gus was driving himself to the utmost to whip the North Side into shape and make it a paying proposition for the syndicate. Hardly an evening passed that did not find him at one of the clubs, either greeting friends in the cabaret, or taking part in the gambling in the casinos.

As a consequence, he became a familiar figure, and by his amiability made many new friends and acquaintances. However, some of these acquaintances were expensive. His reputation for generosity gave rise to multitudes of requests for loans or outright gifts, and he very rarely refused.

This even became noticeable to Murphy, the chauffeur.

Quite often someone who knew Gus would see his car and try to locate him through Murphy, or wait at the car until Gus returned.

Murphy told me he made it a point to know absolutely nothing of Gus's whereabouts.

"Miz Gawge," he said solemnly, "dey catches Mist' Gus goin' and comin.'"

29

A PROMISE KEPT

Gus Winkler's thirty-third birthday was approaching and for the second time I planned a party for him.

It occurred to me as I made preparations that Fate must have had a hand in making such an elaborate affair possible. For I recalled that just ten years had passed since that eventful evening in St. Louis when I gave a party in his honor of his twenty-third birthday.

It was then that he had promised me that in ten years we would have a party that would wipe out the memory of the St. Louis affair.

That had been his determination and his efforts, and as misdirected as they had been, that made it possible for me to carry out his vow.

And this party was to be so much different from the last.

Again his friends were to be invited—not friends of the St. Louis type, but the people he had promised me he would know.

I made arrangements for the dining room at the Chez Paree and issued engraved invitations to about twenty couples, and let me say that every person invited was of good family and recognized as such in Chicago.

I allowed myself a full week to make the arrangements, for the party was to be strictly formal, and consequently must be perfect in every detail. The guests were to assemble at our apartment at 3300 Lake Shore Drive and go in a group to the Chez Paree.

Expert decorators had been employed to prepare the dining room, and table decorations alone brought a bill that was staggering. Two florists worked an entire half day arranging the table decorations and flower baskets. The birthday cake with its thirty-three candles was a masterpiece of pastry art.

I used every precaution to prevent Gus from learning of the birthday party, for I intended to take him to the club with a dramatic flourish, to recall to his mind without my mentioning it, just what he had promised me in St. Louis. However, I had informed him that a number of his friends were calling at the house to wish him a happy birthday.

When the guests started to arrive at the apartment the evening of the party, a corsage of orchids was pinned on each lady by the maids in attendance. Gus was very much pleased when he saw the people who called, and I never saw him so affable and friendly.

When every guest had arrived I suggested that we all go to the club and finish the evening. The line of limousines pulled away from the curb, and shortly were emptied at the Chez Paree with a uniformed doorman officiating.

As we entered the club Ben Pollack's orchestra struck up the old familiar tune, "Happy Birthday to You," and we were greeted on all sides by old friends and acquaintances that sent their best wishes to the guest of honor.

The lavishly appointed and decorated dining room was made even more beautiful by stately ladies and perfectly groomed gentleman—all friendly and at ease with that ease that comes only from experience and breeding.

Gus Winkeler was realizing a dream. His face beamed and his eyes were moist.

Here, there was no home brew. Champagne was poured from the chilled bottles into sparking crystal goblets. At each place was an expensive favor, silver cigarette and match cases for the men and hand-painted "coasters" for the ladies.

Smart talk passed back and forth across the table during the multi-course dinner completely lacking in the smut and vulgarity that marked the St. Louis party.

I was completely repaid for my trouble as we swung into the first dance and Gus said in a husky voice: "Honey, this is the most marvelous thing that ever happened to me; it's the very thing I looked forward to all my life. I have always hoped I could reach the place where I could make up to you the suffering you've gone through in being a wife to me.

"I get the idea, and I appreciate the fact that you let me get it myself. You want me to compare this party with that other one you gave? I can't. There isn't any comparison."

I was so happy I could have cried all over the front of his starched shirt.

"I'm happy, too, Gus," I said. "But if I only knew that those old days were gone forever. I wish I could feel that this is permanent. Please, Gus, don't ever go back to the old life."

"Don't worry," he said, and we danced on in silence.

The evening was more successful than I had dared hope. Greetings came by messenger, telegraph and telephone. There was a steady stream of flowers directed to the dining room, until there was no available space left; and the atmosphere was suffocating with their heavy odor.

Friends not invited to the party, casual acquaintances, and those who wished to make a contact with my husband recognized the occasion.

Finally the hour for parting came. The guests departed with more good wishes. The limousines came to the door at the summons of the doorman, and liveried chauffeurs drove the guests to their homes.

As each car approached, I half expected that the next might be a rattletrap flivver, loaded down with wisecrackers and mobsters.

They were gone now—only politicians, attorneys, city officials, brokers, business men and their wives.

So ended the high point in the career of Gus Winkeler.

In his own way he had made good, and whatever doubts he had entertained as to the degree of his success were entirely wiped away. He had been recognized socially.

Thinking back over his hectic and troubled life in which, God knows, there was very little of actual happiness, I thank God that he was allowed to live to realize his ambitions, culminating in that party.

30

GUS AND THE PLANTED GUN

It never fails.

No sooner does a gangland character begin to assume prominence than he becomes a target for police.

This is not entirely due to the ambition of the Police Department. Quite often it is the result of public demand created when newspapers begin to ask, "Why is it?"

Gus Winkeler had become a public figure, and the public and newspapers were demanding an investigation.

Gus was wise enough to keep his operations carefully concealed. He was not personally identified with any of the clubs and syndicate properties on the North Side, although the police were convinced in their own minds of the truth of the situation: that "Big Mike" was the "King-pin."

Failing to get evidence to link him with syndicate business, the police took advantage of the same trickery that got Al Capone the gun sentence in Pennsylvania.

On April 1, 1933, he was stopped by a police squad while he and David "Benny" Goldblatt, his paymaster and personal bodyguard, were walking down the street.

He was "frisked" on the spot and meekly submitted because he had nothing to fear.

The officers found a gun under his coat.

This was extremely odd, for since taking over the North Side Gus had never been armed. That was Goldblatt's duty.

However, it also was Goldblatt's duty not to get caught with a gun, and he was wise enough to dispose of it as he saw the officers approaching.

So actually, no guns were found on either Gus or Goldblatt.

Nevertheless a charge of carrying a concealed weapon was filed against Gus and he went to trial.

The chief witness was Officer William Drury, who told the court he took the gun from Gus' pocket when he was stopped on the street. This testimony was to have been borne out by Officer George C. Kurzwelly, who told his superiors after the "shakedown" that he had seen Drury remove the gun from Gus' pocket.

The state's case was built on this testimony.

Under the cross examination by Gus' attorney, Officer Kurzwelly's testimony began to waver. He said he had not seen Drury take a gun from beneath Gus' coat. And that all he saw was Drury standing beside Gus with a gun in his hand. Asked if he was sure it was a gun, he wavered again and said he wasn't sure—that he saw Drury with "something" in his hand and that it might have been a gun.

He told the court that all he knew about it was that Drury said that he had taken a gun from Gus, and later amplified that by explaining he had been instructed to say he saw Drury get the gun.

Although Kurzwelly told the truth, the authorities were so determined to frame Gus that he was found guilty and sentenced to serve a year in jail.

Of course my husband's attorney appealed the case, and this appeal was pending when Gus was killed.

Because he would not perjure himself on the witness stand and preferred to tell the truth rather than what he had been instructed to tell, Kurzwelly was dismissed from the Police Department.

Many believed that the officer had been "bought off" by Gus' attorney in an effort to beat the case.

Gus supposed that the case would put a stop to further embarrassment by the police, but he was badly mistaken. They continued to harass him.

They knew his car, and they knew Murphy, the chauffeur, and they never failed to stop him when they saw him on the street. This is an old police custom in Chicago. A police character known to have money is stopped by every passing squad car and he is threatened with an overnight sojourn in jail, followed by an experience in the lineup the next morning.

Whether the officers are ordered to make life miserable for men like Gus, or whether it is a private shakedown, I cannot say. But I do know that Gus was too busy to be bothered spending his nights in jail, so he paid off, and each time it cost him from a hundred to two hundred dollars.

The occasion that angered him most was when he was stopped in a fashionable quarter of the city and his captors demanded five hundred dollars, figuring he would pay off in a hurry rather than take a chance being seen by his society friends dickering with the police.

Gus was stubborn and put up an argument, saying he did not have that much money. The officers did not believe him, so he pulled out a roll of bills from a side pocket and showed them he had just a little less than three hundred dollars.

As a matter of fact, Gus was carrying several thousand dollars in a purse inside his coat, but feared a more serious loss if he exhibited it.

However, the officers agreed to reduce the demand to three hundred, which was still a little more than Gus had shown them. When Gus argued the amount was still beyond his reach, they suggested he borrow the difference.

This he finally agreed to do. He entered a fashionable gambling house maintained in a nearby residence and got the rest of the money from his purse.

"I should have reported them at headquarters," Gus said when he told me about it.

Gus felt that his status could be improved if he could get a dismissal of the Louisville robbery charge still booked against him, and the Jefferson, Wisconsin, bank robbery in November, 1929, in which he had been identified while in the St. Joseph, Michigan, hospital. He was not guilty of either of them.

The Louisville case was dim on the records, so it required no great sum to settle it out of court. I believe this was possible largely because the authorities realized they could never get a conviction in a fair trial.

The Jefferson settlement was more difficult. Someone interested in the case apparently was low on cash and determined to recoup out of Gus' pocketbook. As Christmas approached Gus decided to do something which he sarcastically described as "proving his good will."

"I'm going to have to play Santa Claus to those monkeys anyway, so I might as well make it good," he said.

So he bought a large diamond ring and sent it to a man in Jefferson, presumably as a peace offering. The ring was never returned, indicating a tacit agreement that the charge would be "fixed."

The gift was followed by $10,000 and Gus never again heard of the case.

I asked a number of questions of people in Jefferson, a manufacturing town of about three thousand, on a recent visit there. I found to my surprise that Gus Winkeler was not mentioned in connection with the case. People there told me they thought Killer Burke was guilty.

That gave me an idea. I went to the courthouse and looking in the records, failed to find where any charge had ever been filed against my husband. Neither was there any official record that $10,000 had been received; this sum had been taken to Jefferson personally by "Little Bobby," Gus' bookkeeper.

I often wondered how the man who wore the diamond ring ever explained to his friends how he came to own it.

But to get back, Gus and I were highly pleased that the records had been cleared. My husband had an ambitious program for the development of the North Side, and now could proceed with fewer restrictions.

It was about this time that Gus met Judge Thomas A. Green, the judge who had convicted him for carrying a concealed weapon.

I understand he visited Green at his home and they became friends. At any rate Gus told me that he had talked the case over with the judge.

Judge Green is a gentleman, Gus said, and would be as good a judge as politics would let him.

31

LEGAL BEER AT LAST

Gus was indefatigable in his efforts to make the North Side a paying proposition.

He worked day and night managing the affairs of the syndicate to the best advantage, and developing plans of his own for private enterprises.

As I have said before, it was his intention to relinquish the syndicate business as soon as he was sufficiently entrenched in his own interests.

Demands on his time increased constantly, as intricate details of his business increased in volume. The job was too big for one man, but Gus would not entrust the major problems to lieutenants, permitting only the minor details to be handled by employees.

For his convenience in his infrequent visits at the apartment, he had a telephone outlet installed in every room. The bell was ringing constantly, and the butler would hand Gus the phone as often as ten times during dinner.

It was with considerable alarm one evening that I noticed his car was trailed closely by the Lincoln Park Police squad cruiser as he drew up in front of his house.

"Why the cops?" I inquired the instant he entered the apartment.

"Oh, that's just an escort," he explained lightly.

"Do you need one?" I asked pointedly, watching his expression for some sign that might betray a secret fear.

"Don't you worry," he replied, laughing again. "The boys are only trying to protect me from something that won't happen."

"Well, I think it's darn nice of the police to offer you protection, whether you think you need it or not," I said. "After all, lots of little fish have grown up before they've been caught, and I'll never forget what happened to Ted Newberry."

That time I caught Gus napping, for I could detect a shadow cross his countenance. He walked away without answering.

I was sure that Gus feared some impending danger and whether or not he feared it, it was present or the police would not have troubled to protect him. I made it a point to watch after that, and a squad car always accompanied him home.

Gus was enthusiastic over the repeal of the prohibition.

"It's a New Deal for me, Honey," he told me one night. "This will be big business and it'll be legitimate. A man can do business now and hold his head up. No more alky wars, thank God. That's thug stuff and I don't like it. You can't be a gentleman and handle alcohol. It's dirty stuff—dirty as dope as far as the methods in handling it go. There's a big profit and quick money in handling it, that's why all the strong-arm boys have been in it."

It was a fact that Gus had instructed his employees not to get "tough." It was true there were some strong-arm men in his organization, but they were not there to lead raids into new territory. They were hired to protect the property operated by Gus and the syndicate from the marauding bands of guerilla gangsters.

So far as he was able Gus tried to operate like any other business man. I have often heard him say: "I'd rather make a deal than make a mess."

In preparing for the advent of legal "3.2," a beverage which is now history, Gus was inaugurating a new enterprise of his own. It was a beer distributing plant located at 1414 Roscoe Street.

The building had been completely equipped for the business, and a fleet of trucks had been obtained to make deliveries. Gus told me he bore the entire expense of setting up the business, including purchase of the trucks.

Here, again, he took great care that he not be identified with the business for fear he might give it a bad name in some quarters. To make it strictly legitimate he acquired the services of Cook County Commissioner Charles H. Weber, who acted as his "front" and continued to operate the place after his death.

As his share in the operation of the enterprise, Weber received twenty-five per cent of the net proceeds. Charles Conrad, Weber's friend and first assistant, received a smaller amount. I believe it was ten or fifteen per cent.

These two men practically operated the business alone, but at no time functioned without orders from Gus, or without first asking his advice.

Gus and Weber pulled every political and business string available to get the first beer released in Chicago. Gus later told me they succeeded and that the first deliveries in the city were made from 1414 Roscoe Street.

On the first night there was such a demand for the legal beverage Gus found he had not employed enough men. There was no time to employ all the additional men needed. Gus took over operation of a truck, and with Davie Goldblatt at his side, made deliveries like any of the other truck hands.

This was dangerous, for any man high in racket-land is marked. And to have ventured out with even a bodyguard was taking a long chance.

But this act was indicative of Gus' enthusiasm for his business. He came home late the next morning, dirty, bedraggled, almost completely exhausted, but happy as a child with a new toy.

"This place is going to boom," he said as he threw himself on the bed and dropped off promptly into deep sleep.

If it hadn't Gus would have closed it immediately, with as little loss as possible. For when he miscalculated on money-making possibilities of an enterprise, he always closed it up with the remark, "That's that," which to him was the end of it.

Not all of his places of business were closed voluntarily, however. Trouble was always present in the gambling operations at the Chez Paree, 225 Club, or some other casino. The police were always inclined to look with tolerance at these clubs, catering to the wealthy, but occasionally some patron would be trimmed so thoroughly he would put up a "beef" to the authorities.

The police did not object to crooked gambling, but when the games got too raw they could be counted on to put in a prompt appearance and order the place closed.

Gus, too, disapproved of crooked gambling, but in that respect was forced to bow to the syndicate. And he had means of raking their chestnuts out of the fire in such matters. The "rake" was Moe Rosenberg, Gus' "fixer" who waved the magic wand of money and influence, and always succeeded in re-opening a closed club.

Moe had a reserved table at the Chez Paree, just as Gus did, and every Sunday night he would be waiting to talk things over. Gus and Rosenberg were very close, because Gus trusted him.

However, although responsible for the closing of the gaming clubs, the syndicate never failed to kick about the expense of getting them reopened.

Frank Nitti, Frankie Reo, and Lefty Louie Campagna were what are commonly but aptly known as "money hogs."

They wanted everything coming in and as little as possible going out. These three were attempting to fill Al Capone's shoes, and were succeeding very poorly. They lacked Capone's business sense, and were prompted by different motives.

Nitti, Reo, and Lefty Louie were money-crazy. It was not money Capone was after, it was power, and as his influence increased he became drunk with it and fought for more.

Capone had no regard for money except as a business necessity and a personal convenience. Gus told me that on more than one occasion Capone gave handouts to so many panhandlers that when he left his office he had to borrow five or ten dollars from one his employees to get a taxi home.

The income tax agents who finally succeeded in sending him to prison for tax evasion discovered that of the millions he had made, Capone had little left but debts. For months before he finally was arrested he had been pawning his wife's jewels, he owed for two sixteen-cylinder cars he had bought and on which he had never made a payment, and he had to borrow to meet installments on his Florida residence.

The new triumvirate complained loudly as Ralph Pierce, their stool pigeon on the North Side, reported some of Gus' so-called extravagances. Pierce was with Gus every night and knew what took place.

But there was little the Italians could do. The club operators had been tipped that Pierce was a stool pigeon and they treated him as such. And while the Dagoes were bitter, they feared Jack White, Johnny Moore, and others of Gus' American friends.

32

GUS WINKELER AND THE
NEW NORTH SIDE

Returning to the apartment one evening I heard the low hum of men's voices in our sitting room and turned aside into my own room rather than disturb Gus and his guest.

In a few minutes the maid knocked at my door and said my husband wanted me immediately.

I went to the front room and much to my surprise was greeted by George Goetz, Gus' former companion in many escapades, who I had not seen for months. Naturally I was glad to see George and he seemed glad to see me, although it was evident he was laboring under a strain.

I inquired about Mrs. Goetz and we talked over many of our experiences together, recalling trifling incidents that had seemed terribly important when they had occurred.

We were still deep in conversation when the dinner hour approached, and because Gus did not seem to mind, I invited Goetz to stay for dinner. He accepted.

I was mystified at Gus' seeming unconcern that Goetz had called at our home. For as I have already said, when he became Boss of the North Side he gave strict orders that none of the syndicate men and none of his own employees were to call at our apartment.

He considered this absolutely essential in building up his reputation as a gentleman.

This rule was maintained so strictly that as far as I can remember, Goetz was the only man connected with the underworld that Gus ever admitted to our apartment at 3300 Lake Shore Drive.

It was Gus' fastidious attitude in such matters that caused one Chicago newspaper to dub him "a well-mannered gentleman of the clique."

It was the same attention to such apparently trivial details that caused Alexander Jamie, director of the Secret Six, in a series of articles written by himself for a national newspaper syndicate concerning the work of his anti-crime organization, to say: "Gus Winkeler is the smoothest and most suave crook to ever operate in Chicago."

That is why my mystification at the letting down of the bars was with me throughout the evening, and when Goetz left late that night I asked for an explanation.

"I admit I slipped a little," my husband explained. "I don't approve of his coming here, but after all, you can't turn your back on an old friend like George Goetz. I knew it must be a matter of vital importance to George or he wouldn't have dared to come here.

"The truth is," Gus went on, "George is getting into hot water."

Gus seemed inclined to let it go at that, but I pressed him for further information.

"Well, if you must know, George is interested in some stolen bonds," I was told. "He wouldn't have dared touch them if Al Capone were here, but you know how things are now. A gang from the Twin Cities [St. Paul and Minneapolis] has these bonds, and George thinks there's a big turnover.

"Of course, that's George's business if he wants to get mixed up with them, but I've been off that racket for a long time and I don't want to be dragged into it again." That was the last I heard of the bonds until a few nights later when Gus came home, upset and worried.

He paced the floor with one hand in his pocket, the other rubbing the back of his bent head—a gesture that always meant he was faced with a worrisome problem.

"Well, what's wrong now?" I demanded.

Gus literally "blew up."

"Plenty," he snapped. "It's those damned bonds George Goetz was telling me about. That paper is going to get me into a hell of a spot."

"I don't see how," I answered, "you aren't trying to handle any of them, are you?"

"Hell, no, of course not, but that damn fool Eddie Lebensberger is dipping into that deal, and mark my words, he's going to get in one swell jam.

"Lebensberger don't know enough about that racket to try to do anything with it, but he's seen it done by others and he thinks he's going to make some easy money.

"Any money you make with stolen bonds isn't easy. The government is trailing these bonds like nobody's business, and as sure as Fate, Eddie is going to go to jail if he don't bail out in a hurry.

"I can't afford to have him go to jail right now, and if he wasn't such a fool he ought to know that if he gets mixed up in trouble like that it's going to cost him the biggest chance he ever had to make good in his business.

"Right now I need him worse at the 225 Club than I ever did before. On top of that, I've signed a lease for the old Opera Club and have been spending every dime I could lay my hands on to remodel it and decorate it to get it open as soon as I can.

"Here I've been working for months to open a regular cabaret of my own to be run on the level, and Lebensberger was the man I was to going to put in to operate it, for if anyone can make a success of it, he can.

"But, my God, a man running a high class place like this one can't afford to get publicly mixed up in a racket. You can't get decent people in a place they know is operated by a bunch of gangs.

"It burns me up to see Eddie making such a fool of himself, letting me down too, because I have been counting on him and nobody else. If Lebensberger don't run this new place, I've just thrown away all the my money I've put in it, for I'll never open it.

"He's throwing away the best chance he ever had, just to play with hot bonds. You can't fool with that stuff."

Gus knew what he was talking about, but even he did not suspect the serious outcome of the bond deal. Neither did Lebensberger.

But troubles come in different forms, and unknown to Gus, new ones were being forged at that very moment.

33

THE KANSAS CITY MASSACRE

The newspapers of June 17, 1933, were filled with the news of the killing of four officers in front of the Union Depot in Kansas City, Missouri, in a gangland effort to free Frankie Nash, their prisoner. Nash also was killed in the gunplay.

The papers described the massacre as a "Heinous crime," showing gangland's utter disregard for the majesty of the law. Editorially the papers insisted that the slayers be run to earth at any cost. The news stories vouchsafed the opinion of authorities that Harvey Bailey was one of the men who wielded a machine gun.

On the surface this appeared to be the truth, for Nash was one of Bailey's gangsters who had escaped with him from Leavenworth Prison where he had been serving a twenty-five year sentence for attacking a mail custodian.

Naturally, Gus and I were interested in the case since we knew Bailey, and also were acquainted with Frankie Nash, a bald gangster of middle age known affectionately among his friends as "Jelly."

We read everything the papers had to say.

It seems that Nash had fled from Leavenworth to Hot Springs, Arkansas, where he contacted his wife, set up a respectable home, donned a wig and raised a moustache to conceal his identity.

But somebody had squealed, and Nash was arrested in a Hot Springs speakeasy without a struggle.

Officers immediately started to move him to Leavenworth, realizing that in hastening they might avoid an effort by his pals to release him.

But gangland was informed. As the officers left the Union Depot with their prisoner and started across the Grand Concourse in front of the station to enter their waiting auto a fusillade of shots rang out and the officers fell.

Raymond J. Caffery, Department of Justice operative, Otto Reed, McAlister, Oklahoma sheriff, and Frank Hermanson and W. J. Grooms, Kansas City detectives, fell mortally wounded. F. J. Bailey, a government agent, was less seriously wounded. Nash was shot down right in the door of the car.

Amid a hail of bullets from the guns of the wounded officers, a nearby car hurtled away from the curb, and the assassins escaped.

Nobody but the swashbuckling Harvey Bailey would ever have undertaken such a desperate enterprise, the papers maintained.

"What a smear," Gus commented as we finished reading. "I'm glad I'm not mixed up in it."

The telephone rang, and Gus answered it. He talked for several minutes and after hanging up he turned to me with a mystified look on his face.

"That was Joe Bergl calling me from the garage," he said. "He says some woman has been calling him all morning asking how to get in touch with me. Of course he wouldn't tell her, then she asked him to have me meet her at a dress-making shop. He said the woman told him it was very important, so I guess I'd better go."

"Think it over," I begged. "It might be a setup."

"Oh, I don't think so, but it's worth thinking about," Gus said. "Why don't you go and find out who it is and what she wants. If it's really on the level and pretty important, I'll see her."

That was satisfactory to me and I left at once.

Arriving at the dress shop I was surprised to find Verne Miller's wife, Vivian, accompanied by her small daughter. Mrs. Miller was in tears and almost hysterical. She said she had to see Gus, but I told her he was very busy and I would take her message to him.

She was filled with fear, and words flowed over each other as she told me that her husband had engineered the Kansas City massacre, and was fleeing for his life.

"Good gracious woman," I said, moved to pity in spite of the horribleness of the crime, "has Verne gone crazy?"

Then she told me what had happened.

Someone had telephoned Chicago as soon as Nash was caught. They talked to Louis "Doc" Stacci, a personal friend of Nash's, who operated a tavern in Melrose Park, which I have said before was a hideout for criminals.

The first Miller knew of the Nash capture was when Stacci telephoned from Chicago to his house in Kansas City and told him that the officers were bringing Nash through Kansas City.

As far as I could learn from Vivian Miller, the gangland telegraph had been kept hot as the underworld pulled all its strings to learn the route to be taken by the Nash convoy, and the arrival times. Mrs. Miller said Stacci told her husband there was no time to lose if he wanted to catch the guards at the station.

Miller had no time to get help. He seized the guns and was going to undertake the feat single-handed, in spite of tearful protests from his wife.

At that moment, into their house walked the notorious and much-sought Charles "Pretty Boy" Floyd, escaped convict and natural-born killer. Floyd had been living in Kansas City, knew Miller well, and also Nash. Floyd was recently killed by police near Liverpool, Ohio.

The attempt to free Nash appeared impossible even to the calculating and stone-hearted Floyd.

"You're crazy," Mrs. Miller said Floyd told her husband when he had heard the plan. "No one man can pull a job like that and even have a piper's chance. Man, you might just as well forget it."

"Crazy or not," Miller replied as he strapped on his guns, "I'm going to try it. If I catch 'em by surprise maybe I can get away with it."

Floyd tried to argue with him but to no avail.

Seeing that Miller was determined to go through with it, Floyd suddenly said: "All right, you damn fool, I'll go with you."

They drove to the station, spotted the car provided for Nash and the guards, and parked nearby. No sooner had they settled down to wait than the quarry came down across the concourse toward the car. When they were in easy range, Miller and Floyd unleashed murder from the machine guns.

The officers fell, while their blood ran down the curb and into the gutter. Those not killed instantly pulled their revolvers from holsters and started to return the fire. Nash, just preparing to enter the car, appeared to freeze.

Angered at the delay, Miller leaned from the car and shouted in a frenzy, "Run, Frankie, run."

His soul filled with bloodlust, Miller apparently went crazy. His gun belched death again and Nash toppled to the pavement. The gang car raced away and by a winding route returned to the Miller bungalow.

Floyd had been shot in the arm and Miller and his wife dressed the wound. As they worked Verne told Floyd it burned him up because Nash "stalled around" instead of taking advantage of the opportunity to escape, so he "just shot him."

Miller and Floyd "took it on the lam" as soon as the wound was dressed. Mrs. Miller telephoned a friend, who was not connected in any way with gangland, and had him drive her and the child to a nearby town, where she caught a train to Chicago and was to meet her husband later.

However, the friend had noticed the bloodstains in the house and later reported the matter to police, which identified Miller as one of the slayers.

When Vivian Miller's sob-broken recital was finished I said: "What do you want with Gus?"

"I want his help," she replied tearfully, "I want him to do anything he can."

At no time had Mrs. Miller mentioned Adam Richetti, Floyd's companion who was arrested at Liverpool, Ohio, when Floyd was killed, although the police are now trying to prove he was a party to the massacre.

The Kansas City Massacre of 1933

The Kansas City Massacre led to the creation of the FBI.

That's a simplification offered by the Bureau and it skips the politics of the day, but it involved Gus Winkeler to the extent that he knew most of the hoodlums involved in the murders, including the man who staged them and afterward sought his help when on the run in Chicago.

The kidnap-murder of the Lindbergh baby the previous year had so outraged the American public that it forced Congress to make kidnapping a federal crime. This called for action by the Justice Department's little-known Bureau of Investigation, despite a warning by President Herbert Hoover's attorney general that "You are never going to end crime in this country by having the Federal Government step in."

When Franklin Delano Roosevelt became president in 1933 he took the opposite position. He called crime a "national problem requiring a federal solution," and his attorney general, Homer Cummings, used the Kansas City Massacre to declare the country's first "War on Crime." He sent Congress a "Twelve-Point Program" of federalized crime control that took the public's mind off urban gang crime (thanks mainly to the imprisonment of Capone and the repeal of Prohibition with its urban gang wars) and replaced these with an exciting new game of cops 'n' robbers.

J. Edgar Hoover had been appointed acting director of the Justice Department's notoriously corrupt Bureau of Investigation in 1924 on his promise to clean up the agency. He depoliticized it by throwing the rascals out and handpicking eager young lawyers and accountants who

originally had to content themselves with enforcing antitrust
cases, "obscenity" laws (enacted
under the old Comstock Act,
which also banned condoms and
abortion information), the trafficking in prizefight films (a bizarre Congressional response to a
black heavyweight's victory over a
white man in a 1908 World Cham-
pionship fight), and the Mann
Act, which prohibited interstate
prostitution.

Frank Nash.

The Bureau's most conspicuous role before 1932 and the new
"Lindbergh Law" was combat-
ing interstate car theft (the Dyer
Act of 1919), which amounted to
facilitating the return of cars stolen in one state and recovered in
another. At the time the federal
agents were deemed an "inves-
tigative body" and could neither
carry guns nor make arrests without permission of local authorities.

Verne Miller.

The Kansas City Massacre
changed all that. It involved a
bungled attempt to rescue a federal fugitive, and it constituted
the first deliberate killing of four lawmen, including a federal agent, as
well as the fugitive whom the gunmen were supposed to rescue. That
crime—combined with ransom kidnappings by Machine Gun Kelly
and the Barker-Karpis gangs that same year, and the headline-making
bank robberies by the newly formed Dillinger Gang—helped overcome
state's-rights opposition to most of Cummings's proposals. By the sum-

Scene of the Kansas City Massacre.

mer of 1934 federal crimes included the robbing of federally insured banks, interstate flight to avoid prosecution, the killing of federal officers, interstate transportation of stolen property, and other crimes that could be construed as interfering with interstate commerce.

To complicate things at Hoover's end, his "Bureau" soon was expanded into a "Division of Investigation" that included "revenuers" tasked to enforce the country's Dry laws that had thoroughly corrupted both the police and politicians. Until Roosevelt made good on his promise of Repeal, Hoover feared that his few hundred squeaky clean agents would be confused with the thousands of poorly trained, inept, crooked, and trigger-happy Prohibition enforcers who also were "federal agents." He solved this problem through the creation of a Division of Investigation that segregated the Dry-law men from his "G-men," a term supposedly coined by Machine Gun Kelly when he was arrested in Memphis in September of 1933 and cried, "Don't shoot, G-Men! Don't shoot!" (The FBI has since acknowledged that this was cooked up by Hoover.)

Thus was born the "G-Man," immediately celebrated in magazines, in movies, and on the radio, especially when the Division of Investigation became the Federal Bureau of Investigation after taking out not only Kelly but also John Dillinger, Pretty Boy Floyd, Baby Face Nelson, Fred and Ma Barker, and every other interstate desperado of the day. (Except for Bonnie and Clyde; an ex–Texas Ranger got to them first.)

In the case of the Kansas City Massacre, Gus Winkeler knew most of the suspects from his earlier days in the robbery business, including Verne Miller, who had led the rescue attempt. Miller quickly became the object of a nationwide manhunt and was the last person Winkeler wanted anything to do with. Miller's wife, Vivian, contacted Georgette, begging her to ask Gus to help her husband, but he adamantly refused and through Buck Kempster helped G-man Melvin Purvis try to locate Miller.

At the time of the Kansas City killings, Georgette got her information initially from the newspapers and later from Vivian Mathis, Miller's

Police, bystanders, and two victims of the Kansas City Massacre.

"paramour," as the Bureau liked to call women to whom someone might or might not be married. Georgette's version of the massacre was mistaken on several points.

Frank Nash was a fugitive bank robber who had been recaptured in Hot Springs, Arkansas, and was being returned to Leavenworth by a sheriff and several armed guards, including a federal agent, who were attacked at Kansas City's Union Depot. The rescue attempt involved at least two men with Thompsons who may well have thought that such a surprise display of submachine guns would cause Nash's guards, armed only with pistols and shotguns, to say the hell with it, throw up their hands, and let their captive go. The attack might have been bloodless, but evidence later surfaced that the federal agent in the back seat of a

Bureau car had been handed a quirky riot gun by Chief Otto Reed. It was a Model 1897 Winchester whose hammer did not remain cocked if an excited shooter jacked in a round while also pressing the trigger, but would fire the shell it had just chambered.

So when the agent saw the machine-gunners shouting "Up! Up! Up!" he instinctively pumped in a round in the chamber and the gun went off, killing Nash, who was in the front seat, and setting off a roaring gun battle. Moreover, Reed had loaded his shells not with lead buckshot but with steel ball-bearings, some of which were found in other members of the guard team—victims of "friendly fire" that now was being returned by the equally surprised attackers.

Vivian told Georgette that that one of the shooters had been hit in the shoulder and was patched up at their house on Edgevale before the group took flight, and she said it was Floyd. But when Floyd was killed on an Ohio farm in October, 1934, medical examiners found no such wound, raising the possibility that a third gunman had been hit. The other shooter probably was Adam Richetti, Floyd's partner, who eventually went to the chair proclaiming his innocence—insisting he had been too hung-over that morning to participate in the rescue attempt.

In any case, Miller was nearly caught in an FBI trap at the Sherone Apartments in Chicago in November 1933, and on 29th of that same month his nude and beaten body was found in a Detroit ditch—obviously the work of other gangsters.

On the seventy-fifth anniversary of the shooting, in 2008, the *Kansas City Star* revisited the event in great detail that included a new finding by crime-scene investigators who somehow determined that the bloodstains under an upstairs carpet were not Floyd's. The current Edgevale residents remarked that they rather enjoy living in a house that had once belonged to a famous gangster.

34

GUS AND THE "MILLER MASSACRE"

When I told Gus what Mrs. Miller had told me, we discussed the matter from all angles and tried to advance a logical reason why Miller killed Nash.

"Nash didn't ask for help and that's why he didn't run," was Gus' belief. "Nash's friends won't like that a little bit. If Miller knows what is good for him he'd better stay out of Chicago."

When I asked him if he intended to help Miller through his wife, he said: "Of course not, it's no affair of mine. Miller is not only sought by the police, but probably some of the Bailey gang would like to meet him too. Anybody who tries to help him will be on the spot plenty."

Gus dismissed the matter from his mind, and I supposed Mrs. Miller would seek other sources of aid.

Several days later Gus mentioned to me that Joe Bergl had telephoned and told him that someone had been trying to locate him and wanted to meet him in a hotel apartment on Broadway. Gus casually mentioned that he intended to visit the address.

I objected at once.

"That's a setup to put you on the spot," I insisted. "If anyone keeps that appointment it'll be me."

The shadow of Ted Newberry was with me constantly, and I intended to do everything in my power to prevent the same finish for my husband.

Gus tried to laugh away my fears, but I remained firm and we argued for some time.

At last Gus said, "Well, I'll admit this sounds funny, so you go ahead and go, but be careful. You know what to do, just use your head."

He gave me the address of the hotel on Broadway and I drove to the place. I drove past the building, circling the block several times, but could see nothing indicating a trap. Partly assured, I left the car about three blocks away and walked to the hotel, making a mental note of every parked car and every loafing pedestrian. I walked past the building once before making sure it was safe for me to enter.

Satisfied that if there was any danger it was within, I walked directly through the lobby, not wishing to have the clerk announce me. I wanted to have the advantage of surprise. I walked upstairs and sought the room. For several minutes I stood with my ear pressed against the door panel, hoping to hear voices that would give me advance information of the occupants. There were no sounds.

Then I reached for the knob, grasping it firmly in my palm to prevent a rattle or vibration. It turned easily, and a bit at a time I finally disengaged the bolt. Placing the tips of the fingers of one hand against the door and continuing to hold the knob to prevent it from snapping, I pushed gently until the door swung open about an inch and I was able to look into the room.

I could see the entire room. Three men I had never seen before were lounging about reading, unaware they were being watched. None appeared to be armed.

Sure of that fact, I gave the door a quick thrust and stepped in, holding it open with my foot.

"I'm Gus Winkeler's wife," I said shortly as the three sprang to their feet in alarm. "Who wants him?"

"Mrs. Winkeler?" one of the men stuttered, taken off his feet by the suddenness of my appearance.

"That's what I said. Who wants him?"

"Just a minute," the spokesman replied, regaining a degree of his composure. "Verne Miller's wife is here. I'll call her. Won't you sit down?"

"I'll stand," I said, keeping my position in the doorway as the three withdrew.

In less than a minute Vivian Miller appeared through another door and looked at me in surprise.

"Well, what do you want now?" I demanded.

She took a step toward me before she spoke. "I've got to have money and a place to hide, that's why I wanted Gus," she said desperately.

"So that's it," I replied angrily. "Well, you listen to me, and this is straight from Gus to you. Gus Winkeler will not do a thing for you or anyone else connected with the Kansas City massacre. Gus Winkeler does not intend to get mixed up in that mess.

"Gus has only advice for Verne Miller, and that is, stay away from him and out of Chicago."

"Please Georgette," she pleaded, wringing her hands, "have Gus do something for Verne. Oh, if I could only talk to him I'm sure I could get his help. Just tell me where he is."

"Vivian, I've given you Gus' answer and that's all there is to say," I told her. "Gus wouldn't help Verne anyway, he doesn't know where Verne is. That reminds me—where is he?"

"I really don't know," Mrs. Miller said, "but if Gus won't help Verne, maybe he'll do him this favor. At least you can take him this message."

"Oh, alright, what is it?" I said impatiently.

"There's a rooming house just back of the Leland Hotel," she resumed. "You go in the door and up to the second floor, then back to the far end of the hall. There are three steps up that take you to a room on the right. In that room is a man who knows too much. Verne wants Gus to go up to that room and 'take' him. He's always there."

"So that's the favor your husband wants mine to do," I said, white with anger. "There's only one answer to that—Verne Miller is insane."

I stepped backward and pulled the door shut, leaving her alone in the room with her troubles.

My face burned with anger, but deep in my heart I was sorry for her, and more sorry for her little daughter. They were not responsible for Verne Miller's misdeeds. The look of tired suffering on Vivian Miller's face had wrung my heart.

I could not blame her for using every subterfuge to aid her husband. I imagined myself in her place, and I knew to what lengths I would have gone to help Gus.

By the time I stepped into the street, I was certain in my own mind that if Gus Winkeler had gone to that room instead of me, Verne Miller would have put in an appearance.

Gus listened intently and without comment as I recited my visit, but when I told him about the request for him to invade the rooming house back of the Leland Hotel, he flew into a rage.

"The rats," he said, his eyes gleaming and his voice harsh with rage. "The dirty rats. There's only two ways to figure that proposition. They'd either get me in that boardinghouse and slug me for what money I carried, or they'd get me in there and bump me off just go get even.

"I hope they catch that tramp. He's not even a hoodlum, he's a madman." [Presumably it was shortly after this that Winkeler, through his friend Buck Kempster and to the alarm of Frank Nitti, began secretly providing the Bureau of Investigation with leads in its search for Miller, who he believed, from Vivian's account, had simply lost his temper and killed his friend Frank Nash deliberately. When Miller was located at the Sherone Apartments by federal agents, it was their state-liaison man Kempster who used a machine gun to fire at the car in which Miller escaped.]

35

BEGINNING OF THE END

Gus Winkeler's difficulties were pyramiding, and looking back at those last few hectic days, they seem like some vague awful dream—not horrible enough to waken the sleeper, but grimly unpleasant.

My comfortable surroundings, plenty of money, the absence of those underworld figures that once had been an integral part of my daily life, had lulled me into a sense of security that I now realize was completely false.

My husband, in closer contact with gangland than I was, must have felt that his career was reaching a climax. Now that I reflect back over his actions and words, and analyze carefully, I can see that he was not quite himself.

His mounting troubles, only slightly reflected in his attitude when in my presence, came to me only in a hazy, unreal way.

I knew that Gus was having trouble with the syndicate, which he distastefully termed a "bunch of Dagoes" and "greaseballs."

This was brought to me most forcibly when Ralph Pierce, Gus' syndicate "bodyguard," telephoned one evening saying, "Wait dinner on me." This was his customary method of revealing to Gus that he had matters of importance to discuss.

On these occasions Pierce actually would take dinner with us, but would never discuss his business until coffee had been served and the butler dismissed.

"The syndicate had a meeting," Pierce announced after the butler went to the pantry, "and the boys don't like the way Davie Goldblatt is handling his end of the business." Goldblatt was Gus' personal body-guard and "legman."

"They don't like the way he's handling some of the alcohol business."

He went on in this vein until Gus finally stopped him with, "Was that meeting called to put me in the pan or on the spot?"

This sudden question startled me more than it did Pierce. A flood of fear swept over me, and to conceal my agitation I left the table and went to my room. When I did not return Gus came to me saying, "What's the matter, Honey?"

With the shadow of Ted Newberry before me I said in a weak voice, "Gus, can't you realize what Ralph is saying?"

"I'm not afraid," Gus answered, with assumed unconcern. "They wouldn't dare touch me."

"Yes," I said. "Ted Newberry and Ray Nugent talked the same way. Now where are they?"

Gus patted my shoulder and we returned to the dining room to-gether, but I looked at Pierce through different eyes.

I was confident that if he had told all he heard at the syndicate meet-ing he would have revealed that Gus' time was short.

For the Dagoes in the syndicate feared his growing power and influ-ence and were equally afraid of the American boys by whom Gus was surrounded.

While these difficulties were fresh in our minds, Gus was warned that federal agents were looking for him. That was late on Friday, and since Gus did not seem to be much concerned about the warning I did not make very detailed inquiries. However, I got the idea it was in con-nection with stolen bonds.

"I guess I'll lay low over the weekend," Gus said to me. "If I go down and report Saturday, offices will be closed before I get a chance to make bond. I'll just stay in and go down Monday and give myself up. There's no use trying to hide out, because I can't take care of business if have to stay under cover."

I agreed that would be the best course.

So he did not leave the apartment and on Sunday we dismissed the servants and enjoyed our first visit at home in months.

During the afternoon the wife of a prominent Chicago politician, who had become very friendly with us, telephoned to ask if we would be at the Chez Paree that evening.

I explained the situation to her and said we were staying at home so that Gus would not have to spend the weekend in jail.

"I'm coming right over," my friend declared. "I'm too good a friend of yours to stay clear of you when you're in trouble, police or no police."

Not many minutes had elapsed when she arrived, burdened with books, nuts and candy. We were glad to have her and chilled some champagne, her favorite drink, to show our gratitude for her friendliness.

I ordered dinner from the 225 Club and the club caterer laid the table. During dinner my friend repeatedly told us what a good friend of ours she was, and the feeling came over me that she was bragging.

"I'd stand by you if the police were to walk in this minute," she said. "I'd tell them that you were friends of mine and that I was proud of it, and anything they did to you would be a personal insult to me."

None of us realized how soon she would get a chance to prove it.

I had telephoned the drug store for newspapers, and when the solicitors' bell in the kitchen sounded I supposed the delivery was being made and went to open the door.

I threw open the door, expecting the boy, and nearly fainted when a man grabbed my arm and shoved me back in the room, while others pushed in after him with drawn guns.

My first thought was that Verne Miller and his friends had come after my husband, so I screamed, "Beat it, Gus!" before I saw it was the police.

Gus must have thought the same thing, since the men did not enter in the orthodox manner, but he surrendered to the officers with a smile when he saw who they were.

Before the kitchen door swung shut, I could see my boastful friend rushing about the sitting room from one door to another, frantically ringing her hands and not knowing how best to make an escape.

I left Gus and the police and went to her, trying to assure her that there was no danger, telling her to sit down and keep quiet, but she had visions of spending the night in jail and could not be calmed.

I was disgusted at the shallowness of her friendship, but could sympathize with her predicament. So I returned to the other room and put on an act for the officers to hold their attention until my friend could escape.

"What's the idea breaking into the house like this?" I demanded truculently.

When one of the officers tried to explain, I started toward him swinging my fist as if I would strike him, shouting as loud as I could so that the officers could not hear the closing of a door.

I must have been good for I fooled even my husband who held my arms and tried to quiet me. When I was quite sure my visitor had escaped I relaxed.

Even though her friendship was not as deep as she had boasted, I did not want to see her suffer the indignity of going to jail. However, my efforts had been wasted, for while I was in the front room Gus had explained to the officers that we had a guest, and after telling who she was, asked that she be saved any embarrassment. The officers kindly agreed not to enter the room in order to give her ample time to escape.

Sergeant Shoes [this should be Detective Sergeant Al Schuetz, not Chief Shoemaker, whose nickname was "Old Shoes"] who led the raid conducted himself like a gentleman when we were taken to the station, and Detective Chief William Shoemaker was also very courteous. By comparison I was reminded of the treatment accorded us by the St. Louis police, and the mistreatment we had both received at their hands.

It was here that I learned that Gus was being questioned about the quarter-million dollar Loop mail truck hold up on December 6, 1932. [See Loop Mail Robberies in Biographies and Historical Notes.] City and federal officials were combining in their investigation.

I was confident Gus had very little firsthand knowledge of that holdup, but I learned that the bonds stolen were the same bonds that Goetz and Lebensberger had become involved with.

All I knew about the holdup was what I had read in the papers. The armored truck was going through a Loop intersection when a passing car released a fog of smoke casting an impenetrable veil around the scene. When the smoke cleared away, it was discovered the truck had been "sacked." The bandit car, discovered later, had a chemical smoke gun swung from the chassis.

The police matrons were very considerate of my feelings, and learning that I objected to reporters, who appeared to have the run of the place, helped to keep them from me. The only picture they got was when one was snapped as I left the government office, and the photographer saved that one only by running faster to get away than I could run to catch him.

Since I could tell them nothing, the officers released me on Tuesday.

A day or so later Gus was brought back to the apartment, this time by Federal officers. They treated him like a good friend, seemingly not fearing an effort to escape. While the officers lounged about, talking to me and each other over champagne and highballs, Gus bathed and changed clothes.

Every few days the officers would bring him home again. On one of these occasions he asked them if he could speak privately to me. They consented without argument.

"Honey," he said in a low voice after we reached another room, "I want you to help me out a bit with the business. I want you to go down to the Chez Paree and the 225 Club and tell the boys not to issue payoffs to anyone, not to issue any payroll, and above all, not to give the syndicate a single dollar until I get out."

"I'll do it tonight," I promised him.

36

THE SYNDICATE CLOSES IN

I was startled at the change in Eddie Lebensberger when I saw him at the 225 Club.

The usually calm, suave cabaret manager was pale, and deep lines in his face indicated constant worry. Previously I had never seen Lebensberger drinking while on duty—he made it a point to be at his best when taking care of business.

On this occasion he lacked his usual sartorial excellence, he seemed to have clothed himself with very little care, and it was apparent he had been drinking. In fact, in the short time I was with him he drank several additional highballs.

When we were alone I said, "Eddie, Gus told me to come down here and tell you not to pay out a dime, either to the syndicate or the employees, until he can get out to take care of it personally."

Eddie turned to look at me under half lowered lids and the line of his jaw tightened as he said bitterly, "Georgette, I wish the time would come when I would never have to give the syndicate a cent."

"Eddie," I asked confidentially, "what's the trouble anyway?"

"There's plenty of trouble of all kinds," he answered as he shook his head, staring into his highball glass.

"The thing that's got me burnt up right now is something I just heard. The syndicate is trying to bring some Dagoes in from New York to run the Opera Club that Gus is trying to open.

"Now Gus didn't plan it that way, and it isn't fair to me. That is my spot—Gus promised it to me, and he wants me there. They're going to put the pressure on Gus to force him to put some East Coast wop in what is my place, by rights."

This news was startling, not only because it rang a familiar note, but because I could foresee further trouble between Gus and the syndicate.

For some time the newspapers had rumored that there was a deal on between those high in Chicago politics to "sell" gambling rights to an eastern combine for $2,500,000. In fact, the newspapers had said that the New York interests already had made an initial payment of $1,000,000 and that Chicago syndicates had combined to protect themselves. [Such discussions had been going on prior to April 1932, when New York mobsters "Lucky" Luciano and Meyer Lansky were arrested outside Chicago's Congress Hotel in the company of Nitti mobsters Rocco Fischetti and Paul "The Waiter" Ricca.]

Knowing that some of the syndicate men originally came from New York, I wondered if they were a party to the deal. If that were the case, there would be little left for Gus to do but accede to their demands.

But I tried to comfort Eddie, saying, "Don't worry, Gus won't stand for it."

I left the club, and that was the last time I ever saw Eddie Lebensberger.

Now I really had something to worry about, for it looked like a showdown as to whether Gus would run his own property, or whether he would be a mere figurehead while the syndicate ran it.

Not long afterward information came through one of Gus' office employees that added to my uneasiness.

He came to the house with the warning that "Gus had better watch himself."

"Oh, Lord," I said, "what's the matter now?"

"I don't like to bother you about this," he apologized, "but you know it wouldn't do for any of us to go down to the jail to see Gus. But he ought to be told that some of the syndicate boys were in his office in the Lincoln Park Arms looking for the payroll."

I realized at once that this was the result of his order to not issue any pay.

"They seemed to think," the office man continued, "that Gus is leaving the payoffs to Goldblatt. Little Bobbie (the bookkeeper) slipped the payroll in his pocket and they couldn't find it.

"After they looked all over they asked if all the police and federal men were getting their pay, or if Gus was letting that Jew Goldblatt put it over on him. We didn't know what to say, so we just told them everything was being taken care of."

This was really something to worry about, for the syndicate had always let Gus manage his business.

A short time later Gus was released [from what federal agents called "technical custody," meaning he was only questioned] and the first thing I told him was that the syndicate men had been in his office.

He dismissed it with a wave of the hand.

"Forget it," he said, "I've got something more to worry about than those damn greaseballs. It's just like I said it would be. Eddie Lebensberger is in a jam over those bonds taken in the Loop robbery."

He was right; Lebensberger was in trouble. Federal indictments were returned against Eddie and five others, charging them with having the bonds. Eddie could not be located by the police.

I was confident that Gus could straighten things out, but everything was drifting, seemingly out of control. I had never seen Gus so worried.

Gus had surrounded himself with American boys, one of the most dependable of whom was Al Begard. It was on August 18, 1933, while Gus was out of town that the newspapers carried a report that Begard had left his apartment at 2738 Pine Grove Avenue to go to the barber shop and had not returned. When Gus came home and Begard was still missing, I mentioned it to him. He turned pale.

"Good God," he said. "He'll never come back." Then, after a pause, "I wonder who is next?"

I knew syndicate methods well enough to know what was going on. Knowing they could not put their own men in the North Side as long as Gus had Americans employed, they intended to weaken him by removing them one by one.

Still I had confidence in Gus' ability to take up the reins.

But dangerous rumors were afloat. The newspapers were intimating that it was information given to the federal authorities by Gus that led to the return of the mail robbery indictments. In other words, my husband was being branded a squealer.

I could see no logic in this, for squealing would have involved Lebensberger, and Gus had too much at stake as far as Eddie was concerned to see him go to jail. In truth, his immediate future in his business depended on Lebensberger.

To protect his health I started giving him sleeping tablets.

Other people began to add their burdens to his already overweighed shoulders. Louis Cohen, editor of a Cicero newspaper, began telephoning every day, asking him to use his influence with the syndicate.

It seems that Cohen planned to open a gambling establishment in Miami, Florida, but the syndicate was demanding its operation and most of the profits. Cohen was not close enough to syndicate activities to realize what that demand meant. He felt that the enterprise was his and his alone, and in so many words he told them to "go to hell."

He wanted Gus to back him up.

"Why can't they all play square," Gus said in irritation. "Those Dagoes are money mad. Why, Lefty Louie and Frankie Reo were fifty-dollar-a-week flunkies when Al Capone went to jail, and now look at them. Gone crazy just because they've got a little authority and making a little money."

I don't believe Gus ever saw Cohen personally. He probably couldn't have saved him if he had.

Things were going from bad to worse at the 225 Club, owing to Lebensberger's absence. On the night of October 6, Gus said he was going to visit him at his hiding place and urge him to give himself up to the government and get it over with.

He stayed with Eddie late into the night, talking over the possibilities of avoiding a jail sentence, and showing him that he could never operate a club again if he didn't come out in the open, face the music, and clear himself.

Gus promised him his personal support in getting out on bond and freeing himself of the charge.

Gus later told me that he had talked Eddie into a better frame of mind, showing him that there was no use acknowledging his guilt by hiding out.

Lebensberger agreed to give himself up the next day, and Gus and Ralph Pierce returned him to his home.

Gus seemed relieved when he went to bed that night.

"I believe he can beat this rap," Gus told me confidently. "There's no use of him taking it when he didn't have anything to do with the holdup."

Early the next morning the telephone rang and Gus answered it.

He stood silent at the phone for a long time, while someone at the other end of the wire seemed to be explaining something. Gus kept shaking his head as he listened.

Finally I heard him say, "Like hell he did. I'd have to see him do it before I'd believe a story like that."

As he turned away from the phone his shoulders sagged and he dropped into a chair, leaning his head on his hand.

"What's the matter?" I asked.

"Eddie Lebensberger is dead," he said slowly. "They say he committed suicide."

37

THE POLICE CALLED IT SUICIDE

The breath drained out of my throat and I stood in speechless horror at his announcement.

Then I screamed.

"Steady, Honey, take it easy," Gus said, coming over to me.

After a few minutes of tears I said, "Gus, is that what you were talking about when you said you didn't believe it? Did you mean you didn't believe Eddie committed suicide?"

"Yes," he said, "that's what I meant. As good as Eddie felt when we took him home, in the time that elapsed he couldn't have sunk to the point of suicide. Besides that, I had him feeling pretty sure he'd get out of it."

"Do you think somebody shot him?" I queried.

"Maybe yes, maybe no," he answered, "but whether he fired the shot or somebody else did, he was killed just as sure as we're both standing here."

"What do you mean?"

"I mean that somebody got to him—somebody who didn't want him talking to the federal officers.

"Eddie was either killed outright or scared into suicide; it's the same thing either way."

"But Gus," I continued, perplexed, "who knew he was going to give himself up?"

"I did," was the answer, "and Ralph Pierce did. I didn't tell a soul. Murphy brought me straight back home after we delivered Eddie to his house."

"Then Pierce told it," I said emphatically.

"Suit yourself," Gus said. "You know Pierce."

Later that day, I took occasion to ask Murphy, the chauffeur, just what happened after he drove away from Lebensberger's house. He told me he drove directly home with no stops.

Of course, Lebensberger's death threw the bond theft investigation into an uproar, for this was a new clue. It was understood that Lebensberger was about to give himself up, and even the newspapers felt as Gus did, that someone prevented it.

That day Gus was informed that he was wanted at the government office again, presumably for further questioning in the bond case and Lebensberger's death.

"Go right down," I advised him.

"No," he said. "Monday is Chicago Day and the offices will be closed until Tuesday. I don't want to lay in stir that long. I'll wait until Tuesday and give myself up."

To avoid being located he said we would leave the apartment and go to his suite in the Lincoln Park Arms, directly under those where his business office was located.

Shortly after we arrived, Ralph Pierce informed him a syndicate meeting was being held in Berwyn and he was wanted.

I was uneasy, but I knew he had to go, for to refuse would have precipitated a showdown right then. I heaved a sigh when he returned but I couldn't get a word out of him concerning what had happened at the meeting.

That night he said, "Honey, I'm not going out. The police will be on the lookout at the clubs and chances are I'd be picked up. You'd better go on down to the Chez Paree and take care of whatever there is to be done. Explain to the boys why I'm not there."

Before I left for the club, Ralph Pierce came up and asked Gus to go out with him, but he refused. When Pierce insisted Gus said, "No, I go no place until I turn myself in at the 'G' office and see what they want."

There was a strange look in his eyes, and he was unusually thoughtful of me. I supposed that Lebensberger's death was preying on his mind, and that supposition was borne out when Gus mentioned it several times as I dressed.

When I was ready to leave he reached in his pocket and handed me a roll of bills.

"Burn a candle for Eddie," he said quietly, "and order some flowers to be sent to the chapel—something nice."

It was nearly noon before I started home, then I had a strange feeling that someone was following me. I kept a close watch on the rear view mirror, hoping to be able to identify some car that might be trailing, and even turned off on less traveled streets so that my vision would be better. Several times I drove into blind alleys and stopped.

Although I saw no one, the feeling persisted until I got home, where I told Gus about it. He laughed.

"You're nervous," he said. "Lebensberger's death on top of all the other trouble we've been having has upset you."

I wanted to believe him, but it seemed to me there was a false note in his cheerfulness.

That day my husband talked to me as he never did before. He talked about his business.

Right at the time I thought it was perfectly natural that he should, because he was housed up and unable to look after his business, his mind was burdened with troubles, and he had to "unload" to someone.

But thinking back, I realize that Gus had a presentiment of approaching doom. He was too explicit, too insistent on my remembering what he had to say, and I can see now that not one single time did he mention his current troubles, but talked only of the financial and physical condition of the business.

In the afternoon he telephoned the 225 Club and shortly afterward one of the club employees I knew as "Scotty" came to the apartment.

We talked casually for a time, then the conversation gradually turned to the clubs.

"Georgette," said Gus turning to me, "the Chez Paree is completely out of debt now, and is on a good paying basis. I've got a ten per cent reserve there that I keep on hand in case somebody gets 'hot' in the casino. I use that money to back up the bank. The reputation of a place like that is gone for good if anyone ever breaks the bank."

He went on to explain that all the trucks at the Charles H. Weber Distributing Company, his beer establishment at 1414 Roscoe Street, had been paid for, and that this business too was on a paying basis.

He told me exactly how much the men at 20 West Lake Street, a large saloon at that address, were indebted to him. In his anxiety to make me understand he leaned toward me in his chair, his elbows on his knees, talking earnestly and emphasizing each item by tolling it off on his fingers.

How dense I was. It all seemed unnatural and how I failed to understand that Gus was reading me his will, with Scotty as a witness, I cannot see.

Gus discussed all of his property. Finally he leaned back in his chair, turning his head toward Scotty: "Those stocks I bought are paying well, but I don't want to sell them," he told the man from the club. "I'm saving them for her," waving his hand toward me.

Scotty started kidding him.

"What are you going to give to the rest of your women?" he said. "You can't buy blocks of bonds for all the women you're supporting."

This joking was too serious to please me. Gus had a hard and fast rule, of which I believe Al Capone was the originator. If any of the men were killed while doing their duty to their employer, their regular pay was turned over to the wife or sweetheart until they either married or found some source of income.

But Gus laughed.

"Several of the North Side boys were killed when Ted Newberry was running things up here," he said. "I never knew them, but when I found their wives' names on the payroll I went right ahead sending them the money. The syndicate kicked to beat the devil, but the widows got theirs first, before there was any split."

Quickly he attempted to change the subject, commenting about his plans to open the Opera Club, but the morbid subject he had just discussed apparently was uppermost in his mind and he came back to it.

"When that place opens, Eddie Lebensberger's wife is going to get a cut out of it," he declared. "She'll get a cut out of the 225 Club, too, as soon as it reopens."

"Remind me of that, Honey," he said pointedly to me.

It looks so simple now. Even the reader of this book, knowing the circumstances, can see that he was acquainting me with facts so that I could look out for my interests. And Scotty was there to hear, and to aid me, for Gus trusted him.

Another one of the boys from the club came over soon, and both he and Scotty went out to bring us some dinner. When they were gone Gus remarked, "There are two fine boys and I'm going to do something for them. They'll both get better jobs when I get the new place open."

When dinner was finished, the four of us sat down and played bridge.

Ralph Pierce came in a little later, but did not bother to remove his coat.

"Ride over with us to take a look at Lebensberger," he suggested to Gus.

Gus stared at him for a minute before replying: "Do I look that damn dumb? You can run my wife over if you care to."

There was a hidden play of word meaning here that I did not catch at the time, although I recall seeing a peculiar look cross Pierce's face.

Now I think I understand. Pierce was trying to take Gus from cover.

"No, thanks," I said. "I don't care to go."

Pierce left and the bridge game continued until one o'clock in the morning.

When the game broke up Scotty and the other man from the 225 Club spoke to Gus in low tones.

"Don't you think we'd better stay all night?" Scotty said. His face was tense, his eyes earnest and his voice sincere.

Gus patted him on the shoulder and laughed a little.

"I'll be all right," he said. "I'm not afraid. You boys go on home to bed."

Both boys realized Gus was near the finish. It was just like a death-bed scene and I didn't know it.

When we were alone again Gus pulled me down in a chair, and again repeated everything he had told me about the clubs, saloons, his money, the distributing plant, the new club and several other things.

"Honey," he said when we had talked until nearly three in the morning, "if you're ever in trouble the best friend you can have is Father Dwyer. You can tell him everything, and you can count on him."

Many, many times since I have wished I had remembered that advice.

38

"THEY'VE TAKEN HIM
TO THE MORGUE"

Gus asked me to go to our Lake Shore Drive apartment and get some fresh clothing.

"Get some rest while you're there," he said. "I wouldn't come back until about eight o'clock if I were you."

He seemed restless and kept moving about through the rooms.

"You're the one who needs rest," I said. "Why don't you go to bed and try to get some sleep."

He said he didn't want to sleep.

I prepared a sedative, but he tried to avoid taking it.

"What are you trying to do, make a ninny out of me?" he complained as he finally took it.

"I'll be back between seven and eight o'clock," I promised. "Don't open the door for anyone until I get here."

As I left I took the key and locked the suite from the outside.

The maid had just returned to the apartment when I arrived. She made coffee, after which I went to bed and tried to sleep. But my mind was a maze of whirling thoughts. Eddie Lebensberger, his wife Alice, clubs, dollar signs, roaring beer trucks—then the pale face of Ted Newberry, and finally, "Do you want us to stay all night?" whispered over and over again in my mind.

What was happening? What was taking place just beyond the grasp of my understanding? I was vaguely uneasy.

I finally gave up all attempts to sleep, rose and packed some clothes for Gus, prepared a lunch, and rang for the chauffeur. On our arrival at the Lincoln Park Arms, I told Murphy that Gus would not need the car that day. It was October 9, 1933.

While coffee was being sent up from the café below, Gus bathed and dressed while I laid out his clothes—green suit, tie to match, and other of his favorite accessories, including a jewel studded belt, a gift from Ted Newberry.

What I am about to relate may sound ridiculous to some, but it happened, and it left its mark on my mind, a mark that remains today. It was not imagination—it was too real.

Gus entered the room, clothed in his usual excellence. He was talking about some trivial thing as he approached.

I looked away for an instant, and when my eyes turned back to my husband, they widened in terror, and my hand flew to my lips to suppress a scream.

Gus stood before me, not in his green street suit, but in a tuxedo, with the formal black bow tie instead of the green four-in-hand. His face was set, one hand was across the front of his waistcoat, and wrapped around his fingers was a rosary.

I shut my eyes and swayed, putting one hand against his chest to keep from falling.

"Honey," came his voice, "what's the matter?"

I opened my eyes. Gus Winkeler was standing before me in his green suit, supporting me by the elbows. "Are you ill?" he said with concern. He led me to a chair and brought me a glass of water.

"You're as white as a ghost," he continued with a shaky laugh. "What's wrong?"

I wish I had told him. I wish I had said: "I have just had a vision." I wish I had passed that warning onto him. Possibly he would have been more cautious, for he had faith in what he termed my "hunches."

But I only said: "Nothing is wrong, I'm just a little faint, that's all. I guess Eddie Lebensberger's death is getting on my nerves. I'll be all right in a minute."

But I wasn't. I had just had a vision of death, a vision that mere words could not dismiss from my mind.

About an hour before noon Benny Goldblatt [also referred to as Davie] came in, accompanied by a man I knew only as "Red," who was employed by Gus. Shortly after their arrival Ralph Pierce came, then "Little Bobby."

I felt there was no occasion to worry with Goldblatt and Red around, so I told Gus I would drive out to Cicero to get my hair washed and dressed.

"Okay, Honey, run on," Gus said. He handed Goldblatt a roll of bills and told him to pay for the flowers used to decorate the Vanity Fair, another of the clubs he operated. Just before I left the suite Goldblatt handed me the money and asked me to pay the florist, since the shop was in Cicero. I consented.

"What are you getting dolled up for?" Pierce bantered as I opened the door.

"Why for me, who else?" Gus said. "Isn't that right, Honey?"

I laughed and went out, but everything seemed wrong. A weight pressed on my heart. Goldblatt accompanied me down the hall where I rang for the elevator. When the boy opened the door and I started to enter the lift, I had a sudden sensation of stepping into a bottomless void from which I could never again reach the world.

"Wait a minute," I ordered, my breath coming short.

I ran back down the hall to our suite, and flung the door open. Little Bobby and Red were sitting on the divan at one side of the room, while Gus sat in a chair at the other side. Pierce was leaning over the back of the chair, whispering in his ear.

They looked up at the sound of my entrance, and somehow I was embarrassed.

"Is there anything you want that I can bring back?" I said to my husband as an excuse for my return.

"No, I guess not," he said with a smile. "Just run on and hurry back. I'll be waiting for you."

"I'll be waiting for you"—my husband's last words to me.

The papers later said I went to the home of my mother, but that is not true. My mother passed away when I was a child too young to remember her. I went to the hairdresser's establishment.

All the way out to Cicero I was depressed. Everything was so unreal. I was unaccountably nervous.

The cold water of the rinse cleared my head somewhat, and it was while the tiny needle wash was sending streams of water coursing behind my ears that Benny Goldblatt telephoned.

When I heard the girl who answered the phone say "Mr. Goldblatt calling," I rushed to the phone with water running down my neck. Already apprehension was upon me.

"Hurry to the office," was all Bennie said as I answered.

Cold fear crystallized in my brain. I was blinded by water streaming down my face, and a swimming sensation in my head. I staggered out of the shop into a street that stood on end. Cars parked at the curb seemed to shuttle back and forth until I couldn't locate mine. I gave up.

I stood at the curb waving my arms, crying for a cab, until one came.

The ride to the Lincoln Park Arms cleared my head a little, but left but one thought—to see my husband.

Most of Gus' boys were gathered in the lobby. From a great distance their voices tried to stop me, and their hands reached forth, but I eluded them and without waiting for the elevator rushed panting up the steps and down the hall.

I threw open the door of the suite and ran in, calling "Gus, Gus," but my only reply was from the empty rooms.

Some of the boys followed me and stood quietly at the door as I wheeled and demanded, "Where is he?"

Little Bobby spread his hands placatingly and said, "He was shot, they've taken him to the hospital," then at my look of terror, he quickly added, "but he's not hurt bad, don't worry. Come on Mrs. Winkeler, I'll take you to him."

I was in frantic haste. I led them down stairs and into Bobby's car. Someone followed in another machine—I think it was Red. He drove to the John B. Murphy Hospital, and as soon as the car pulled up at the curb I had the door open and was running across the walk into the building.

At the information desk I gasped out, "Where is he, my husband, Gus Winkeler?"

The girl at the desk surveyed me curiously as if to study my reaction before she replied.

"They've taken him to the morgue."

39

GUS GOES HOME

The brutal announcement paralyzed my mind and body.

Before an impenetrable fog settled around me, I remember lifting my hand to my mouth. I did not speak, but I felt the world crumple silently into dust around me.

I do not remember the ride home, or who talked to me and what was said. I did not know when my husband's relatives came to the apartment that night, or did I know who sent for them.

The night was interminable, while I floated bodiless in a haze, devoid of any feeling but numbness.

The next morning someone put my nerveless arms through the sleeves of a coat, pulled a hat over my disheveled hair, led me to the street and into an automobile.

I do not remember the ride. The cold wind that blew across my face did not blow away the mist that enshrouded me. Ages later I was led into a room where there were many voices—voices that came in a monotonous babble from a great distance.

My nurse told me later that I sat motionless in a chair with my hands in my lap, while newspaper photographers lifted my veil and snapped pictures of my grief.

Through the veil came the serene, kind face of Father Dwyer. Father Dwyer, who held my hand, talked to me in a low voice, a Father Dwyer who offered sanctuary in his strength. I could not understand what he said, but his voice and his touch comforted me.

It was Father Dwyer who led me to the casket for my first view of my slain husband. It was his arm that held me when I looked at the torn body,

Killers Get Winkler

SINCE that scarlet day in 1929 the score of gang murders has mounted steadily. And, by no means strange, the list of victims includes some of those very men who, chattering "typewriters" in hand, entered that Clark street garage and dealt wholesale death.

Take Gus Winkler, for instance. Investigators place him in the Valentine execution squad. Always in more or less trouble, Gus was in his final jackpot on October 9, 1933. Driving alone, unarmed, he left his car and started across the street to offices of a beer distributing firm. Paid killers, concealed in a small truck, let him have it in the back.

The immediate reason for his rubbing out was believed by underworld observers to have been fear that Winkler was preparing to "sing" about a quarter of a million dollar mail robbery. But those who went deeper into the background of the dapper gangster's life declared that the history of the case went back farther than that—in fact, that it reached back to that crimson fiasco when Gus and his mob marched into the Chicago garage, shooting as they went.

Freddie Goetz, reputedly another member of the execution squad, later went on to figure in the kidnaping of Edward G. Bremer, St. Paul banker. But retribution overtook him, too. University educated, possessed of a keen mind, Goetz went wrong. Only a few months ago he succumbed to a bad case of lead poisoning. The story of Fred "Killer" Burke, is well known and need not be repeated here except to state that he was trapped by officers, taken to Michigan to face trial for the slaying of a policeman, and now is serving a life term in that state. He, too, was fingered as a member of the Valentine murder detail.

Byron Bolton, a minor hoodlum attached to the fringes of the Capone gang, came to Chicago from a small Illinois city. He worked for a time in a garage operated by Goetz, did jobs for members of the mob and worked himself into their good graces. At best he was little more than a punk. But, apparently, he did know what happened in the Valentine fiasco and, years later, came forward with a story that placed himself near the scene of the seven-fold killing in the role of finger man. Bolton, now, is serving a long term in an Illinois prison.

The scene outside the Charles H. Weber Distributing Company following the shooting of Gus Winkeler.

the patched hands that held the rosary, resting over the still breast where once was the battleground of man's strongest emotions. A husband who in appearance was the fulfillment of my vision of the day before.

Then the babble again, and finally the voice of Ralph Pierce penetrating the cloud about me, saying in so many meaningless words how sorry the syndicate was that Gus was gone.

Then over and over again, low and tense, that I must be careful not to tell anyone that I knew Commissioner Charles Weber, not to tell anyone that Gus was associated with the cabarets, and promises that the syndicate would settle with me for every cent Gus had invested.

Dimly I heard, but the words made no impression. But the nurse heard, and it was the nurse the syndicate paid—not the doctor and the undertaker.

Night again, my grief written and pictured over the pages of the papers. Jesting words, cold analytical words, words deriding my conduct and my remarks.

But the pictures served a purpose. A flood of telegrams and night letters came to the apartment, offering sympathy, aid, and revenge. They were followed by hundreds of letters from people I never heard of, people who sent condolences. I could not read them—only appreciate them all for the spirit in which they had been sent.

Then more men from the syndicate with their whispered sympathy and their veiled threats as they continually intoned: "You don't know Weber, you don't know anything about the clubs."

Back to the undertaker's chapel, where the last of the thousands who streamed past "Big Mike's" bier were shut out, and where other syndicate men whispered threats in sympathetic voices.

Then the train and the long ride to St. Louis as Gus returned home.

Arrival, with the silent ranks of the American Legion standing at attention as the body of their old comrade-at-arms was lifted from the train. Photographers snatching off my veil, voices, thousands of the curious.

To the chapel of another undertaker, then to the Catholic Church, where the same priest who said the last words over Ben Winkeler and his wife repeated them over the body of the son.

The final resting place in Park Lawn Cemetery, near the graves that housed the father and mother.

"Ashes to ashes—" as the rose petals fell.

Then the ranks of silent, respectful uniformed men, moving into the distance, the shuffling of the departing crowd, and a woman in a black veil left in a fog of unreality, alone above the body of a departed husband, alone to face the only world she knew, a world that waited with bared fangs.

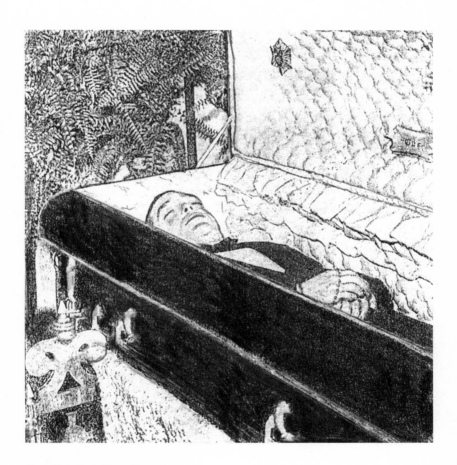

Gus Winkeler in his coffin.

40

WHO KILLED MY HUSBAND?

On the long train ride back to Chicago the fog began to lift and I was capable of thought. But my brain seemed closed to all but one thought—who killed my husband?

I brooded on this for the entire trip, and by the time the train pulled into the Chicago station, I had determined to find out.

I was comparatively certain that the syndicate was responsible for his death, and had taken him just as Newberry and many others were taken. But the possibility that it might have been some outside interest, possibly a gambling trust, or an organized gang of bond thieves, kept intruding.

I was dumbfounded when I entered my home on Lake Shore Drive, for to put it bluntly, the place had been "sacked." The finest items from my wardrobe were missing, including some very valuable furs. Some expensive tapestries were also gone. On second thought I was not surprised, for I had heard of such methods before.

The hirelings of the syndicate had taken them as gifts to wives, sweethearts and plain "molls." When they were taken I do not know—possibly while I was in the stupor induced by my husband's death—possibly while I was in St. Louis.

The first thing I did was to accumulate all the newspapers of the previous few days, and read what was said about the assassination of Gus Winkeler.

Gus was shot by unseen killers about one o'clock in the afternoon as he started up the steps of the Charles H. Weber Distributing Company at 1414 Roscoe Street.

Several witnesses said Gus drove to the curb on the wrong side of the street, left the machine and started up the steps of the establishment just as a small green panel truck cruised slowly down the street.

There was a fusillade of shots and Gus fell, mortally wounded. The truck sped away. Edward Conrad, distributing company clerk, heard the shots and ran out to find "Big Mike" face down on the sidewalk.

Gus asked to be moved over on his back, just as the Town Hall police cruiser arrived. Officer Roy Coutrie recognized Gus and asked who fired the shots. Gus told him "never mind."

He was taken to John B. Murphy Hospital where surgeons found that seventy-four shotgun slugs, commonly known as "shrapnel," had pierced his body. Gus asked for a priest and Father James Fitzgerald, hospital chaplain, was just starting to lead him through the prayer for the dying when the last breath left his body.

Mystified, the police arrested Benny Goldblatt, who said that the car my husband drove was the property of Mrs. Goldblatt, and that Gus had borrowed it. He said that Gus had asked for it at 9 o'clock in the morning, and he had delivered the car to him at Pine Grove Avenue and Addison Street, a half block from the Lincoln Park Arms.

Goldblatt said Gus told him he wanted to see his attorney, William Waugh. The attorney partially bears out this statement, saying Gus had asked for an appointment for two o'clock.

Goldblatt denied any dealings with my husband except that he once peddled alcohol with him. He denied that Gus had any dealings with Charles H. Weber.

The papers said the police were balked by several apparent inconsistencies. In the first place, Gus was known to have been planning to surrender to the government on Tuesday, and would not have risked arrest by appearing publicly on Monday.

In the second place, they could not understand what induced him to take the risk to get to a distributing company where apparently he had no connection.

But their best clue was the fact that no automobile keys were found in Gus' pocket, and neither were they in the car, indicating that someone had accompanied him to drive the car.

Davie (Benny) Goldblatt.

This struck me as my best clue, and one I determined to follow up later.

The newspapers advanced some rather interesting and widely divergent theories concerning the motive for the slaying.

One was that he had betrayed George "Machine Gun" Kelly, notorious killer, to the authorities. Kelly had just been captured at Memphis, Tennessee, and it was said that he had conferred with Gus a few days before, and that Gus knew his whereabouts. Gangland exacted its toll for this doublecross.

Another was that gangland had learned that Gus had aided Ted Newberry in the plot to kill Frank Nitti, and had meted out its own justice.

The newspapers, however, conceded most generally that "Big Mike" was killed to prevent him from surrendering to the government. This was borne out by the fact that Lebensberger had died just before he was to surrender. There was an intimation that Lebensberger was not a suicide.

Most papers believed that Gus had given the government valuable information in the quarter-million dollar Loop holdup, and that principals feared that he would give more the second time.

Out of the maze of conjecture two ideas of my own were born. Gus had either been betrayed into venturing out where he would be an easy mark for the gunmen, or tiring of the strain and worry, had deliberately taken his life in his hands, thereby committing suicide as surely as Eddie Lebensberger was alleged to have done.

Considering Gus Winkeler's astuteness in such matters, I could not fathom why he should risk his life to make an unimportant visit at the distributing plant.

In the seclusion of my stripped apartment, still numb from shock and grief, I was yet unable to draw up a plan of action.

41

THE WIDOW AND HER WORLD

While I was still grasping for an answer to my problems Benny Goldblatt came to call on me.

In spite of my suspicions, I greeted him as a friend, but the news he brought nearly stopped my heart.

"Georgette," he said, "you've got to watch yourself. The syndicate boys have been talking it over and they think you know too much, and you know they don't trust women very far anyway. Now be damn careful or you'll get what Gus got. And the boys are all set to take you to the cleaners if they have to bump you off to do it. They'll get everything they can lay their hands on, and my advice to you is not to go out by yourself. Why, they've already issued orders not to pay you a dime.

"I argued against this but they had made up their minds and they talked me down. Then I tried to stop it by saying that I had written a letter in which I outlined all of Big Mike's interests. I told them that this letter was to be opened only if I were killed or disappeared. I figured if I could make them believe it they would be afraid to harm me.

"Then they wanted to know right away where that letter could be found, and the best thing I could think of is tell them was that I had entrusted it to Abe Marovitz." [As a young lawyer, Abraham Lincoln Marovitz represented his share of racketeers, usually in civil cases, but ultimately he became a respected federal judge whose large private office eventually acquired many hundreds of photographs, busts, documents, and nearly anything else related to Abraham Lincoln. Before his death in 2001 he was helpful in the preparation of this work.]

Marovitz is a well known Chicago criminal attorney with offices in the Engineering Building at 200 West Wacker Drive. I know that my late husband was one of his clients.

I had very little faith in Goldblatt, although I told him how much I appreciated the warning. However, I could not bring myself to believe that the ex-bodyguard had come to me in a spirit of friendly personal interest.

I felt reasonably sure that he was attempting to ingratiate himself into my good graces, possibly for the same reason that he had been so friendly to my husband. But I could only guess at his designs.

When Ralph Pierce came to call I had an opportunity to investigate further. I related to Pierce everything that Goldblatt had told me and asked him point blank if it were true.

"Goldblatt is a dirty liar," Pierce said angrily when I had finished. "We'll get that damn Jew," he continued. "He talks too much."

Knowing Pierce as I did I had very little reason to trust him, so I did not let him get away without attempting to force from him some statement of the syndicate's policy in regard to my future.

"You can call Benny a liar if you want to," I said, "but what are you going to do about the Charles H. Weber Distributing Company? You know as well as I do that Gus Winkeler owned that place, lock, stock, and barrel, and you know how hard he worked to get it on a paying basis.

"Now what I want to know is: Is Charley Weber going to steal that place from me?"

Ralph Pierce looked at me and a sneer twisted his mouth as he raised an eyebrow and said, "Can you prove it belonged to Gus?"

Then I knew. The syndicate was all set to strip me of everything Gus had earned. Goldblatt had told me the truth.

"You know damned well Gus didn't keep any records on that place," I said, white with fury, "but you know I know he owned it. Even our chauffeur knows that. He drove Gus to the place two or three times a week."

I went on to recite other proof of Gus' ownership, and the more I talked the more enraged I became. I raved at Pierce and the syndicate.

When I was so exhausted I could no longer speak Pierce was leaning toward me and his face was set in hard lines of anger.

"You better forget that stuff," he hissed. "You better forget it if you know what's good for you."

"You mean, keep my mouth shut and take a cleaning," I said bitterly.

I was limp with strain and emotion and could not go on. I could see the finish. The syndicate would have its way and I was helpless to prevent it.

Construing my silence as acknowledgment of defeat, Pierce said, "Where's the equipment and furnishings taken out of Sky High when it was closed? We want that."

What was the use, I asked myself; they'd get it anyway. So I told him where the stuff was stored.

Pierce swaggered out of the apartment, victor in a battle that was his from the start. He had every advantage, the backing of the most powerful crime syndicate in the world pitted against one woman, and that woman not yet recovered from the effects of the greatest shock she had ever known.

That night there was further evidence that Goldblatt had told me the truth.

Marovitz' law office was broken into and ransacked from ceiling to floor. When I read of it in the paper I knew at once what prize was sought. Gangland wanted the letter Goldblatt had said I had written. Of course there was no such letter.

I can see how Marovitz would believe that the robbery was committed for the sole purpose of getting the $2,500 which his safe contained. That theory was borne out by the fact that an office of the New Jersey Zinc Sales Company directly above also had been ransacked.

However, police did not delude themselves. They pointed out that in the sales office the safe had been chiseled open and nothing else molested.

They believed that the yeggs had made a mistake and broken into the Zinc Company first, then discovered their mistake and had gone to Marovitz' office.

Officials advanced the theory that the looting was the direct result of Gus Winkeler's death. They believed gangland thought the safe contained gambling records compiled by my husband.

They also said it might have been because Gus had left information concerning the quarter-million dollar Loop holdup in the safe, to be used when he surrendered to the government.

Then too, it was possible that the safe had contained records and depositions drawn by Detective Sergeant Harry Lang, accused of assault to kill Frank Nitti. After being suspended from the Police Department, Lang had threatened to "blow the lid off."

But all these theories did not bewilder me, for I knew. The syndicate was building its case against the widow of Big Mike Winkeler.

In the meantime the law was busy trying to find the slayers of my husband.

The federal government was making a determined effort to round up those indicted in the Loop robbery. They knew what had happened to Eddie Lebensberger when he was about to give himself up, and as a last example they had the death of Gus Winkeler.

The witnesses summoned in the robbery inquiry also were the object of considerable concern. It was evident that if the perpetrators of the robbery would resort to assassination, every witness was in personal danger.

As a matter of fact, the witnesses themselves were more aware of this than the government. Every man subpoenaed feared for his life. John J. "Boss" McLaughlin, prominent Chicago politician, gave up efforts to float a $50,000 bail bond and expressed perfect willingness to accept the safety of jail. Other witnesses were known to be under police guard in some remote hotel on the outskirts. The newspapers even said that some witnesses, who already had made bond, were quietly having them cancelled and going to jail for safety.

Personally, I knew that Benny Goldblatt was in mortal terror of losing his life, and Joe Bergl, Gus' old friend, was not daring to venture out.

All this time preparations were moving forward for a coroner's investigation of the death of Gus Winkeler. Technically it was an inquest; the district attorney, goaded by slighting remarks by the members of the jury selected, had promised a thorough sifting of the facts in regard to gangland operations in Chicago. It was known that men both high and low in the gambling and whiskey interests had been summoned to appear.

The most extensive examination of Chicago crime activities ever planned was ready to be launched.

The coroner's jury probably was the most outstanding body of its kind ever assembled in Chicago. It included Henry Barrett Chamberlin, managing director of the Chicago Crime Commission; Bertram Cahn, president of the Kuppenheimer Clothing Corporation, who was to act as foreman; Professor Ernest Putkamner and Professor Ernest Burgess of the University of Chicago; and William Schlosman and Charles W. Berquist, both prominent Chicagoans.

The list of witnesses summoned was a startling roster of leaders of the old Capone syndicate and illegitimate interests all over Chicago. Included were Commissioner Weber; Frank Nitti; Billy Skidmore, Chicago gambling king; Charles Conrad, Weber's partner; Marty Guilfoyle, interested in North Side gambling enterprises; Goldblatt; Detective Chief Shoemaker; a couple of newspaper reporters, and politicians and police officers from all over the city.

In addition to all these, there would be one more witness—"Big Mike's" widow.

This I knew was the showdown for me. If I was not killed to close my mouth at the coroner's investigation, I most certainly would be killed if I undertook to tell what I knew.

Without exaggerating the facts, I was "on the spot."

42

"THE GAS LISPED ITS
SONG OF DEATH"

I faced this crisis absolutely alone. There was no strong arm to lean on. For fifteen years, I had depended utterly on the fearless resourcefulness of my husband. On the occasions when circumstances forced me to act on my own initiative, I had always had the assurance that someone was either in a position to spring to my assistance or to profit by my activity.

The last had always been my incentive when I was forced to act without his aid. Now there was no incentive but self preservation.

That sense had always been as strong in me as in any other normal person, but the shock and grief of the last few days had undermined my strength, and I did not feel able to meet the ordeal alone.

In the solitude of the empty apartment I paced the floor in nervous agitation, or slumped in a chair, exhausted of thought. In my condition, I could see no solution to my problem.

I could not tear the thought of Gus from my mind. He became an obsession with me. In every vacant chair I saw him. He stood in doorways and sat across from me at the table. In my tortured mind he finally became almost real.

"I'll be waiting for you," those last words he said to me, became a whispering symphony ever present in my ears.

In desperation I finally went to Benny Goldblatt's home.

"My God, woman, why don't you stay out of sight?" was his startled greeting. "I saw two Dagoes in front of your house last night and they're watching my house too. Good God, it'll be your finish if you don't quit gadding around all over town and it'll be mine too if you get caught coming in here."

Rebuffed, I left him, got into my car and drove aimlessly all day, trying to clear my head. I stopped only when I needed to refuel. But Gus rode in the car with me; the whispers followed me.

It was comfort and strength I needed and I knew not where to turn to find it. I was too proud to go to those friends Gus had made when he reached the top ranks.

Just before dark I drove to the home of the only true friends I felt that I had—honest, hardworking people. They were shocked at my appearance, and in the peace and quiet of their home an apathy settled over me that left me in much the same condition I was in after Gus' death.

When it was time for me to go they would not permit me to drive my car and insisted that one of their boys drive me home.

Too dazed to object, I consented. At 48th and 22nd Streets I witnessed the worst auto accident I ever saw. Two cars filled with children crashed in a head-on collision, and witnesses were gathering up their bloodstained bodies.

I was so absorbed in my own troubles that I was not even sickened at the sight.

As my driver stopped the car to look I only gazed at the scene without emotion and murmured: "Poor little things. I hope they're dead, then they can escape all this misery."

The boy apparently was alarmed about me when we arrived home and offered to stay at the apartment, but I sent him home to his mother.

And Gus was with me again, and so were the whispers. The curtain of apathy drew closer and closer about me, and suddenly sanctuary opened before my eyes.

With no emotion whatever I went about the house, seeing that all windows were tightly closed, and that the doors were locked.

Then I dressed carefully in a plain black frock.

As I turned on every jet in the stove I reasoned that the whispers would become the firm voice of my husband, who would lift the veil around me so that once more I could lean on his strong arm.

As the gas lisped its little song of death I went to the telephone intending for the last time to hear the voice of a friend. Possibly it was courage I sought.

I telephoned Bonnie White, the wife Killer Burke had married before he was captured in Missouri.

"I have just called to say goodbye," I said, trying to assume a natural tone. "I'm going on a long, long, trip, and will never return to Chicago."

She asked me where I would go, but I merely said goodbye again, and returned the receiver to its hook.

I switched off all the lights, then pulled my chair to the stove where I rested my head on my bent arm.

Already the odor of gas filled the apartment. It whispered in the kitchen with the voice of my husband, saying, "I'll be waiting for you."

I took a deep breath, then another, and another. I was floating motionless in the air, rising higher and higher.

Another breath, not so deep this time, then I hurled outward into the black void of oblivion.

Something tugged at my lungs, an unseen hand grasped my heart, wringing the blood into my tortured bosom. There was a roaring in my ears, and my breath tore in my throat. I sank from a great height, falling rapidly and still more rapidly.

Then voices, and I opened my eyes. People, swimming crazily before me, and out of the mass came the frightened face of Mrs. Edward Sherman, who lived in our building.

Something had gone wrong. This was not death. This was rescue—rescue for what?

"You're not doing me any favor," I said sleepily, as I closed my eyes again and tried to drift back into the void.

But the tugging at my lungs lifted me back to consciousness.

They would not let me die.

The doctor came and treated me against my will. My world steadied, and friends came.

Bonnie White had been alarmed at the tone of my voice. She knew that I had been at the breaking point and feared for me.

She lived so far away she did not dare waste the time to come to the apartment herself. She telephoned Mrs. Sherman. Mrs. Sherman had come to my floor, detected the odor of gas, then ordered it shut off in the basement. She summoned the Fire Department, and the crew broke

Fred Burke's wife, Bonnie.

down the door of the apartment, found me drifting from life, and brought me back to the world with a pulmotor.

Although the curtain had been torn asunder by my experiment with death, with a madness I could not understand I schemed to finish what I had started at the first opportunity.

43

REBIRTH AND REVENGE

In my insane desperation and self-pity I scorned the attempts of friends and acquaintances to ease my state of mind.

My only excuse is that I was weak and ill from both the mental and physical shock of my experience. A bleak world was before me; life held nothing but misery.

Then, into the misery again came Father Dwyer.

The good man was born to be a leader. With a wave of his hand he cleared the room, then sat at the side of the bed and took my hand.

"Tell me all about it," he said in his low, kind voice.

And I did. I began at the first, in St. Louis. The jumble of events, housed in my brain, poured from a tortured soul. Sometimes I paused from weakness, but he only sat quietly and waited for me to continue.

I talked for hours, and related to him most of the incidents in this book, the horror, the fear, and my struggles. I told him of my efforts to make Gus go straight, and often my emotion made me pause.

I told him how Gus had always advised me to go to Father Dwyer when I was heavy in spirit, and he only smiled, and the tears gathered in his eyes.

My self pity must have been evident.

"Dear child," he said when I had finished, "you should not want to die, for now you are ready to live.

"Everyone has a cross to bear in life—Gus Winkeler was yours. Now the cross has been removed. You have served your penance. What you have told me is your reason for living, and you must fight for life. You owe no obligation to God and humanity, for your life is an example of human errors. Your mission should be to teach others. If you could convince only one boy or girl who has dreamed of money, and money alone, that money and power is the least thing in life, then these years in your life were spent for a purpose.

"Let me tell you my story," he continued.

And Father Dwyer did tell me his story, his early life, his own trials. He told of the cross he had to bear, and how he finally turned to the robe, that in his experience he might be able to lead others.

And as his story was unfolded I realized how pitifully insignificant were my own troubles. I was concerned only with myself—Father Dwyer was concerned for all humanity. As he talked I painted a new picture of Georgette Winkeler, a picture of a coward, an unflattering picture in every respect.

And when his story was finished late in the day, he talked not to the Georgette Winkeler he had come to visit, but to a new woman born of his wisdom.

In the gathering darkness of the room, he turned his face to the last light of the autumn day seeping through the windows, and he said a prayer for me and for the world.

When he was gone I shed tears—not the tears of selfishness, but tears of remorse at my own littleness.

My emotion passed, I looked with new eyes at my situation. How trivial it all seemed—death, the syndicate, the coroner's jury, clubs, cabarets, casinos, money.

The syndicate would get it all, for I would make no effort to stop them. I would live. My life, the thing I had held so cheaply, now was as dear to me as ever.

I was not afraid.

The coroner's inquest was being held up pending my recovery. After Father Dwyer left an officer came from the coroner's office, and although the doctor had told the nurse not to admit anyone, the officer pushed her aside and entered my room. It was apparent he had been drinking. The other officers in the house had made no effort to bother me.

"I've come to run these cops out," he leered confidentially.

He started using the telephone and called the various government agencies that had officers in my home. He said the coroner wanted the men removed. The Lincoln Park police squad, all friends of my husband, objected, but finally were ordered to leave.

Left in sole charge, the officer made himself at home and rambled on in aimless conversation.

My distaste was so evident the man finally said, "Say, what are you afraid of? You don't even know who sent me here."

Then he started telling me how well he had known my husband and what a fine fellow he always thought Gus was. Since I was trying my best to forget, his remarks were entirely unwelcome, and furthermore, they bore not the slightest ring of sincerity.

In exasperation I finally raised up and said: "Lay your cards on the table. Who sent you here and what did they send you for? Either tell me at once or get out, and if you don't leave under your own power I'll call Chief Shoemaker and have you thrown out."

At my mention of Chief Shoemaker he sobered somewhat and backed out of the room.

Much to my surprise Ralph Pierce came up the next day.

"Well," he said with a confident smirk, "you're doing alright so far. The syndicate is convinced you aren't talking."

"What do you know about it," I snapped.

Then he repeated almost word for word what I had told the officer who had been in the house the night before. Even on my sick bed I could not escape the syndicate.

Murphy, the chauffeur, overheard what went on, and when Pierce departed he came close to me and said, "Miz Gawge, watch yo'self. That police man who came in heah las' night he know Mist' Gus, 'cause I done drove 'em, and he's plenty friendly with them Dagoes."

44

END OF THE EMPIRE

The entire complexion of the Gus Winkeler inquiry had been changed.

Starting out as a thorough sifting of Chicago's wide-flung gambling empire, it had simmered down to an investigation of the ramifications of the enterprises in which my husband was involved, and appeared likely to fail in that.

There was very good reason for this change of motive.

Of all of the witnesses summoned at two previous hearings, held earlier in October, there was a conspicuous absence of most of them. Those who showed up were mostly lesser lights who had so few irons in the fire they had very small chance of losing anything, least of all their lives.

My attempt to quit this world had caused postponement of a third session of the jury, and it was during my period of recovery that I studied in the newspapers what already had transpired at the hearings.

Considering the nature of the testimony, it is not unusual that I was deeply interested. In fact, quite a bit of the testimony would have been downright amusing if I had not been in such desperate straits.

On October 9, Charles Weber, Charles Conrad, and Arthur Schroeder, their associate in the distributing establishment, and the Streets of Paris and other concessions at the Century of Progress fair, were in Miami, Florida, when the assassination had occurred.

When they testified at the investigation, none of the three knew my husband, even by sight.

Weber had no idea why "Big Mike" Winkeler was entering his distributing company office when he was killed.

Other employees said they had never seen him about the place—some hadn't even heard of him until his death.

Frank Nitti and other members of the syndicate could not be found at all.

I was ordered to appear on October 30, and many of those interested in the investigation were literally on tiptoes with expectation, half expecting a "blowup."

I was still weak and ill when I took the witness stand, but determined that my testimony would in no way contribute to the general endeavor to learn the truth.

My attitude could be attributed to one major reason: I was in fear of my life. I was suspicious of everyone in the courtroom.

Under questioning I told the coroner's jury that I knew nothing of my husband's affairs and thought he was connected with an automobile selling concern. Asked if I knew Charles Weber, my answer was "No."

I told them that my husband had never discussed his affairs with me, and since he seemed to do well, I had never asked any questions except on one occasion when I inquired why he carried a gun, and he told me to "mind my own business."

I fabricated some minor untruths concerning the last time I had seen my husband, and under what circumstances, before being asked to explain why my husband was in a borrowed automobile.

I explained that Gus had been harassed by police every time they saw his car, and on this occasion he must have borrowed a car to avoid detection.

Fortunately, they did not press me far on this testimony, or I might have become involved in my own falsehoods. Those conducting the questioning seemed to take cognizance of my physical condition and were not insistent.

After escaping photographers, who swarmed in the court room before and after I left the stand, I became an interested student of further developments in the last phase of inquiry.

At this point the inquiry had practically disintegrated from a gambling investigation to a meager effort to ascertain facts in connection

GARAGE OWNER FACES TRIAL FOR POLICE SLAYING

Seek Evidence Linking Bergl with Crime.

Chief of Detectives Schoemaker said yesterday that police and federal agents are still holding Joseph Bergl, owner of a garage at 5346 Cermak road, Cicero, in the expectation of bringing him to trial on a charge of accessory before the murder of Policeman Miles Cunningham. The policeman was slain on Sept. 22.

Bergl was arrested when it was learned that he had ordered bullet-proof glass, armor plate, red and green headlights, a short wave radio set, and a police siren installed on the automobile used by the slayers of Cunningham. This car was abandoned at Halsted and Adams street, the scene of the murder, as its five occupants, armed with machine guns, fled with loot obtained a few minutes earlier in a robbery of four federal reserve bank messengers at La Salle street and Jackson boulevard.

Meets with Prosecutor.

Chief Schoemaker discussed the prosecution of Bergl yesterday with Assistant State's Attorney Wilbur Crowley. The prosecutor told Schoemaker that he expects to obtain additional evidence linking Bergl with the Cunningham murder and that "Bergl will get everything the law can give him."

Lieut. Frank John of the state's attorney's office recalled yesterday that a year ago he had seen Bergl in the company of Frank Nash, a notorious criminal, who was killed in the Kansas City massacre. Three policemen and a federal agent were victims in the same shooting.

Bergl told police that his partner in the Cicero garage was Gus Winkler, public enemy, who is known as the Chicago agent for criminal gangs of other states. Winkler, who was an associate of Fred [Killer] Burke, now serving a life term in a Michigan prison for the murder of a policeman, has been in custody since Sunday, when he was arrested in his Lake Shore drive apartment.

Communicates with Criminals.

According to Schoemaker and the federal agents, Winkler has been in communication at various times with Harvey Bailey, George [Machine Gun] Kelly, Verne Miller, and others implicated in the Urschel kidnaping in Oklahoma. Kelly was captured Tuesday in Memphis. Miller, who was the machine gunner in the Kansas City massacre, has been identified as one of the gunmen in the Cunningham slaying. He is still a fugitive.

Winkler was known around the Bergl garage as Mike, Schoemaker said. Records found there indicate that the garage had done work on many cars owned by criminals.

Schoemaker has also learned that the car which Bergl had had armored was used several weeks ago in a federal reserve bank holdup in St. Paul, during which a policeman was killed.

Machine Gun Kelly had been linked with the murder of Cunningham in two ways, Schoemaker disclosed. An auto owned by Kelly was given in part payment for the Cunningham death car. Also Kelly is known to have been in Chicago on the night of the holdup and murder, fleeing to Memphis after the crimes had been committed.

with my husband's death—a very ordinary procedure. The entire matter was becoming what is commonly known as a "frost."

Lieutenant Otto Erlanson, homicide officer, confessed his inability to discover any reason for Gus' murder and said that Goldblatt, who he believed was in a position to know more than anyone about the case, had been of no help whatever.

Joe Bergl said he knew nothing of my husband's business, and his only connection with him had been in auto sales deals.

Bergl was under arrest for alleged implication in the Loop holdup.

Jack Rubens, the public administrator's chief investigator, told the jury he had visited the 225 Club, but had found nothing there indicating that my husband had had any connection with either the operation of the club or the late Eddie Lebensberger, who managed it.

So it went—an amazing lack of information. The names of witnesses were called by the dozen, and no one answered. Nitti was out of town; no one knew where. Saloon operators, tavern keepers, and many others had evinced a sudden interest in other places and could not be found.

The investigation had struck an impassable obstacle and dissipated into thin air.

And is it any wonder?

Knowing the methods of the underworld, is it logical to believe that anyone valuing his life would risk it, even to deal a death blow to gangland?

Is it natural to believe that the men in the position of Joe Bergl and Benny Goldblatt would tell of their connection with Chicago's crime syndicate, knowing that they themselves might become involved, unless gangland retribution came first?

Is it reasonable to believe that men who had broken every law of God and man, who had ignored every rule of established order, who had defied society and the regulations imposed on it, would heed the summons of a mere subpoena?

No, the contrary would be natural.

The far reaching tentacles of crime organization cannot be so easily trapped.

No one can say that the law is weak in these respects. The law is there—the enforcement is weak. Henry Barrett Chamberlin of the Chicago Crime Commission, who was one of the jurors, summed up the situation when he said concerning the investigation, "It's apparent that under such circumstances such a procedure is useless. The easiest course is to have a medical examiner certify the cause of death."

The examination in no way was of benefit to me except to establish the perfidy of the witnesses. Many questions of vital interest to me remained unanswered.

Chief among them was the failure of the investigators to learn what had become of the keys in the Goldblatt car to which Gus had ridden to his doom.

I was determined to find out.

45

"DO YOU SEE THIS GUN?"

Working on the theory that Benny Goldblatt was the weakest link in the chain of untold evidence, I laid a trap for him.

I summoned him to the apartment.

When he entered the door he was surprised and alarmed to find me sitting at a table on which lay a revolver, with a vacant chair before me. I beckoned him into that chair.

I talked casually for awhile, at no time taking my hand from the gun. I handled it carelessly, but at all times made sure he could look into the barrel.

I made no threats, indicated no displeasure, but I was sure he was unpleasantly aware of the weapon in my hand. Benny kept glancing nervously at the gun, and finally couldn't sit still in his chair. Automatically he would keep leaning out of range.

"Benny," I said finally, "do you see this gun?"

"Hell, yes," he exploded, "who wouldn't? I wish you'd let the damn thing alone; you're giving me the jitters."

Benny was on the witness stand and didn't know it.

"When I find the man who has the keys to the car Gus Winkeler was driving the day he was killed," I continued as if I had not been interrupted, "I'm going to unload this thing in his filthy carcass."

"For God's sake, Georgette," he pleaded, livid with fear, "don't do that. Put the gun down, Georgette, and I'll talk to you."

"Okay," I said, placing it within easy reach. "Get going."

"I've got the keys," he announced. "I've had them all the time."

"Get busy," I said through clenched teeth as I grabbed the gun again. "Explain that away before this thing goes off."

Goldblatt was standing and shaking in fear.

"Don't shoot," he begged. "I didn't drive Gus over there. Someone else did, and they gave me the keys later."

"Don't hand me that stuff," I said, resorting to a bluff. "I happen to know you left the Lincoln Park Arms with Gus."

"Yeah, that's right, I did," he stammered, backing toward the door, "but I left him."

"Sure you did," I said in a low voice, pointing to the gun. "Sure you left him—after he got out of the car and someone filled him full of lead. Then you left him. Now get out of my sight, you dirty rat, and if I ever see you again, I'll blow you to hell."

But I never did see him again.

Only a few days later I received a telephone call from the man named Jack, sometimes called "Schnozzle," who has been mentioned before. He was one of Gus' most trusted employees.

He said he wanted to see me, but since most of the boys were laying low I would have to meet him someplace, as he did not want to be seen. I agreed to meet him in Cicero.

Jack had always been a mystery to everyone, and I do not believe that even Gus knew his last name. He never discussed his past.

When I met him he was partially disguised, dressed in laborer's clothing.

"Georgette," he began, "who do you think killed Gus?"

"Why, Verne Miller," I replied, since I had never revealed my real opinion to anyone.

"You're wrong," he replied, "and we'll prove it to you in a few weeks. Them damn Dagoes took him, and we can prove it. We've been watching Lefty Louie Campagna's house, and we've found out plenty, but right now there's nothing much we can do because Jack White and the rest of the American boys are hiding until the heat cools off.

"But don't you worry; we'll get some of those Dagoes yet. Now you just watch yourself, and above all, be nice to Ralph Pierce—he's dangerous.

"Why, do you know, Pierce tried to put Gus on the spot that Saturday he took him to the syndicate meeting, just before he was killed."

"Are you sure?" I gasped, as a flood of recollections swept over me.

I remembered how anxious Pierce was to get my husband away from his friends! I recalled my own agitation, caused largely by Pierce's behavior and the growing danger to my husband.

"Positively," he replied, "and they'd have done it too but they couldn't get rid of the chauffeur. You ask Murphy what happened. He knows all about it."

When we parted I thanked Jack and promised to meet him the following week.

As soon as I got home, I summoned the chauffeur.

"Murphy," I began, "you thought a lot of Gus, didn't you?"

"I sho' did, Miz Gawge," he said, starting to cry. "Mist' Gus was the bes' friend I evah had."

"Well, then Murphy," I continued, "I want you to tell me just what happened when you took Gus and Ralph Pierce to that syndicate meeting on the Saturday before he was killed."

And Murphy did.

He said they drove out to Berwyn and stopped at the address where the syndicate always held its meetings. They parked directly in front of the entrance, and when Gus got out he told Murphy under no circumstances to move the car until he returned.

Murphy said he waited in the car, but before long Pierce came out of the building saying, "Murphy, things look funny to me across the street. I think I saw someone looking out of the window. You drive on down the block and park just around the corner and wait for Gus there."

Murphy said he told Pierce that Gus had instructed him not to move the car and to wait in that spot, and right there is where he would wait. The colored man told Pierce that if there was any danger he would meet Gus at the door as he came out and walk in front of him to the automobile.

Pierce argued with him and tried to make him move the machine, but Murphy said he did not answer.

Eventually my husband and Pierce came out to the car, and they drove back to Chicago. Neither mentioned anything suspicious across the street from the meeting place.

"I wish you had told Gus, or at least told me," I said to Murphy when he finished his story. "We might have saved him."

"I know it," he sobbed, "but dat's de las' time I evah drove him. I nevah saw 'im agin."

That was true, for Gus was killed the following Monday.

It was easy to see through Pierce's plot. Someone had been concealed in the house across the street and had intended to use Gus as a target as he left the meeting place.

The car was parked between the entrance and the opposite house, making a good shot impossible.

While Murphy was still in the room, I tried to explain to him that I wouldn't need him anymore because I couldn't afford a chauffeur.

He broke into tears again and pleaded for my permission to stay. He said all he wanted was just something to eat.

"You ain't got no bizness bein' alone, Miz Gawge," he argued. "When you is yo'self agin I'll get me a nuther job. But you's in danger, Miz Gawge, and ol' Murph stays right heah. I owe that to Mist' Gus. I'm only a nig-gah, but I wanta help you all I kin."

All the servants were the same way. I discharged the butler outright, but every day, when I would be gone, he would slip back to the house and take the dog for the customary daily walk.

I finally escaped them by giving up the apartment and moving to Berwyn without their knowledge, leaving no forwarding address.

46

CONFRONTING THE MOB

Secluded in a house at Berwyn, with only Murphy and my maid, I had plenty of time to think over the most recent events.

They preyed on my mind. The future appeared blank, for I had no income, and now I valued my life too much to go to the syndicate or attempt to explain my position to the proper authorities.

I marveled that during the investigation, the things that had appeared so plain to me could not be uncovered for the jury.

Many of the facts were common knowledge, even to the newspapers. I could not help but believe these facts had reached the jury, but I could not understand why, if they had, there were no disclosures made.

In the very first place, if Goldblatt did not drive Gus to his doom, then how did he get possession of the keys to the car?

If what Goldblatt said was true, that the keys had been returned to him by another individual—then who was it?

If Goldblatt convinced the authorities that he had no connection with Gus other than to peddle alcohol for him at one time, then why were they seen constantly together in public places, most often at the clubs on the North Side?

If Charles H. Weber did not know my husband, what kind of enterprise were they in together before the return of legal beer?

Why was Gus Winkeler a daily visitor at Weber's real estate office at 2922 Southport Avenue, where Arthur Schroeder and Charles F. Conrad also made their headquarters?

What was the office on the floor above that real estate office, and if Gus, Weber and Goldblatt did not sell illegal beer to North Side speak-easies from that office, then what did they sell?

If it wasn't beer that was stored in the small garage which still stands at the rear of that office, then what was it used for?

If Weber did not know Gus Winkeler, how was it he never saw him when he daily went through the real estate office to get to the office above it?

Why was the office and garage vacated when the new place opened at 1414 Roscoe Street, where my husband was killed?

If Gus Winkeler didn't put up the money to open the Charles H. Weber Distributing Company—then who did?

If Weber owned it, then why did Gus ride the trucks the night beer came back?

If Gus had nothing to do with the distributing company, why was he always allowed to go through the books whenever he put in an appearance?

Why did the employees always put on such a great display of being busy when Gus called, unless they knew he had the power to discharge them?

Why did office manager Edward Leisk say, "If he (Winkeler) don't quit coming around here everyone will know he's got a slice of this"?

If Gus had nothing to do with it, why was he able to order beer bought by the Charles H. Weber Distributing Company, then have it sent to branch distributors in surrounding towns?

Why weren't the employees at the distributing plant asked why they had never seen Gus when he made an inspection of the place every time he went there?

Why was it necessary to finally arrange a private office for Gus at the distributing company?

Thinking it over, I could see that the same questions, if answered truthfully, would have revealed much in connection with a startling number of cabarets, clubs, and saloons on the North Side.

In all of them Gus was almost a daily visitor. He came and went in the business offices as he wished and made inspections of the books whenever he felt it necessary.

He gave orders, and employees would hasten to obey.

Why weren't these employees asked about his visits? Why weren't they asked why they took orders from Gus Winkeler?

Of course, Gus never kept records of his business. He took his share in cash, he did not write checks, and in all cases he took great care to remain in the background.

But surely, in the presence of so many facts, some truth could have been found that would certainly have identified him with the properties he owned.

In asking myself these questions, I was not malicious. I entertained no hope of recovering the property, but was only amazed that the facts could have escaped the investigators.

It was not surprising that the operators of the places he owned would keep a close guard on their tongues, but surely the dozens of the minor employees could have shed some light on the matter.

It was fortunate for me that they had not. For had I been recognized as the succeeding owner of the property, it is certain from facts I have before mentioned that I would never have lived to have a share of the profits.

And even now I realized that I was not safe. I knew that as long as I lived in Chicago, I would be under constant surveillance in anticipation of the time when I might undertake to assert myself.

47

ON THE SPOT

Temporarily I was safe, but I knew it was a matter of only a few days before I would be located.

Lefty Louie Campagna saw Murphy and asked my address, but the faithful colored man refused to tell.

Lefty wheedled him on the grounds that the syndicate men wanted to talk to me about a settlement, but Murphy knew that if they had any such intentions they would have done so before.

It wasn't long before Murphy and I realized that we were being followed whenever we were seen on the street. Syndicate men recognized the car and trailed it in the hope of finding where I lived. Murphy was too clever to be caught in such a fashion and was always able to shake his pursuers.

But such tactics made me nervous. I could not get over the fear that, failing to learn where I lived, they might end the chase with a hail of bullets, with me as the target.

So in desperation I telephoned Lefty Louie and gave him my address, but no one came to see me.

Then I was certain they were not interested, except in keeping track of me.

Jack White, still in hiding, sent one of his boys to my house to learn if I had seen Jack "Schnozzle," who appeared to be missing.

I explained to this man that Schnozzle had come to see me with an offer of aid, and that I had agreed to meet him the following week to learn further details of Gus' death, but he had failed to keep the appointment.

The matter began to worry me, and I telephoned a friend of Schnozzle's in East St. Louis, Illinois, asking if he had seen him. He said he had not heard from him in some time. I reported this fact to Jack White.

A few days later I was surprised when Ralph Pierce telephoned. I never learned how he got my phone number because it was installed under an assumed name.

"I just found your number," Pierce began. "I thought I'd better call you and give you the dope since I understand you have been trying locate Schnozzle. You can take it straight from me that you can't locate him now. He won't bother you anymore."

I was so shocked that I could not even answer—just returned the receiver to its hook.

I knew what had happened. Jack had been disposed of, taken for a ride because he had dared try to befriend me. Blown to ribbons, probably, because he represented the North Side machine set up by Gus Winkeler—a machine that was being torn down.

It occurred to me that I might learn something from Louis Cohen, the Cicero editor who was trying to get Gus' help at the time he was killed.

I asked Murphy if he had heard anything more of Cohen, and he said he hadn't.

We had talked it over—how he wanted to open an establishment in Florida, and how he had defied the syndicate when they demanded control of it.

"Well," I said, "I guess he had to do just like we all do, bow down to the syndicate. I suppose it's all settled now."

I asked Murphy to get the papers for me before he went home.

When he returned with the papers, he was rolling his eyes. "Miz' Gawge," he said seriously, "don't you ever talk me to death."

"What's the matter, Murphy?" I said smiling.

He laid the papers in my lap and there was the answer to my question in black headlines:

LOUIS COHEN MURDERED
Shot in Car; Killers Escape

A day or so later Jack White sent another of his men to my house to see if there was anything I needed.

I thanked the men and told him I was getting along well enough, but warned him that Jack ought not to send his boys to the house, citing what had happened to Schnozzle.

"You might be followed here," I told him, "and that would be your finish."

I explained that several strange cars had been parking along the street, and that Murphy and the maid were positive they had seen men watching the house.

"Oh, that's all right," Murphy said. "The syndicate don't know me, and Jack has a safe hiding place where no one could ever find him."

"That's all right, too," I said, "but you make sure you don't lead them right to Jack. I know these Dagoes."

That was the last time he ever was sent to see me.

Jack White was killed that night.

From friends I learned that George Goetz was trying to locate me, and tried to get him word of my whereabouts, but I never knew what he wanted.

He was shot down on the street March 20, 1934. [Goetz was mortally wounded outside a café in Cicero about 11 PM on March 20 but died in a hospital a few hours later, on March 21.]

He was almost the last of the American boys who had been with Al Capone and later with Gus, and their elimination meant the downfall of the last underworld opposition to the syndicate. I knew Louie Campagna's methods well enough to know that those who remained would go one at a time, until there was no remnant of the old regime.

They wanted a clear field. I understood that they had stepped into the North Side and taken over everything, running it their own way. Frank Nitti was the apparent leader, but I suspected that Lefty Louie had more to do with it than anyone realized.

In the meantime I had read with considerable interest the newspaper accounts of the slaying of Verne Miller. His unclothed body had been found November 29, 1933, in a ditch near Detroit, Michigan. He had been stabbed in the head.

48

RESOLUTION

My efforts to lead a retired and normal life seemed to be in vain, for I had no difficulty seeing that I was still being watched and therefore figured the syndicate must attach some importance to my presence in Chicago.

In a final attempt to reach some kind of understanding with the syndicate that would free me of their surveillance, I determined to go to Lefty Louie Campagna personally and attempt to persuade him to let me alone.

So one night I drove to his home on Maple Avenue in Berwyn in an effort to have it over with once and for all.

I was shown to the second floor of the house, for apparently there was some kind of a gathering downstairs.

It was plain Lefty couldn't figure out why I had come, but he attempted to appear unconcerned. I made no effort to alarm him, but after greetings let him do most of the talking.

He mentioned Jack White, George Goetz, and the other boys who had been Gus' friends, but I made no comment. This seemed to make him nervous, for it was evident he believed I had some purpose in visiting him.

He went on to explain that the syndicate now controlled the distributing company, and that Weber would continue to run it.

"You got everything, didn't you?" I said finally.

"What would you expect?" he came back.

"Nothing from you," was my reply, "but I'm wondering what became of the 225 Club."

"Oh, that went to Eddie Lebensberger's wife," he answered with a smile. "Why don't you claim it?"

It was my turn to smile.

"Lefty," I said in all sincerity, "all I want is peace."

His brows knotted in perplexity. He did not know what I meant; no one wrapped in the business of the underworld could understand.

Lefty Louie Campagna could not understand that the peace I wanted was peace of mind, and a complete separation from the kind of life that had claimed fifteen of the best years of my existence.

Such a man could not understand that a woman who had been in my position might want to atone for the sins of her husband. But surely he could see that the woman who sat before him was not the woman who had been the wife of "Big Mike" Winkeler.

Lefty still groped for something to say that might bring out the reason for my visit. He spoke aimlessly on various subjects for a time, then came out with what he probably considered would be a bombshell that would shatter my calm.

"You figuring on trying to even up with us?" he asked, watching me closely. "You know, a lot of people make confessions and statements, but nothing ever comes of it."

I raised my eyebrows as if I did not understand what he was driving at as he continued: "You know, you must see a crime committed to prove it."

"That's right, Lefty," I nodded in perfect agreement, "you have to see it done to prove it."

I knew I had no chance against the syndicate, and Lefty Louie knew it, but he had learned that I was not afraid of him.

"Just forget about me," I remarked as I left the room.

After I got downstairs I walked directly into the room where the gang was sitting. There was talking and laughter before I came in—dead silence as I came through the door.

As I walked within arm's reach of Tony Paseo his eyes narrowed as they followed me over his shoulder. This hired killer of the syndicate would not entertain the least compunction at killing me, but I felt perfectly safe.

MRS. WINKLER GIVES UP FLAT ON THE DRIVE

Mrs. Georgette Winkler, whose husband, Gus, north side gang leader, was slain Oct. 9, yesterday moved away from the apartment they occupied at 3300 Lake Shore drive. Her new a̶ ̶ ̶ ̶ closed.

Ra̶
ment
term
kler
an F
Chic
"
a p
her
alw
gel
me
pa
sa
w
al

FORCED TO SELL FURNITURE, GIVE UP APARTMENTS

Lebensberger and Winkler Estates Nil.

BY KATHLEEN McLAUGHLIN.

There's a yawning emptiness, these days, behind the impressive facade of 1258 Lake Shore drive, until recently the home of the late Edgar Lebensberger. There's an apartment available" notice outside swanky 3300 Sheridan road.

I stopped for a moment and spoke to them, but none seemed overjoyed to see me. They were too mystified by my visit.

I have seen none of them since.

A short time later I went to St. Louis to visit members of the Winkeler family and was forced to try to explain to them that I had been stripped of everything Gus had owned. They could not understand how I could be left almost penniless when Gus was known to have been one of the most influential figures in the underworld. Making them understand entailed an explanation of how the syndicate worked.

I went out alone to visit my husband's grave.

A cross had been placed there at my direction.

Somehow I felt, as I stood leaning against the heavy cross, that I was very close to my husband. A feeling I could not understand swept over me that if I knew, he was there for me to talk to.

I sat down on the sod and shed bitter tears.

My emotion spent, I sat down near the grave and began to ponder my course. Father Dwyer had since died, but his advice to me lived on. I had something to live for—and I turned this over in my mind, trying to see the light. I had something to do that would show my life as a lesson to others.

When I looked at my watch I was surprised to learn I had been at the grave for over two hours.

But I had seen the light, and as I walked from the cemetery I was filled with high resolve.

I would write this book.

GEORGETTE TALKS TO THE FBI

By 1933 Gus Winkeler had acquired a degree of respectability by way of elegant nightclubs and casinos in what had formerly had been Bugs Moran's Near North Side. He was also a good friend of Buck Kempster, a former bodyguard to two governors who worked both sides of the fence and then was assigned to act as liaison between the State of Illinois and the Justice Department's Bureau of Investigation. This arrangement also kept Winkeler apprised of the Bureau's activities.

Then in June of 1933, Verne Miller, a former Winkeler accomplice, led a bungled rescue attempt at Kansas City's Union Station that cost the lives of a federal agent and three other officers, as well as their captured fugitive. This was the first time outlaw gunmen had deliberately attacked lawmen, and it made banner headlines that shocked the entire country. It also provoked U.S. Attorney General Homer Cummings into declaring a national "War on Crime" that would soon transform the Bureau of Investigation into the FBI.

Miller was quickly identified and zoomed to the top of the Bureau's most-wanted list, and when Miller's frantic girlfriend tried to contact Winkeler in hopes of finding him a hiding place, the answer was an emphatic No. Winkeler had little affection for Miller who, he then believed, had deliberately killed their fugitive friend Frank Nash as well as a federal agent and three other cops. Newspapers called it the Kansas City Massacre.

So Winkeler had personal reasons for wanting no part in that mess or with the federal hornet's nest it was stirring up. Through Buck Kempster he indicated to Melvin Purvis, special agent in charge of the Chicago office, that Miller had crossed the line. He then provided the feds with "intelligence" as to Miller's other Chicago friends and his possible whereabouts.

Frank Nitti was aware of Winkeler's earlier cooperation with the Chicago Crime Commission's "Secret Six" in recovering the loot from the Nebraska bank robbery, and now he worried about what Syndicate information Winkeler might be spilling to the feds. On top of this, he had since learned that Winkeler's friend Ted Newberry was party to the police raid on Nitti's downtown office in which he was nearly killed. And when the bungled Loop mail robbery on September 23, 1933, led both the police and the G-men to visit Winkeler because of his connection with car dealer Joe Bergl, that may have been the last signal Nitti needed to send out his killers, who shotgunned Winkeler on October 9.

After Gus's burial, the burglary of their apartment, and Georgette's suicide attempt, she moved to Indiana to write her expose of the Chicago Syndicate. And when pressure from the mob forced her publisher to break their contract in October 1934, two months later she contacted Melvin Purvis, the federal agent she believed she could trust. She was unaware that Purvis himself had since run afoul of J. Edgar Hoover over the personal publicity he received after the killings of John Dillinger, Pretty Boy Floyd, and Baby Face Nelson, and that he would soon decide to leave the Bureau.

Because Georgette had moved to Louisville, Kentucky, Hoover assigned her case to Indianapolis agents. They listened politely to her recounting of her late husband's crimes, none of which were federal offenses at the time. Moreover, Verne Miller already had been killed by other mobsters, and his known partner, Pretty Boy Floyd, was in deep hiding; so they clearly were more interested in what light she could shed on the kidnappings of brewer William Hamm and banker Edward Bremer, which now involved two "American boys," Fred Goetz and Byron Bolton, who had joined up with the Barker-Karpis Gang.

Many of the names she mentions to the federal agents do not appear in her memoirs; and it was entirely by coincidence that she gave her manuscript to them about the same time that Byron Bolton's role in the

(G   (● LOUISVILLE KY
                                      12/14/34

MR. MELVIN PURVIS.   101185
            DEAR SIR.:-
                        I AM TAKING THE LIBERTY OF
WRITING YOU, AS I WOULD LIKE TO GET IN TOUCH WITH YOU PERSONALLY.
            I HAVE SEVERAL THINGS I WOULD LIKE TO TELL YOU, BUT
WHAT I HABE TO SAY IS FOR YOU AMD YOU ONLY I WILL NOT TALK TO
NO ONE ELSE, ALSO REQUEST YOU NOT TO TELL ANYONE I AM TRYING
TO GET IN TOUCH WITH YOU, I KNOW YOU WILL UNDERSTAND THIS REQUEST
WHEN YOU HAVE TALKED TO ME.
            PLEASE LET ME KNOW JUST WHEN AND WHERE I CAN SEE YOU
I RELIZE YOU ARE BUSY, BUT THIS IS IMPORTANT, I WILL MEET YOU
ANY TIME OR PLACE YOU MAY STATE, OR BE, BUT PREFERABLE SOMEWHERE
OUT OF CHICAGO,
            RESP. YOURS

                    Mrs Gus Winkeler

                MRS. GUS WINKELER
                % GENERAL DELIVERY
                LOUISVILLE KY.

                                    DEC 15 1934

62-000000 -2311

St. Valentine's Day Massacre (which he denied releasing) made front-
page news in the *Chicago American*.

In her interviews with the Indianapolis agents she corrects the mistakes in the newspaper account, as did Bolton when being questioned
by the FBI.

                    *   *   *

January 30, 1935
Director
Division of Investigation
U.S. Department of Justice
Penn. Ave. at 9th St., N.W.
Washington, D.C.

Dear Sir:

Reference is had to Division letter dated January 19, 1935 which enclosed photostatic copies of letter dated December 14, 1934 to Special Agent in Charge Melvin Purvis by Mrs. Gus Winkeler, c/o General Delivery, Louisville, Kentucky, and instructing that Mrs. Winkeler be located and all information in her possession be secured if possible.

Special Agent F. E. Hurley located Mrs. Winkeler, who is now Mrs. Walter Marsh, 113 South Western Parkway, Louisville, and there is attached hereto in triplicate a memorandum submitted to me by Special Agent Hurley covering his interview with her.

There is also enclosed a page from the Evansville, Indiana, Press, dated October 14, 1934, which contains an article pertaining to a book written by Mrs. Winkeler.

Enclosed also herewith are three copies made at the Indianapolis Office of the manuscript of the book Mrs. Winkeler has written. The original manuscript has been returned to Agent Hurley for return to Mrs. Winkeler in accordance with her request. She did not specifically authorize the making of copies of this manuscript but it was presumed that if she were willing that it might be read by Agents of this Division that copies might be made for that purpose.

In view of the fact that this manuscript contains a great deal of information applicable to conditions in the Chicago territory one copy of it is attached to the Chicago Office copy of this letter.

H. H. REINECKE
Special Agent in Charge

Louisville, Kentucky,
January 31 1935.

10-14-34   THE EVANSVILLE PRESS

Book Written in Evansville About Slain Gangster "Too Hot" To Print

* * * *

Publishing Company Turns Down Life Story of Gus Winkeler, Chicago Racketeer; His Wife Was Author

Notorious Mob Characters In Story

Mrs. Gus Winkler

By ED KLINGLER

AN EXPOSE book by the wife of a slain Chicago gangster, written and printed in Evansville during the last 11 weeks, will not be released to the public.

The printing company, which contracted to complete the book in September, definitely refused Saturday to let go of it. Even proofs were recalled.

The author of the book is Mrs. Gus Winkeler, whose husband was killed Oct. 9, 1933, in a Chicago Loop gun battle.

The printery gave only one reason for refusing to release the book: "It's too hot." By this they apparently meant they feared the story might involve them in court action or in libel charges.

Mrs. Winkeler left the city Saturday for her home. For fear of gangland reprisal she said she is keeping her place of residence a secret.

Succeeded

However, she said that she will expose her residence thru court action, if necessary, in order to get her work published.

Mrs. Winkeler was assisted here in writing the book by Dr. P. X. Hollinberger, who, says he also collaborated in writing "The Strange Death of President Harding" by Gaston B. Means, and "The President's Daughter," by Nan Britton. Hollinberger's pen name is Marla P. LaCrona.

Gus Winkeler, the chief character of the book, rose from petty crime in St. Louis to succeed Al Capone as gang baron of Chicago after Capone was sent to federal prison for income tax evasion.

In her book, which was completely printed before the refusal to release it, Mrs. Winkeler traced her husband's career of crime over a period of 15 years.

Didn't Spare Husband

However, according to the prologue, the book is addressed to girls who have "taken up" with gangsters. Through the book she never allowed the reader to get far from the shadow of terror under which she lived constantly, and which led to a series of nervous breakdowns which eventually caused her to attempt suicide shortly after her husband's death.

Her story did not spare her dead husband. She charged him with the crimes of which she knew he was guilty, and undertook to explain away the crimes with which he was charged and had no connection.

Among the major crime events she told about were: The holdup of the Portland Bank in Louisville; the $3,000,000 bond holdup of the Lincoln City, Neb., National Bank; the Kansas City Depot massacre in which four federal officers and Gangster Frankie Nash were shot; the St. Valentine's Day massacre in which the Bugs Moran gang was wiped out, besides a number of minor offences.

Many of these crimes never have been solved by police.

Pretty Boy Mentioned

She told of the flight after the St. Valentine's Day massacre and the auto accident in St. Joseph, Mich., which led to Winkeler's capture.

She charged that a man now in Alcatraz Island Prison plotted to kidnap Winkeler from the St. Joseph hospital to prevent a "squeal," and how she thwarted the attempt by going directly to Capone.

Among those mentioned intimately in the manuscript were: Harvey Bailey, Verne Miller, Pretty Boy Floyd, Fred "Killer" Burke, Frank Nitti and dozens of others, both living and dead.

She told of the operations of the crime syndicate and how she was forced to give up her husband's interest in syndicate property after his death.

This section, which included serious charges against men still living and not in jail, is believed to have been the deciding factor in "killing" the book.

"Since the old St. Louis days Gus was constantly striving for respectability," Mrs. Winkler said before leaving the city. "He thought the only way he could get it was with money—and in a way he achieved it. After he rose to position in Chicago his underworld life was entirely divorced from his home life.

"Father Dwyer of Chicago, who died recently, urged me to write this book. I'm going to do it—one way or another. I don't expect to make money out of it, but there's a lesson in it that every girl in the world should learn."

MEMORANDUM TO SPECIAL AGENT IN CHARGE:

RE: MRS. GUS WINKELER

Louisville, Kentucky.

(Crime and gangsters, Chicago, Illinois)

Agent returned Mrs. Winkeler's manuscript to her in accordance with the suggestions contained in your letter of recent date. The title of her proposed book is, "A Voice From The Grave." She seemed well pleased over the fact that her offer to cooperate with the Division is appreciated. She again advised that she will be pleased to meet with any authorized representative of the Division at any time if an interview is desired. She promised to give details as to past and pending crimes in the Chicago and St. Louis districts. She maintains her willingness to appear as a witness if necessary. In this connection, she advised that she is not afraid to die; that she would like the opportunity of testifying against such mob men as Frank Nitti and "Lefty Louie" Campagna, Chicago gangsters.

She feels that her cooperation could be extended and that she can reach women and men that the Division, perhaps, cannot contact successfully. She seemed to resent the intimation that she might be used as an informant. Agent's conversation with her was entirely satisfactory so far as personal considerations are concerned. She mentioned the fact that Special Agent Smith of Chicago has interviewed her in the past. In this connection, Mrs. Winkeler intimated that she would like to have him represent the Division in the future; that she has a kindly feeling for the manner in which Agent Smith handled her in the past. However, Mrs. Winkeler stated that any well informed person from Chicago, or one that knows Chicago gangsters and crime conditions, would be welcome to her home. Briefly, she likes Agent Smith.

Mrs. Winkeler appears to be a well educated, strong minded person. She admits brooding over the death of her former husband, Gus Winkeler. She is very bitter toward the gangsters of Chicago, particularly toward those whom she terms "the syndicate." However, her desire to whip the Nittis, the Campagnas and such does not get the better of her good judgment. She appears to be very courageous but reasonably careful.

Agent questioned Mrs. Winkeler with reference to the authorship of her manuscript. She claims to have written it; that she did not employ any person to collaborate with her or act as a "ghost writer"; that she has collaborated with one Dr. Francis X. Hollenberger, PhD., a resident of Lake Wandawega, Elkhorn, Wisconsin, on a former occasion; that at the time she wrote a manuscript covering much the same matter as contained in her present manuscript; that Dr. Hollenberger, however, ruined it with too many details and direct accusations and insults to Government officials, State, City and Federal; that she and the doctor quarreled vigorously and the doctor has threatened her repeatedly. She claims that Hollenberger, a well educated German, was arrested during the late World War as a suspected German spy and held in prison; that she knows that he is now a German spy, at least an energetic, tireless Hitlerite and Nazi enthusiast; that she knows that Hollenberger has received coded messages of great importance from his brother in Germany; that he read her the code and explained it in part to her. Mrs. Winkeler further advised that Dr. Hollenberger is undoubtedly an enemy of the United States, that is, politically; that he is a dangerous man in other particulars; that she can furnish facts to prove her contentions. She referred Agent to a Miss Martha Grabowski, 1331 West Florence Street, Evansville, Indiana, as a young woman whom the doctor deceived; that she has an affidavit from Miss Grabowski in which the latter explains her relations with the doctor; that she claimed therein that the doctor had promised to "knife" Mrs. Winkeler with reference to the manuscript; that he would go to the gangsters in Chicago and betray Mrs. Winkeler; that she, Miss Grabowski, could act as his intermediary in the betrayal; that Miss Grabowski could claim $15,000.00 from the syndicate in Chicago; that they could then go to Germany and become man and wife. Mrs. Winkeler showed the affidavit to Agent. This was done only to corroborate her statements to some extent. She admitted that perhaps the Division would not be interested in such matters; that she does feel, however, that the Division may feel interested in Hollenberger, the German spy; that the records show that the United States Government was very much interested in him during the War, according to the doctor's own admissions to her. She gave Agent a photograph of the doctor, same to be forwarded to the Division. The fact of real interest to the Division at this time is that while the doctor collaborated with Mrs. Winkeler in the writing of a manuscript on Chicago crime in the past, he did not do so when she wrote the present manuscript; that she wrote it herself and did not employ a "ghost writer."

Informant, in referring to Dr. Hollenberger from time to time, advised that he formerly resided at 1217 N Street, Washington, D.C.; that he has not been a resident in Washington for some time; that the doctor advised at one time that he did not dare go to Washington; that she jumped to the conclusion that either the authorities knew of his deviltry or that his superiors in office did not want him in that area fearing that he might complicate matters for them. She is not definite on this score.

Agent also met Mr. Walter Marsh, the present husband of Mrs. Winkeler. Marsh is a former resident of Chicago where he was employed for seventeen years as a foreman in a steel construction concern. He is now engaged as a lecturer, from time to time, on religious subjects. He is not steadily engaged at any occupation. He is not identified with any religious house or organization as a preacher or lay worker. His serious pleasure, he claims, is uplift work among the unfortunate. He is not engaged in any line of work at the present time. He and his wife purchased their home at 113 South-Western Parkway, Louisville, Kentucky, about one year ago. They are permanently located there. Her sisters and brothers are also residents of Louisville. A sister, Mrs. Lee, lives with the Marshes and their two children, a girl about 10 years of age and a boy of 14 years. Both attend public schools at Louisville near their home. Mr. Marsh has been engaged for some time in the renovation and decoration of their home. He is a skilled mechanic and artist. Their home is remarkably comfortable and tastefully established. Mr. Marsh seems to be in hearty agreement with his wife's plan. He seems to encourage, rather than to block, any prospective move she may make against gangsters. He also appears to be a well educated, keen minded person. Their attitude toward Agent was decidedly friendly, respectful and apparently sincere. They repeatedly stated that they would welcome any Division representatives should the Director care to send one to their home. Apparently they do not care to seek favors or ask for protection. They did request, however, that inasmuch as they have met the reporting Agent and have held conversations relative to Chicago crime matters, it is only proper that this agent introduce them to any Division representative that may care to interview them in the future. They reminded Agent that they fully trust the Division and are willing to meet representatives at any time. However, they want to feel assured that any other Special Agent that might call on them is so authorized to discuss Chicago matters with them; that his call is directly due to the report that this Agent has submitted to his official superiors.

F. E. Hurley
Special Agent

ADDENDUM: Mrs. Winkeler added that anyone who converses with Dr. Hollenberger, sometimes spelled Hollnberger, can induce him to expand provided they appear to sincerely praise Hitler.

*   *   *

U -
FEDERAL BUREAU OF INVESTIGATION

Form No. 1
THIS CASE ORIGINATED AT St. Paul, Minn.   FILE NO. 7-34:3

REPORT MADE AT	DATE WHEN MADE	PERIOD FOR WHICH MADE	REPORT MADE BY
Louisville, Ky.	5/19/36	5/15,18/36	JOHN L. MADALA JLM/moh

TITLE	CHARACTER OF CASE
CHARLES JOSEPH FITZGERALD, with aliases, et al; WILLIAM A. HAMM, JR., -- VICTIM	KIDNAPING

SYNOPSIS OF FACTS: Mrs. Walter Marsh, formerly Mrs. Gus Winkeler, advises that "Old Gus", whom she also knows as "Schnozzle" and "Jack", was close associate of Charles J. Fitzgerald and Gus Winkeler. Does not know his correct name nor has information regarding his history and background. States that "Old Gus" formerly had a farm in vicinity of Chicago, on which he raised Doverman Pinscher dogs. Left this farm to his wife after their divorce in 1932 or 1933. Later became associated with young Bohemian girl, identity unknown. Mrs. Marsh definitely indicates "Old Gus" slain by syndicate in Chicago, Illinois shortly after Gus Winkeler's assassination by that outfit in October, 1933. "Old Gus" well known to Charles Fitzgerald, Joe Bergel, "Buck" Kempster, and Louis "Doc" Stacci, and all can furnish valuable information as to him. Mrs. Winkeler partially identifies photograph of Jack Pfeiffer as visitor to her apartment in Chicago some time after Hamm kidnaping. Purpose of his visit was to have Winkeler get him in touch with Fred Goetz. Pfeiffer was accompanied by small woman, presumably his wife. Further information relating to activities of the Al Capone Syndicate, Fred Goetz, Charles Fitzgerald, and Bryan Bolton set forth herein.

- P -

REFERENCE: Letter from Chicago Bureau office dated May 5, 1936.

APPROVED AND FORWARDED: O.C. Dewey   SPECIAL AGENT IN CHARGE   DO NOT WRITE IN THESE SPACES
7 + 77 - 1738   MAY 26 1936
MAY 27 19..

COPIES OF THIS REPORT
(3-)Bureau
2-St. Paul   COPIES DESTROYED   MAY 25 A.M.
2-Chicago   135   MAR 15 1965
2-Cincinnati
1-USA, St. Paul
2-Louisville

U. S. GOVERNMENT PRINTING OFFICE   7-8094

FEDERAL BUREAU OF INVESTIGATION

(Report made on 5/19/36 by Agent John L. Madala at Louisville, Ky., for period 5/15–18/36.)

Mrs. Walter Marsh, formerly Mrs. Gus Winkeler, advises that "Old Gus," whom she also knows as "Schnozzle" and "Jack," was close associate of Charles J. Fitzgerald and Gus Winkeler. Does not know his correct name nor has information regarding his history and background. States that "Old Gus" formerly had a farm in vicinity of Chicago, on which he raised Doberman Pinscher dogs. Left this farm to his wife after their divorce in 1932 or 1933. Later became associated with young Bohemian girl, identity unknown. Mrs. Marsh definitely indicates "Old Gus" slain by syndicate in Chicago, Illinois, shortly after Gus Winkeler's assassination by that outfit in October, 1933. "Old Gus" well known to Charles Fitzgerald, Joe Bergl, "Buck" Kempster, and Louis "Doc" Stacci, and all can furnish valuable information as to him. Mrs. Winkeler partially identifies photograph of Jack Pfeiffer [variously spelled in other books and documents but should be Peifer] as visitor to her apartment in Chicago some time after Hamm kidnapping. Purpose of his visit was to have Winkeler get him in touch with Fred Goetz. Pfeiffer was accompanied by small woman, presumably his wife. Further information relating to activities of the Al Capone Syndicate, Fred Goetz, Charles Fitzgerald, and Bryan Bolton set forth herein. [The man Georgette calls "Schnozzle" or "Old Gus" has never been firmly identified.]

REFERENCE: Letter from Chicago Bureau office dated May 5, 1936.
DETAILS: AT LOUISVILLE, KENTUCKY

Reference letter requests that Mrs. Walter Marsh, who formerly was the wife of Gus Winkeler, now deceased, be interviewed regarding her knowledge of one "Schnozzle," whom it is believed is identical with "Old Gus," alias Gus Stone, alias Gus Stevens, prominently mentioned in the instant case, as well as the Brekid Case [FBI shorthand for Bremer Kidnapping Case], and that a definite inquiry be made concerning his past acquaintances, associates, and activities which might assist in establishing his identity.

Mrs. Walter Marsh was interviewed by Special Agent Z. J. Van Landingham and the writer at her husband's place of business on May 15, 1936, and thereafter was again interviewed by the writer and Special Agent in Charge, O.C. Dewey, also at her husband's place of business, on May 18, 1936. For the information of the file, Mr. and Mrs. Walter Marsh own and operate the Triangle Restaurant located at 1804 [then listed in city directories as 1605] Bardstown Road, Louisville, Kentucky, and their residence address is 113 S. Western Parkway, Louisville, Kentucky. [In a separate report to Hoover from Louisville agent John L. Madala covering interviews on May 15–18, 1936, he advises that an edited version of her story—with names changed—recently appeared in *Famous Detective* magazine and that she has no objection to the Bureau using her original in any manner it sees fit.]

With particular reference to the letter from the Louisville office to the Chicago office dated August 6, 1935, which is mentioned in reference letter and which refers to "Schnozzle," thought to be identical with the said "Old Gus," Mrs. Marsh at this time furnished considerable additional information, which, it is believed, might be of some value in establishing his identity.

Mrs. Marsh stated that the individual whom she knows as "Schnozzle" and also as "Jack" is also known to her as "Old Gus." She stated that this individual has a Jewish appearance, in view of the largeness of his nose; that he is approximately 45 or 50 years of age; five feet, eleven inches tall; weighs 165 pounds; hair dark; eyes dark; complexion dark. It will be noted that this description is substantially identical with that of the Gus described by Arthur "Red" Johnson as set out in reference letter.

Mrs. Winkeler advised that she has known "Old Gus" since 1931; that he was a close associate of Charles J. Fitzgerald, Fred Goetz, and her late husband, Gus Winkeler. She was unable to furnish any information concerning his history or background but stated that it is her belief that he is from the vicinity of Chicago, Illinois. Mrs. Marsh further stated that "Old Gus" participated in the Lincoln, Nebraska, bank robbery in September of 1930, and that he subsequently was instrumental in recovering a portion of the bonds taken in that robbery, which bonds were thereafter turned over to the Lincoln, Nebraska, authorities for the release of Gus Winkeler, who was being held for that crime. Mrs. Marsh stated that "Old Gus" was married and that in 1932 or 1933 he obtained a divorce from his wife and thereafter kept company with a young Bohemian girl who comes from either Cicero or Berwyn, Illinois. She was unable to furnish any information regarding "Old Gus's" first wife nor could she be of any assistance in the identification of the latter girl.

Mrs. Marsh further stated that it is her information that "Old Gus" at one time within the past five years owned a farm outside of Chicago,

Illinois, exact whereabouts unknown to her, on which farm he raised Doberman Pinscher dogs; that "Old Gus" spent considerable time on this farm attending to his dogs and very few persons were allowed to visit him thereon; in fact, only a few persons know of the location of this farm. She stated that Gus Winkeler, whom "Old Gus" trusted implicitly, visited this farm on several occasions, and at one time he was accompanied there by Joe Bergl, who owns and operates the Chevrolet Agency in Cicero, Illinois, this individual being well known to the Chicago Bureau Office. Mrs. Marsh further stated that it is her information that when "Old Gus" divorced his wife, he left the farm in her possession, and that as far as she knows, she, "Old Gus's" wife, is still residing on this property.

Mrs. Marsh further stated that "Old Gus" likewise is well known to "Buck" Kempster, a former Illinois State Highway Police Officer who also is well known to the Chicago Bureau Office; that "Buck" Kempster and Gus Winkeler were very close friends; and that through this association "Buck" Kempster became affiliated with Charles Fitzgerald and "Old Gus." She stated that subsequent to the time Charles Fitzgerald was wounded in the fall of 1933—this being the South St. Paul payroll robbery on August 30, 1933—"Old Charlie" was taken to the cottage of "Buck" Kempster at Mt. Sterling, Ill., where he was laid up for a considerable period of time; that "Old Gus" made frequent visits to this cottage, as did Gus Winkeler and Joe Bergl.

Mrs. Marsh also indicated that "Old Gus" likewise is well known to Louis Stacci, who is presently serving a two year sentence at Leavenworth, Kansas, in connection with the Kansas City Massacre Case. In this connection she stated that "Old Gus" as well as other members of the Harvey Bailey Gang frequently visited the O. P. Inn at Melrose Park, Illinois, which rendezvous was formerly owned and operated by Stacci. Mrs. Marsh was unable to furnish information regarding whether "Old Gus" and Mrs. Frances Nash ever kept company together.

Mrs. Marsh further stated that around the time Gus Winkeler was assassinated by the Capone Syndicate in October, 1933, Charles J. Fitzgerald, and her late husband operated together; that shortly after Gus Winkeler was killed she made frequent contacts with "Old Gus," who at that time was endeavoring to secure for her certain debts which were owed to Winkeler at the time; that on one occasion, while she was in the office of Abie Merowitz [correct spelling Marowitz], Attorney, Chicago, Illinois, who represented Joe Bergl at the time he was arrested in connection with the smoke screen killing of Chicago Police Officer Myles Cunningham ... [September 22, 1933]. "Old Gus" called her at Merowitz's office and suggested that she immediately meet him at a flower shop in Cicero, Illinois. She stated that this flower shop is owned and operated by a very good woman friend of hers named Dombrow, which name also identifies the instant florist's shop above mentioned. Mrs. Winkeler stated that her business at Merowitz's office at that time was to secure her share of the Chez Paree Night Club, which the syndicate was trying to wrest from her. She stated that she met "Old Gus" at the above meeting place, at which time he told her that he believed he could get a large portion of the money which was due Gus at the time of his death, and that she should meet him again at a designated spot outside of Chicago, Illinois, a week hence. Mrs. Marsh stated that when she saw "Old Gus" on the above indicated occasion he was wearing a pair of coveralls over his clothes to more or less afford him a disguise. In this connection she stated that this was not unusual, for "Old Gus" was a very "cagey" individual and was very much afraid of the law. She stated that "Old Gus" never had persons meet him at his home and that whenever he arranged to meet with someone, such meeting place would always be either on a street corner or at one of the gang's hangouts. She stated that she recalls that on one occasion "Old Gus" mentioned that he never served any time and that the law does not have a photograph of him; that he very seldom visited any night clubs or public places, and on only rare occasions did he visit anyone in their home.

Mrs. Marsh further stated that "Old Gus" did not get along with Fred Goetz and Bryan Bolton very well in 1932 and 1933; that he never trusted Bolton and he always was against Goetz for associating with Bolton.

Mrs. Marsh stated that a day before she was to meet "Old Gus" outside of Chicago, as above indicated, she received a telephone call from Ralph Pierce, whom she refers to as the "rat" and stool pigeon of the syndicate, advising her that it would be best for her not to meet "Old Gus" the next day. He further informed her that "Old Gus" could not be trusted and that if she continued to contact him he would get her into trouble. Mrs. Marsh stated that she was very incensed by this telephone call because of the fact that she deemed "Old Gus" as one of her best friends and that he was apparently the only one who was trying to assist her in any way after Gus Winkeler was killed. She, however, gave Pierce's telephone call considerable thought, and on the day she was to meet "Old Gus" she sent her negro chauffeur, named Murphy, to the designated spot to arrange a meet with him for her for the following day. She stated that when Murphy returned he reported that he waited for approximately an hour at the appointed place for "Old Gus," but that he never showed up. Mrs. Marsh stated that thereafter she did not hear from "Old Gus" any more and naturally became alarmed over him. She made frequent telephone calls to "Three-Fingered" Jack White's apartment and various other places to ascertain whether he had been around those places, but with negative results. She stated that some time thereafter Ralph Pierce confidentially informed her that "Old Gus" would no longer trouble her, and in the conversation which followed Mrs. Marsh definitely gained the impression that "Old Gus" was slain by orders of the syndicate, possibly because they believed that he was meddling into their affairs in trying to collect the debts for Mrs. Winkeler due her husband at the time of his death. In this connection Mrs. Marsh stated that "Old Gus" had ascertained from the underworld that Gus Winkeler was killed by Fred Goetz, Tony Capezio, and a third party, whose identity she had never been able to ascertain, by orders of the syndicate; that shortly after Al Capone was sent to the penitentiary, the Italian element of the syndicate took over the reins of the organization and were more or less trying to force out the American element; that the latter faction was more or less headed by Gus Winkeler and during the years following Al Capone's conviction, Winkeler was gaining considerable power and backing within the syndicate; that those who stood behind him strongly were "Three-Fingered" Jack White, Ted Newberry, "Old Gus," and several other of the American boys, all of whom have since been slain by the Italian element.

Further information advanced by Mrs. Marsh indicates that "Lefty Louie" Campagna, also known as "Little New York," together with Gus Winkeler and Fred Goetz, were sent to New York in the spring of 1931 to kill Frankie Uale [more commonly spelled Yale]; that in this killing Gus Winkeler drove the car and Campagna and Goetz did the shooting.

She further stated that Campagna was almost put on the spot by Al Capone after this killing, inasmuch as while he was in New York Campagna made several telephone calls to his girl friend at Cicero, Illinois, which calls were subsequently traced to her home; that at that time there was considerable heat in Chicago, in view of the tracing of these calls and Al Capone was very much incensed over Campagna's indiscretion in making these calls.

Mrs. Marsh further stated that "Old Gus" frequently hung out at the saloon in Cicero, Illinois, which was operated by a man whom she only knows as "Big Six"; that this saloon is located on the south side of Twenty-second [Street] in the 5200 block; that "Old Gus" frequently visited Louie Cernocky's place at Fox River Grove, Illinois, and also at Joe Bergl's cottage at Cary, Illinois, which town is only two miles north of Fox River Grove. She stated that if Joe Bergl would talk he could tell the Bureau the entire history and background of "Old Gus."

Further information advanced by Mrs. Marsh disclosed that "Old Gus" never learned to drive an automobile and on each job in which he participated he always took the part of a lookout. She stated that in either 1931 or 1932 "Old Gus" had some plastic surgery work performed on his nose, and that this work was done by Dr. Otto Von Borries, a plastic surgeon in Chicago, Illinois, who likewise did similar work on the face of Gus Winkeler and Fred "Killer" Burke; that Dr. Von Borries' services were obtained through the effort of Dr. Omens, also of Chicago, who for a long time attended members of the syndicate. Both of these doctors are well known to the Chicago Bureau office.

Agent questioned Mrs. Marsh as to whether she is acquainted with Jack Pfeiffer or any night club owner from St. Paul, Minnesota. In this regard she stated that she definitely recalls that possibly a month after the Kansas City massacre she came home after playing a game of golf and that her maid told her that a man and woman had been there on several occasions, who desired very much to get in touch with her husband. She stated that around 6:30 on this particular occasion she received a telephone call from the desk clerk downstairs advising that a man and woman desired to see her. Thinking that they were friends of hers, she requested that they come up to the apartment. Mrs. Marsh stated that the man introduced himself as a good friend of Gus Winkeler, stating that he was a night club owner in St. Paul, Minnesota. Mrs. Marsh stated that in the conversation which followed, she learned that Gus Winkeler had been to the Mayo Brothers Clinic Hospital in Rochester, Minnesota, two weeks previous and that while he was there he traveled to St. Paul, Minnesota, and frequented this man's night club. Mrs. Marsh continued that this party advised that he had come in from St. Paul and that he was very much in need of a drink, so Mrs. Marsh offered him some beer, but he asked for whiskey; that both the man and the woman drank a large quantity of whiskey and shortly thereafter Gus Winkeler entered the room. Mrs. Marsh stated that she noted that Gus Winkeler was very much aggravated over the fact that these people had come to their apartment, as at that time he was trying to keep such type of persons away from there. She stated that this gentleman and Gus Winkeler went into another room and talked privately for approximately ten minutes, after which time Gus Winkeler left the apartment to make a phone call from a pay station to Fred Goetz. She stated that Fred Goetz came to their place about a half hour later, at which time this man and woman left with him; that prior to their leaving, the man borrowed $500.00 from Gus Winkeler, which he still owes. She further stated that the man invited both Gus and her to his place at St. Paul, Minnesota, remarking that they would be safe up there, as he had the proper connection with the St. Paul police. He also at the time offered to send her a white ermine neckpiece, stating that he had a large quantity of these on hand, but did not advance the information as to where he got them. Mrs. Marsh further related that when this party and woman left with Fred Goetz, she overheard the latter remark that Irene would certainly to glad to see them again.

The foregoing information was given by Mrs. Marsh to the writer and Agent Van Landingham on May 15, 1936, and when Mrs. Marsh advised that she does not know Jack Pfeiffer of St. Paul, Minnesota, but would be able to identify the photograph of the man who visited them as above related, a telegram was transmitted to the St. Paul Bureau office, requesting that they forward to this office immediately the latest photograph of Jack Pfeiffer for display to Mrs. Marsh. On May 18, 1936, when the writer, together with Special Agent in Charge, O. C. Dewey, again interviewed Mrs. Marsh, the photograph of Pfeiffer, which the St. Paul Bureau office had in the meantime forwarded to this office, was exhibited

WINKLER WIDOW TELS BOAST OF 'FIX' IN ST. PAUL

Protection Talk Related at Hamm Trial.

(Pictures on back page.)

St. Paul, Minn., July 21.—[Special.]
—How Jack Peifer, night club oper-
ator, boasted that he had police protection in St. Paul was related today
by the widow of Gus Winkler at
Peifer's trial for conspiracy in the
$100,000 William Hamm kidnaping.

Appearing as a government witness, Mrs. Georgette Winkler Marsh
told how Peifer and his wife called
at the apartment of the former Capone li_____ in Chicago the day
before _____ split up.
Winkle_____ his
wife _____
that t___
"Big____
ways____
Chic____

Th__
"__
got___
T___
sh___
sta___
er___
ad___
b___

HAMM CASE 'DEAL' TOLD

Widow Testifies to Gangster Boast of Having St. Paul Police Protection

ST. PAUL, July 21. (*P*)—Mrs.
Georgette Winkler, widow of Gus
Winkler, slain Capone lieutenant,
testified in the Hamm kidnap trial
today that John (Jack) Peifer told
her she need not worry about coming to St. Paul with her husband
"because we have police protection
there."

Mrs. Winkler first detailed how
Peifer and his wife came to her
home to see "Big Mike" as her husband was known, and, in the
absence of Winkler, talked about
her coming to St. Paul.

AFRAID OF TH___

to Mrs. Marsh, but she was unable to make a positive identification of the same. She stated, however, that the photograph looked very familiar to her. She denied that she ever visited St. Paul, Minnesota, nor could she recall where and under what circumstances she had previously met Pfeiffer, stating, however, that it is entirely probable that he is the man who visited their apartment at the above indicated time.

It should be noted that the foregoing incident in some respect corroborates Bryan Bolton's story, in that Jack Pfeiffer learned of Fred Goetz's address through Gus Winkeler at the time he, Bolton, accompanied Pfeiffer and his girl friend to Chicago, Illinois, and en route left the plane at Madison, Wisconsin, after he recognized Hamm on the same plane with him.

It is believed that if it becomes necessary to use Mrs. Marsh as a witness in the coming trial of Jack Pfeiffer and others for the instant kidnapping, she can be induced to testify.

With reference to Irene Dorsey, the paramour of Fred Goetz, Mrs. Marsh stated that she has known Irene for seven or eight years, that Irene is a self-educated girl and holds the respect of nearly every member of the syndicate; that Fred Goetz was the type of person who told Irene everything; and that if Irene could be made to talk she would be able to tell the entire story of both the Bremer and Hamm kidnappings, that is, if Fred Goetz participated in those crimes. She stated that Irene on several occasions related to her information which she deemed highly confidential and that Gus Winkeler on numerous instances criticized Fred Goetz to her for his indiscretion in this respect. She stated that it is her belief, and she is almost positive as to this, that Irene Dorsey is presently receiving a monthly monetary tribute from the syndicate; that this is the policy which the syndicate has always followed; and possibly it is for this reason that Irene Dorsey is reticent to furnish any information.

Mrs. Marsh furnished the following information, which relates to Gus Winkeler's advent to Chicago and his subsequent affiliation with the Capone syndicate.

She stated that she and Gus Winkeler came to Chicago, Illinois, from St. Louis, Missouri, in May, 1927; that prior thereto, Gus Winkeler was associated in St. Louis, Missouri, with Fred "Killer" Burke, a member of the old "Egan Rats" and who is presently serving a life sentence for murder in the Michigan State Penitentiary; Tommy O'Connor, now serving a 25 year sentence in the Nebraska State Penitentiary, for participation in the Lincoln, Nebraska, bank robbery; and Ray "Gooseneck" Nugent, who it is believed, was slain . . . some years ago. Upon Winkeler's arrival in Chicago, he became associated with Fred Goetz, Bryan Bolton, Bob Newberry [a.k.a Bob Carey], also known as "Gimpy," "Old Charlie" Fitzgerald, "Old Gus," Harvey Bailey, Frank Nash, and Slim Morris. Thereafter he connected with Al Capone, "Lefty Louie" Campagna, and other prominent members of Capone's criminal organization, and it was not very long before Winkeler was on their regular payroll and doing their killings. This association subsequently led up to the commission of various crimes by him and his companions which will be hereinafter captioned and described.

TOLEDO AMERICAN EXPRESS ROBBERY

Mrs. Marsh stated that this robbery took place on October 16, 1928, and that over two million dollars was taken; however, all of this money was subsequently recovered by the authorities, due to the carelessness of Fred Goetz. Mrs. Marsh went on to relate that the job was cased from the home of Ray Nugent, better known as "Gooseneck," who had established his residence in Toledo, Ohio. The participants were Fred Goetz, Gus Winkeler, Ray Nugent, Bob "Gimpy" Newberry, Bob Carey [this Newberry and Carey are the same person under different names], and "Old Charlie" Fitzgerald. The loot was contained in a safe which was stolen from the express company. The men later had difficulty in opening this safe, and while they were in the act of prying it open in the garage of Nugent at Toledo, Ohio, they were confronted by police officers who had gained entrance into the garage. A gun battle ensued and during the battle Fred Goetz mortally wounded a Toledo police officer. In the confusion which followed, Goetz left his coat at the garage. The coat was subsequently found by the police and it contained bills and other papers bearing the address of Bryan Bolton, with whom Fred Goetz was living at Chicago, Illinois at that time.

Mrs. Marsh further stated that a subsequent investigation by the police never solved this case, and that no one was ever prosecuted for the same. However, Al Capone was very much incensed with Fred Goetz for the latter's participation in this robbery, and as a result was nearly put on the spot. It seems that Al Capone did not approve of robberies of this kind, as nearly all of his and the organization's enterprises at that time consisted for the most part of so-called "rackets."

MURDER OF FRANKIE UALE AT NEW YORK CITY

Mrs. Marsh advised that Frankie Uale [or Yale] was murdered at New York City on July 1, 1928, by Gus Winkeler, Fred Goetz, and "Lefty Louis" Campagna upon orders from Al Capone. She stated that Uale was recognized from his photograph and that Goetz and Campagna did the shooting while Winkeler drove the car. According to Mrs. Marsh, Winkeler later told her that Uale was ordered slain because of the fact that suspicion lay on him for the killing of Dion O'Banion and "Big Jim" Colosimo. [Misheard or mistaken, as Gus reached Chicago in 1927 and may not have known of these killings in any detail.]

It will be recalled that during prohibition Ollie Berg, convicted in the Bremer kidnapping case, was closely associated with Dion O'Banion, above mentioned. [Dion was O'Banion's baptismal name.]

Mrs. Marsh further stated that some time after the Uale killing Tony Lombardo, a good friend of Al Capone, was slain in gangland fashion in Chicago, Illinois, and it has always been said that this killing was in retaliation for the Uale murder.

ST. VALENTINE'S DAY MASSACRE

Mrs. Marsh stated that this massacre took place in Chicago, Illinois, on St. Valentine's Day, February 14, 1929, and was effected upon orders from Al Capone. The object of this wholesale killing was to eradicate "Bugs" Moran and his mob, who at the time were threatening the dominance of the Capone criminal organization, especially in the booze dominance and beer racket. Mrs. Marsh further stated that about a month prior to the massacre Bryan Bolton and Jimmy "The Swede" Morand [frequently spelled Moran] rented an apartment across the street from the North

Clark Garage where it was learned that the Moran mob had frequent meetings. From this spot Bolton and Jimmie the Swede and occasionally "Gimpy" Newberry [Bob Carey, a.k.a. Robert Newberry] maintained a surveillance of the said garage with the orders that should they observe "Bugs" Moran enter this garage to immediately telephone Rocky DeGrazia's residence in Melrose Park, where other persons were stationed and who were to do the killing. At this latter place were Fred Goetz, Fred "Killer" Burke, Gus Winkeler, Rocky DeGrazia, and Ray Nugent. Mrs. Marsh stated that contrary to Bolton's supposed confession of this crime [in the *Chicago American*], Claude Maddox and Murray Humphries did not participate in this killing.

Mrs. Marsh stated that Bolton and Jimmie the Swede on the morning of February 14, 1929, upon observing a number of men enter the garage and thinking that "Bugs" Moran was one of the group immediately telephoned the other place, whereupon all of the above named individuals hastily drove to the said garage, Gus Winkeler doing the driving. [Given newspaper reports that a second car entered the alley and that two men disguised as policemen entered the garage through the rear doors, this may have been the car driven by Winkeler and later destroyed in Maywood, where it was found to contain a notebook belonging to Massacre victim Albert Weinshank.] Fred Goetz and "Killer" Burke wore police uniforms which had been previously furnished to them by a Chicago police officer friend of theirs, and it was these two individuals who in reality did the shooting with Thompson submachine guns. The other boys, namely Rocky, "Gimpy," the Swede, Bryan Bolton, and Ray Nugent acted as lookouts.

When it was later discovered that "Bugs" Moran was not one of the group who were killed Al Capone ordered Bryan Bolton and Jimmie the Swede killed for this blunder, and it was only through the continuous efforts of Fred Goetz that they were saved. A further blunder on the part of Bolton, in that he left a bottle of medicine in the apartment [police reported finding a letter to Bolton from a family member], which the police subsequently traced to him, made him the object of a nation-wide police search. Since that time Bolton had been "on the lam" and was being supported by Fred Goetz, who morally felt responsible for his predicament.

The persons killed in this massacre were six men of the "Bugs" Moran mob and an innocent person who happened to be at the garage at that time.

Later Fred Burke killed a police officer at St. Joseph, Michigan, in an argument over an automobile accident and some time thereafter he was arrested and given a mandatory life sentence, and he is now serving this sentence in the Michigan State Penitentiary.

THE LINCOLN, NEBRASKA, BANK ROBBERY

Mrs. Marsh stated that this robbery took place in September, 1930, and that over two million dollars of bonds were taken, in addition to an indefinite amount of cash. She stated that Charles J. Fitzgerald and his wife, Belle (this being Belle Born) cased this job and prepared the getaway chart. Employed in this robbery was a large enclosed moving van. After the robbery the holdup car was driven into this large van and the same, together with the men, was driven in this truck. Mrs. Marsh advised that the following men participated in this crime: Charles J. Fitzgerald, "Old Gus," Harvey Bailey, Slim Morris, Big Homer, Verne Miller, and a man known to her only as "John" and who has a wife whose first name is Console.

Mrs. Marsh stated that some time after this holdup Gus Winkeler had an automobile accident and was confined to a hospital at St. Joseph, Michigan, for several months; that while at this hospital several witnesses of the instant robbery viewed him and positively identified him as one of the participants. Subsequent thereto and after he became well, the Nebraska authorities removed him to Lincoln, Nebraska and committed him to the State Penitentiary there pending his trial. His bond was set at one hundred thousand dollars and thereafter, mainly through the efforts of Al Capone, the amount of this bond was posted and Winkeler was released.

Mrs. Marsh stated that thereafter it was agreed upon by the Nebraska authorities that if Winkeler returned a major portion of the bonds he would not be prosecuted. She stated that Gus Winkeler had knowledge that his friends committed this robbery and in view of his close association with them he ultimately was successful in recovering a portion of these bonds, which were valued at approximately one-half million dollars. She stated that he later turned these bonds over to the Lincoln, Nebraska, bank officials in the office of the Secret Six in Chicago, Illinois, which organization at that time was headed by Alexander Jamie. Mrs. Marsh stated that Harvey Bailey, Verne Miller, and "Old Gus" were mainly instrumental in assisting Gus Winkeler as above related.

Regarding Slim Morris, Mrs. Marsh stated that he was subsequently slain in Red Wing, Minnesota, for reasons unbeknown to her. It is the writer's belief that this individual is identical with Slim Moran, who, together with Charles J. Fitzgerald, committed the Estherville, Iowa, bank robbery, for which crime the sheriff of Emmet County, Iowa, issued a reward circular for the arrest of Fitzgerald.

Mrs. Marsh stated that Tommy O'Connor and Hal "Pop" Lee, in view of their prior association with Gus Winkeler, were tried and convicted for [the Nebraska] robbery, but that they are innocent. She stated that they are presently serving a sentence of 25 years in the Nebraska State Penitentiary. As a point of interest Mrs. Marsh advised that Tommy O'Connor and "Old Gus" are very similar in appearance and have the same type of nose, which as heretofore indicated is very prominent; that Tommy O'Connor was identified as the lookout man in the Lincoln job, which part was in reality played by "Old Gus." She stated that at the time of Winkeler's death he was negotiating with someone to vindicate Tommy O'Connor and Hal "Pop" Lee of this charge.

KANSAS CITY MASSACRE

It will be recalled that this killing took place on June 17, 1933. Mrs. Marsh advised that either the day or two days after this crime, she received a telephone call from Joe Bergl advising that Vivian Mathis, the paramour of Verne Miller, was in town and was very anxious to get in touch with Winkeler. Mrs. Marsh stated that she thereafter went to Cicero, Illinois, and as prearranged met Vivian at a dressmaking shop on Twenty-second Street. Vivian was accompanied by her young daughter, Betty. At this time Vivian told her that she desired to get in touch with Gus right away, inasmuch as she expected Verne to come to Chicago in the next few days, and that she wanted Gus to hide him out. She further indicated to

Mrs. Marsh that Verne Miller engineered the massacre and he at first wanted to deliver Frank Nash himself. She stated that Frank Nash and Verne Miller were the best of friends. Vivian further indicated to Mrs. Marsh that shortly after Frank Nash was taken at Hot Springs, Arkansas, someone phoned Doc Stacci at Melrose Park, Illinois, who in turn got in touch with Verne Miller at Kansas City, Missouri, advising him of Nash's apprehension.

She further indicated that "Pretty Boy" Floyd was in Kansas City on the eve of June 17, 1933, and when he learned that Miller was going to take Nash alone, he volunteered to accompany him; that they met the train the next morning at Kansas City, Missouri. Mrs. Marsh further stated that according to Vivian, after Verne Miller and "Pretty Boy" Floyd fired upon the officers, Verne yelled to Nash to run, and Nash was supposed to have said, "Verne, have you gone crazy?" This statement aggravated Miller to such an extent that he thereupon turned his gun on Nash and killed him. Mrs. Marsh further stated that "Pretty Boy" Floyd was wounded in the shoulder and upon his return to Verne's bungalow in Kansas City, Missouri, Vivian and Verne dressed the wound. Mrs. Marsh stated that at no time during her conversation with Vivian regarding this crime, did Vivian mention the name of Adam Richetti, or that a third person had assisted Miller and Floyd.

Mrs. Marsh stated that after the underworld learned that Miller was responsible for the instant killing, no one wanted to have anything to do with him. Gus Winkeler especially was very much aggravated with Miller, mainly for the reason that he killed Nash, a very good friend of his, along with the officers. [Evidently it was the Kansas City Massacre that prompted Winkeler to help the FBI in its efforts to track down Miller.]

Mrs. Marsh was unable to state how, why or where Verne Miller died, but conjectured that he was killed by persons connected with the syndicate.

KILLING OF CHICAGO POLICE OFFICER
MYLES CUNNINGHAM

It will be recalled that the shooting of this officer was precipitated by the robbery of a postal messenger in downtown Chicago on September 22,

1933, in which two sacks of mail were taken. Mrs. Marsh advised that this robbery was staged by Fred Goetz and Bryan Bolton and whomever they were operating with at that time [which suggests that the Barker-Karpis Gang was yet to be identified]; that the car used in this holdup, which was equipped with a smoke screen and oil-spray arrangement, was so equipped through Joe Bergl at a garage on West Washington Boulevard in Chicago.

It should be noted that other information later received concerning this robbery and killing indicated that [it was committed by] the Barker-Karpis mob, including Harry Sawyer, assisted by Fred Goetz and Bryan Bolton.

KIDNAPPING OF THE LINDBERGH BABY

Mrs. Marsh advised that she has no information whatever concerning the abduction of Lindbergh's son; however, she does know as a positive fact that Al Capone issued orders to the various members of his organization to "shoot" every angle in the underworld to find the baby and to learn who kidnapped him; that Al Capone believed that if his men could have found the baby, some consideration would have been given him in connection with the 11-year sentence which at that time had already been imposed upon him by the Federal Court at Chicago, Illinois.

MURDER OF FRED GOETZ

It will be recalled that Fred Goetz was killed on March 21st, 1934, as he emerged from the Minerva Restaurant at 4811 West Twenty-second Street, Cicero, Illinois. [Goetz was shot the night of March 20th, but died after midnight.] Mrs. March was questioned concerning her knowledge of the identity of the persons who killed Fred Goetz and as to the reason for his assassination, and she advised that shortly after Goetz was killed she talked with "Lefty Louis" Campagna regarding the same and he indicated to her that the St. Paul outfit put him on the spot for unknown reasons. Mrs. Marsh stated, however, that it is her belief that the Italian element of the syndicate were in fact responsible for this murder. She could or would not furnish any other information regarding this murder.

Fred Barker	Alvin Karpis, a.k.a. "Ray"	Arthur "Dock" Barker	Kate "Ma" Barker	Fred Goetz, a.k.a. "Shotgun George Ziegler"
Bryan Bolton	Volney Davis	Harry Sawyer	Harry Campbell	Delores Delaney

The Barker-Karpis Gang.

Mrs. Marsh was also questioned regarding her knowledge of the Barker-Karpis gang, and she advised that she has never met Alvin Karpis, Fred Barker, Doc Barker, Harry Campbell, Volney Davis, William Weaver, and Harry Sawyer, nor does she know any of their girl friends. She stated that she has never been in St. Paul, Minnesota.

With reference to Willie Harrison, Mrs. Marsh stated that she has known Harrison for a considerable number of years; that the boys used Harrison more or less as a "stooge"; and that while Harrison operated his saloon at Calumet City, Illinois, in 1932 and 1933, the whole outfit used to hang out and spend considerable money there. Mrs. Marsh stated that Harrison was quite a drinker and when in an intoxicated condition he was uncontrollable. She stated that she is well acquainted with Willie's wife, Ruth, and in fact Willie and Ruth were married on the same day that she and Gus Winkeler were married in the Catholic Church at Chicago. Mrs. Marsh also knew Dickie May, who lived with Willie Harrison after he separated from Ruth; that Willie and Dickie May paid them frequent visits at their apartment in Chicago, Illinois, and on several occasions accompanied them to the Chez Paree Night Club, also in Chicago. She stated that she is also acquainted with May Green, with whom

Willie consorted after Dickie May left him. Mrs. Marsh was surprised to hear that Willie Harrison was killed in the manner he was. [His body was later found in a burning barn in northern Illinois.]

Continuing, Mrs. Marsh advised that she is likewise well acquainted with Johnny Patton, the boy mayor of Burnham, Illinois. She stated that this town, through Patton, is controlled by the syndicate and that in 1931 and 1932, when things were too hot for the boys in Chicago, they used to hide out at Burnham; that the Coney Island Night Club in this town is a great rendezvous for the criminal element of Chicago. The name "Eddie O'Hare" was mentioned to Mrs. Marsh, and she advised that this individual is likewise a member of the syndicate, and is their front man in the operation of the Hawthorne Race Track at Cicero, Illinois. With reference to the summer home built by Fred Goetz [near Cranberry Lake in Wisconsin] many years ago which, according to information received, was sold to Eddie O'Hare, Mrs. Marsh advised that this place was in fact purchased by Al Capone, and that as far as she knows, he still owns the said property. She further stated that if Eddie O'Hare's name is shown as the purchaser of this property, he undoubtedly fronted for Al Capone in the deal.

Mrs. Marsh was also questioned concerning her knowledge of the Hamm and Bremer kidnappings, but she was unable to furnish any information concerning these crimes.

Agent questioned Mrs. Marsh as to whether she knew where "Old Charlie" Fitzgerald and Belle Born were residing in Chicago, Illinois, during the summer of 1933, and she advised that she does not know the exact address, but that they had an apartment somewhere on Sixty-seventh Street near Stony Island Avenue in Chicago; that she recalls that the Illinois Central Interurban trains ran past the building in which they resided.

With reference to Winkeler's colored chauffeur, whom she has referred to as "Murphy," Mrs. Marsh advised that his correct name is Marion Murphy; that he performed errands and worked for various members of the syndicate long before Gus Winkeler hired him as his personal chauffeur; that Murphy is in possession of considerable information regarding the past activities of the syndicate and can tell a very good story if he could be made to talk. She further stated that she has no idea where

Murphy is residing at the present time, but believes that he could be located through the Chicago telephone directory.

It is left to the discretion of the Chicago Bureau office and the office of origin as to what investigation should be conducted from the information submitted, in determining the identity of "Old Gus." For this reason no definite leads are being set out.

PENDING

May 20, 1936
Director
Federal Bureau of Investigation
Washington, D.C.

On May 18, 1936, Mrs. Walter Marsh, who formerly was the legal wife of Gus Winkeler, notorious Chicago gangster, now deceased, was interviewed by Special Agent John L. Madala and myself, regarding her knowledge of the Hamm kidnapping case, and with more particular reference to the identity of an individual known to the Bureau as only "Old Gus," who according to Byran Bolton, was originally a party to the conspiracy to kidnap Mr. Hamm.

As you will recall Gus Winkeler was a strong henchman of Al Capone and a prominent member of Capone's organization, commonly known in Chicago as the "Syndicate." Just prior to Winkeler's assassination in Chicago, in October of 1933, the latter made frequent trips to the Chicago Bureau Office, ostensibly for the purpose of assisting the Bureau in the location of Verne Miller, who at that time was being sought in connection with the Kansas City Massacre case. The contact with Gus Winkeler was presumably made through Buck Kempster, a former Illinois State Highway Police Officer, who at that time was assigned to the Chicago Bureau Office, at the sanction of Governor Horner, to assist in the investigation of the Jack Klutas and the Kansas City Massacre cases. Gus Winkeler's contacts at that time with the Chicago Bureau Office were usually with former Special Agent in Charge M. H. Purvis. It has been the talk among the underworld since that time that these trips to the Chicago Bureau Office contributed largely to Winkeler's demise.

Mrs. Marsh, sometime after her husband's death, married Walter Marsh, her present husband, and at the present they are operating a restaurant in Louisville, Kentucky, known as the Triangle Café, which is located at 1805 [city directories of the day have it as 1605] Bardstown Road. She stated that she has seen so much of the criminal side of life that she is willing to assist in any way within her power to eradicate this type of individual. She is very friendly toward the Bureau and made the statement that it is admirable the manner in which the Bureau has served the public in spite of the many obstacles which she knows for a fact have confronted the Special Agents in the field. She made particular reference to the crooked politicians, police officers, and fixers in Chicago, Ill., all of whom she stated, at times during her experience, proved themselves available and valuable in this respect.

Mrs. Marsh was closely questioned as to this situation, and she related that an individual known to her as Bartholomus [Edward Bartholmey], or some such name, has in the past fixed cases for Gus Winkeler and other members of the "Syndicate" to such an extent that now, one could not even locate a record of the crime in which they were involved. She made particular reference to the Portland Bank job in Louisville, Kentucky, and the Jefferson Wisconsin bank robbery of which crimes Winkeler was accused. She stated that this fellow Bartholomus cleared Winkeler on both of these jobs, for which Winkeler paid a consideration which ran into thousands of dollars.

Mrs. Marsh further stated that just prior to, or during the prosecution of Al Capone in Chicago for income tax evasion, Gus Winkeler was negotiating with Bartholomus to clear Capone of this charge, and it resulted that Bartholomus could possibly have effected the "fix" through one of his connections in Washington, D.C., for a consideration of $100,000. In this regard Winkeler went before the Board of Directors of the "Syndicate" with the above proposition, but they refused to advance the money, or aid in any way, and, in conclusion they told Winkeler to mind his own business. At that time Winkeler asserted that the boys, namely Frank Nitti, Rocky DeGrazia and "Lefty Louis" Campagna, apparently were in favor of Capone going to jail in order that they could carry on the operation of the "Syndicate" for their own profit.

Mrs. Marsh at first was reluctant to give the name of the fixer whom she frequently advised could reach Washington on any type of case, but, after considerable questioning she furnished the name Bartholomus, and added that he spends considerable time in the office of W. W. Smith, a Chicago attorney. She stated that Attorney Smith is, as far as she knows, an honest attorney, and that he on only one occasion handled a case for Gus Winkeler.

Mrs. Marsh further stated that another fixer in Chicago, Illinois, is an individual by the name of Bill Finuty, or some such name, who is a politician affiliated with the present administration; that this party is on the regular payroll of the "Syndicate," and has in the past fixed many cases which involved certain members of this criminal organization. She also stated that former Chief of Detectives William Shoemaker, of the Chicago Police Department, was one police officer whom the "Syndicate" could never touch, and it was for this reason that he was ultimately ousted. Just prior to his release, Ralph Pierce, a member of the "Syndicate," told Winkeler, in the presence of Mrs. Marsh, that Shoemaker was going to be replaced by one of their (the "Syndicate's") own men. A short time thereafter, John Sullivan, former Chief of Police of Cicero, Illinois, was made Chief of Detectives in Chicago. It should be noted that Cicero, Illinois, was over a long period of years, and still is, a haven for this organization and its members.

Mrs. Marsh stated that she also knows of her own personal knowledge that the "Syndicate" likewise had on their payroll several other high officials of the Chicago Police Department, none of whose identity she knew. In this regard, Agent Madala informed me that he recalls Byran Bolton's statement, in which he advised that Captain Stege, who had charge of the so-called Dillinger Squad in Chicago, Illinois, received a tribute of $5,000 a month from the "Syndicate." [In his later memo to Acting Attorney General Joseph B. Keenan on August 27, 1936, J. Edgar Hoover gave the amount as $5,000 per week, but even $5,000 per month at that time would now be the equivalent of over $70,000 per week or $840,000 per year, suggesting a mistake in the payment time period or the zeros or both.]

Along this line, Mrs. Marsh also definitely stated that the police uniforms used in the St. Valentine's Day Massacre, and which were worn by Fred Goetz and Fred "Killer" Burke, were supplied by a detective connected with the Chicago Police Department and were delivered to her home by this officer.

With further reference to Buck Kempster, mentioned above, Mrs. Marsh advised that he supplied Winkeler with bullet proof vests, a bullet proof shield, several Thompson sub-machine guns, and a dictaphone set, which Winkeler utilized in his apartment. She stated that all of this equipment was removed from their apartment by their chauffeur, Marion Murphy, upon orders of Winkeler, after he was taken into custody by the Chicago Bureau Office, for questioning, sometime in September of 1933; that the colored chauffeur, Murphy, moved this equipment to a home occupied by another colored family who were friends of Murphy's, and, as far as she knows, this equipment is still there.

Mrs. Marsh stated that Gus Winkeler and Kempster were very close friends, and it was always her belief that Kempster was placed in the Chicago Bureau Office to keep Winkeler and the "Syndicate" posted as to the Bureau's activities. She, however, could furnish no definite information along this line.

She went on to relate that former Special Agent in Charge Melvin H. Purvis forestalled certain investigations which involved members of the "Syndicate," and when questioned for details regarding these charges, she was unable to furnish any definite proof other than to state that she told Mr. Purvis the whereabouts of the bullet proof vest and Thompson machine guns, and other equipment, which guns Winkeler had removed from his apartment, and Mr. Purvis took no action to recover same.

Mrs. Marsh also stated that Charles Fitzgerald was wounded during the commission of a crime in the fall of 1933—it is known as a positive fact that Fitzgerald was wounded in the South St. Paul payroll robbery on August 30, 1933—and that sometime thereafter he was removed to a cottage of Kempster's at Mt. Sterling, Illinois, where he was kept for recuperation for a period of time. Mrs. Marsh asserts that while Old Charlie was at this cottage, Mr. Purvis visited there with Kemptster, as did Gus Winkeler, and the individual known as "Old Gus." She continued that shortly after Winkeler's death, and while Fitzgerald was at Kempster's cottage, she called Kempster at his place, over long distance telephone, in an effort to locate "Old Gus," who, at that time, was assisting her in collecting some of Winkeler's debts, and who had seemingly disappeared, and, in conversation with Kempster, who was very much intoxicated, he told her that Mr. Purvis was there with him. She did not know of her own accord that Charles Fitzgerald was at the cottage at the time she made the telephone call.

Mrs. Marsh was closely questioned regarding everything she knew concerning Mr. Purvis, but was not able to give a great deal of information in detail. She plainly stated that she disliked Mr. Purvis very much, and thought that he was "stuck up," for the reason that when she would call at the office he was always so busy that he could not see her. [By this time Purvis had his hands full with the search for Verne Miller (the Kansas City Massacre), two unsolved kidnappings, and the killings of John Dillinger, Pretty Boy Floyd, and Baby Face Nelson, each of which increased the resentment of J. Edgar Hoover, who made Purvis's life sufficiently unpleasant that he was deciding to resign from the Bureau.]

When questioned as to other individuals who were on the payroll of Gus Winkeler and the "Syndicate," Mrs. Marsh mentioned the name of Al Lehman, whom she advised was a former Prohibition Agent of Chicago, Illinois. She stated that Lehman kept Gus Winkeler posted on the activities of the Prohibition Bureau. She also stated that on one occasion Al Lehman exhibited a report to Gus Winkeler and her, which contained information relative to their investigation of Mrs. Marsh's family, showing that she had a sister who was manager of the Cafeteria at the Belknap Hardware Company, at Louisville, Kentucky; that along with this report, Mr. Lehman had a photograph of Mrs. Marsh's sister, and considerable information concerning her background. She stated that this report was not retained by Gus Winkeler, and Al Lehman presumably returned the same to the files of the Prohibition Bureau on that same date. She further stated that whenever she telephoned Al Lehman, she used the name of Marion, or some similar name, and that he paid them frequent visits. She also stated that Al Lehman was running around at that time with a girl who was employed in the office of the U. S. District Court, in Chicago, Illinois, from whom he was able to obtain any information desired regarding Winkeler and his associates. She added that Gus Winkeler paid Al Lehman $300 a month for his services in this respect.

Further information advanced by Mrs. Marsh indicates that the Jake Factor kidnapping was just a hoax, and was conceived to keep Factor in this country, and also to lay the suspicion of his abduction on the Touhy gang, which organization the "Syndicate" at that time was trying to eradicate. She stated that around the time of the Factor kidnapping, every effort was being made to extradite him to England. She went on to relate that the Touhy mob in fact kidnapped Factor's son, and when questioned for details stated that on the night the boy was taken, Al Capone called Gus Winkeler, and told him that the Touhy mob had taken Factor's son, and to get several other members of the "Syndicate" and do everything possible to get the boy back. Jake Factor at the time was in good standing with the "Syndicate." She stated that she was absolutely positive that the Touhy mob did not kidnap Jake Factor, as the boys frequently sat around her apartment and laughed over the fact that the Touhy mob was so strongly suspected in connection with this kidnapping, and likewise made the remark that it looks like Factor would stay in this country after all.

Mrs. Marsh talked very freely to Agent Madala and myself, and, should there be any other details desired from her, further contact will be had in an effort to secure all the information which you might desire to secure.

Your attention is called to report of Special Agent John L. Madala, which contains valuable information concerning Jack Pfeiffer and "Old Gus" in connection with the Hamm kidnapping case. This report is presently being typed and will go forward to the Bureau within the next few days.

Very truly yours,
O. C. Dewey
Special Agent in Charge

*   *   *

June 5, 1936
Mr. D. W. Ladd,
Federal Bureau of Investigation,
U.S. Department of Justice,
Post Office Box 812,
Chicago, Illinois

For your information, I am attaching hereto copies of a Personal and Confidential letter addressed to me under date of May 20, 1936 by Special Agent in Charge O. C. Dewey of the Louisville Office which pertains to information recently furnished Mr. Dewey and Agent Madala by Mrs. Walter Marsh, former wife of Gus Winkeler. I desire that a very thorough investigation be given to all of the matters outlined in Mr. Dewey's letter, which pertain to items of interest to the Bureau. I am particularly interested in ascertaining complete information concerning Bartholomus who is reported to be the "fixer" for members of the Syndicate, it being noted that Bartholomus spends considerable time in the office of W. W. Smith, a Chicago attorney. Any data pertaining to corruption or bribery on the part of the Chicago Police Department should of course be obtained, together with data concerning Marion Murphy, described as chauffeur for Gus Winkeler.

With reference to the first paragraph beginning on Page 4 of Mr. Dewey's letter, you advised that a careful review of the Bureau Files does not disclose any interview conducted by former Agent in Charge Melvin Purvis with Mrs. Marsh, and no data are contained in the Bureau files indicating that Mr. Purvis knew the whereabouts of the bullet-proof vest and Thompson machine guns which Gus Winkeler was alleged to have removed from his apartment.

You should endeavor to obtain any information possible to indicate the association of Buck Kempster with Charles Fitzgerald and other persons, including the former Agent in Charge of the Chicago Bureau Office, Melvin Purvis. No direct approach should be made to Mr. Purvis upon this matter. . . .

Very truly yours,
John Edgar Hoover, Director

August 27, 1936

MEMORANDUM FOR MR. JOSEPH B. KEENAN,

ACTING ATTORNEY GENERAL

With reference to your inquiry as to information furnished by Bryan Bolton concerning the identity of the persons perpetrating the St. Valentine's Day Massacre in Chicago, Illinois in 1929, you are advised that Bolton was questioned concerning this offense. Bolton stated that the persons who actually perpetrated this massacre were Fred Goetz, Gus Winkler, Fred Burke, Ray Nugent and Bob Carey. Bolton stated that he personally purchased the Cadillac touring car which was used in this massacre, having been furnished with the money to make this purchase by Louis Lipschultz. Bolton claims that he purchased this car from the Cadillac Company on Michigan Avenue in Chicago sometime before the massacre happened and assumed at the time that he purchased the car that it was to be used in hauling alcohol. Bolton believes that he used the name James Martin in purchasing the car. The object of this massacre, according to Bolton, which was planned by members of the Capone organization, was for the purpose of eliminating "Bugs" Moran from the bootlegging racket in Chicago. Bolton claims that the plot to perpetrate this killing was initially developed at a place on Cranberry Lake, six miles north of Couderay, Wisconsin, where one George operated a resort. Al Capone, Gus Winkeler, George Zeigler, Louis Campagna, Fred Burke, Bill Pacelli (reported to be an Illinois State Senator) and Dan Saratella [should be Serritella]are reported to have been at the resort operated by one George on Cranberry Lake at the time the killing was first planned, this being in October or November of 1928. Bolton states that Jimmy McCrussen and Jimmy "The Swede" Moran were selected to watch "Bugs" Moran's garage, since they both knew Moran by sight, in order to learn his movements.

Bolton states that Al Capone went to Florida before the Massacre was perpetrated and left Frank Nitti in charge of the operations and that one Frankie Reo, now dead, was Nitti's assistant in the transaction. Bolton claims . . . that when the killings took place the persons actually perpetrating therein did not know the identity of each of their victims but rather than risk the possibility of missing Moran, killed all of the persons found in the garage. [This may have been one of the mistakes to which Georgette refers when she overheard Gus and others discussing the killings afterward.]

As indicated above, Bolton states that Fred Goetz, Gus Winkler, Fred Burke, Ray Nugent and Bob Carey were the actual perpetrators of the Massacre. According to Bolton, Claude Maddox of St. Louis, Tony Capezio of Chicago and a man known as "Shocker" also of St. Louis, burned the Cadillac car after the Massacre.

Bolton has consistently denied that he personally participated in the Massacre and has expressed willingness to confront anyone of the individuals named by him, accusing him of participation in this offense.

In discussing this matter, Bolton has informed Special Agents of this Bureau that at the time of the St. Valentine's Day Massacre, Chief of Detectives Stege of the Chicago Police Department was on the payroll of the Capone Syndicate, receiving $5,000 per week, and kept the members of the Syndicate informed as to the whereabouts of "Bugs" Moran.

Respectfully,
John Edgar Hoover,
Director

BIOGRAPHIES AND
HISTORICAL NOTES

*Persons and events mentioned by Georgette in her
memoirs and in later interviews by FBI agents*

"AMERICAN BOYS"

Al Capone's original "American boys," as Georgette Winkeler calls them, were Gus Winkeler with his two St. Louis friends, Ray Nugent and Bob Carey. They were soon joined by Fred Burke, also from St. Louis, and Fred Goetz and Byron Bolton, all of whom constituted a special-assignment crew unknown either to the Chicago police or to Capone's gangland rivals. Some were involved in the 1928 murder of New York gangster Frankie Yale, Capone's one-time employer at a dive in Brooklyn, and all participated in the St. Valentine's Day Massacre on February 14, 1929.

BAILEY, HARVEY

In his autobiography, *I Rob Banks,* Harvey Bailey provided a pretty lame alibi for Fred Burke on the morning of the St. Valentine's Day Massacre. He claimed the two of them were drinking beer in an Indiana tavern— probably Willie Harrison's—at the time of the killings, but the heat that immediately came down on prime-suspect Burke made it impossible for them to continue their bank-robbing operations.

Bailey was born in Jane Lew, West Virginia, in 1887. During the twenties, when state police were mostly paper organizations and local lawmen could rarely identify their "motorized bandits," Bailey became

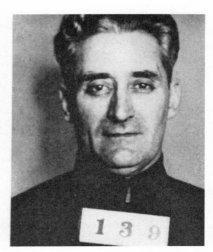

Harvey Bailey.

the country's premier bank robber, knocking over something like seventy banks without acquiring notoriety. He didn't head up a specific gang but knew nearly everyone in the business and occasionally worked with Fred Burke, Frank Nash, Verne Miller, Gus Winkeler, the Barker-Karpis Gang, Wilbur Underhill, and Machine Gun Kelly. He denied any part in the Denver Mint robbery of 1922, but he was somehow involved in the Lincoln National Bank Robbery of 1930 that would cause much grief for Gus Winkeler when Winkeler later was identified as a suspect.

Bailey's phenomenal luck ran out when he made the mistake of laying over at the Shannon farm near Paradise, Texas, where wealthy Oklahoma oilman Charles had been held after he was kidnapped by small-time bank robber Machine Gun Kelly on July 22, 1933. Kidnapping had been made a federal crime the previous year, following the kidnap-murder of the Lindbergh baby, and with Urschel's help—and probably some tips from Oklahoma City detectives—federal agents honed in on the Shannon farm and arrested Bailey with Kelly's submachine gun lying under his cot. Bailey was convicted for his presumed part in the Urschel kidnapping and spent the next thirty years in federal and state prisons. He finally was paroled on March 31, 1965, and died in Joplin, Missouri, on March 1, 1979.

BARKER-KARPIS GANG

Of the Barker-Karpis Gang, by far the best known is Arizona Clark "Ma" Barker, thanks largely to J. Edgar Hoover. The Barkers were from Oklahoma and little known to the press until they went into kidnapping. Doc (also called Dock) Barker was arrested in Chicago on January 8, 1935, the same day Bolton and others were captured in a firefight at an apartment on Pine Grove Avenue. There police found a map that pointed the way to Ocklawaha, Florida. Eight days later, on January 16, G-men laid siege to the house where she was staying with her son Fred, who answered with a submachine gun.

The Feds poured the place full of bullets and then sent in a black gardener (there were no black G-men) to see what was left of the occupants. Fred was dead in an upstairs bedroom and so was "Ma." Hoover must have been perturbed that his men had killed somebody's mother and immediately turned her into a ferocious harridan who had led her sons in their lives of crime. In his own book, *Persons in Hiding,* Hoover wrote: "The eyes of Arizona Clark Barker, by the way, always fascinated me. They were queerly direct, penetrating, hot with some strangely smoldering flame, yet withal as hypnotically cold as the muzzle of a gun."

The Barker Boys (mainly Doc and Freddie) had formed a major crime ring in the twenties, robbing banks and payroll messengers with something like ten killings, but they had attracted little attention until they began snatching wealthy individuals in violation of the "Lindbergh Law."

Alvin Karpis in handcuffs.

By this time the Barkers had been joined by Chicago's Alvin Karpis and now were known as the Barker-Karpis Gang. In 1932 they recruited former "American boys" Fred Goetz and Byron Bolton through mutual connections in St. Paul.

With the Feds now determined to nail the kidnappers of William Hamm Jr. in 1933 and Edward Bremer the following January, the Nitti Syndicate was starting to worry about federal heat, especially when it became known that Gus Winkeler had been talking to Special Agent in Charge Melvin Purvis (probably because Winkeler been approached by Verne Miller, looking for a hideout after the Kansas City Massacre that took place in June). When Chicago G-men captured both Byron Bolton and Doc Barker in January 1935, they suspected that a tip-off had come by way of the Syndicate.

Karpis himself had continued his own crime spree and eluded the G-men for more than a year, during which time Hoover had been chafing under criticism that he only manned a desk in Washington while sending his men into battle. Hoover believed this obliged him to make some headline arrests himself. When Karpis was located in New Orleans, Hoover rushed there to capture him personally on May 1, 1936.

Later Karpis poked fun at this episode, saying that Hoover stayed out of sight until Karpis had reached his Plymouth coupe and found himself covered by federal guns. Then Hoover was told he could safely come out of an alley. No G-man had thought to bring handcuffs, however, so Karpis's hands were bound with an agent's necktie. And when no one knew where to find the federal lockup, he wisecracked that he would show them because he was planning to rob the post office there.

With the capture of Karpis, Attorney General Cummings's "War on Crime" virtually petered out as Hoover shifted his sights to communist agitators and the German-American Bund.

BARTHOLMEY, EDWARD

The "Bartholomus, or some such name," mentioned to FBI agents by Georgette Winkeler, was Edward Bartholmey of Bensenville. He was tight with the Chicago mob and claimed to have Washington connections who, for $100,000 that Nitti refused to provide, might have mitigated Al Capone's 1931 prison sentence.

Bartholmey was politically active and became the Bensenville post-master. His house had been used by the Barker-Karpis Gang to stash their first kidnap victim, St. Paul brewer William A. Hamm Jr., who was grabbed on June 15, 1933. (It was the participation of Goetz and Bolton in the Barker-Karpis Gang's bungled mail robbery the following September that landed Joe Bergl and Winkeler in hot water.)

In January of 1934 the Barker-Karpis Gang kidnapped St. Paul banker Edward Bremer and transported him also to Bensenville. Bolton blamed the Nitti Syndicate for tipping off the Feds to their respective hiding places in Chicago. G-men arrested Doc Barker on Surf Street on January 8, 1935, and that same evening captured Bolton and killed Russell Gibson in an apartment-building gun battle on Pine Grove Avenue. It was while Bolton was being interrogated on kidnapping charges that the *Chicago American* mysteriously acquired his secondhand (and somewhat garbled) confession to being one of surveillance team for the St. Valentine's Day Massacre. A greatly irritated Hoover, having just "solved" a major kidnapping case, did not want it overshadowed by a front-page newspaper story and immediately declared it false.

For some unknown reason, the FBI reports Bartholomey's first name as Edmund, which was the name of his son.

BERGL, JOE

Joseph P. Bergl owned a car dealership and a garage in Cicero, one of them next door to Ralph Capone's Cotton Club, and he "fixed up" cars for any number of gangsters and outlaws. Al Capone himself would use Bergl's office to conduct private business, and Bergl's list of customers included (under various names) Machine Gun Kelly, Frank Nash, Verne Miller, James "Fur" Sammons, Tommy Holden, Francis Keating, and Fred Burke, to name a few.

Bergl's absentee partner was Gus Winkeler, occasionally described in newspapers as his brother-in-law, which now appears unlikely; but when Winkeler was badly hurt in car wreck in 1931 Bergl would prove to be one of Georgette Winkeler's most dependable friends.

An unsolved mail robbery in downtown Chicago on December 6, 1932, baffled police, and when they found the abandoned getaway car it had a smoke-screen device that could have been installed by Bergl. The

Joe Bergl, Chicago car dealer.
Photo courtesy of Joe Bergl Jr.

police speculated that this robbery may have been the work of "amateurs"—no one was caught—but when the stolen bonds began showing up in Chicago, Gus Winkeler remarked to Georgette that the robbers were from Minneapolis and St. Paul and might have been the yet-unknown Barker-Karpis Gang, which had been hard on banks and their messengers. The same could be said of the gang led by Tommy Touhy, brother of bootlegger Roger Touhy, although both were considered Chicagoans.

On September 23, 1933, the Barker-Karpis Gang definitely pulled a mail robbery in the Loop, crashed their escape car, and killed a police officer, but their loot consisted only of letters. In that episode the wrecked car—equipped with armor plating, bulletproof glass, red and green headlights as used on squad cars, a police radio, a siren, and a smoke-screen device—was traced to Joe Bergl's shop and thence to Winkeler. Bergl disappeared for several days and apparently beat the rap, since armored cars with police-type accessories were not illegal, and Winkeler was killed two weeks later.

Bergl had married Marie Jiruska about 1925, and they separated in the early thirties. In 1936 she would die in an auto accident near Fox River Grove, a hamlet north of Barrington where Baby Face Nelson had made his last stand. Louis Cernocky had two taverns at Fox River Grove that catered to Chicago gangsters and outlaws, and in 1934 he had sent the Dillinger Gang to Wisconsin's Little Bohemia Lodge, where they shot their way out of an FBI trap.

In 1938 Bergl had an exceptionally short marriage to a woman named Claire, from whom he sought a divorce in February of 1939 on the grounds she had hit him with an ashtray on Christmas Eve, had bopped him with a lamp on New Year's Eve, and a week later had punched him with her fists. However, the judge ruled that Bergl wasn't hurt very much and that "if a couple rushed into divorce courts every time they exchanged slaps and words on Christmas and New Year's eves we'd be doing nothing but hearing divorce cases."

Joe and Claire continued to squabble until they found a judge who would grant them a divorce. In 1943 he married Dorothy Johnson, one of the "Adorables" working at the Chez Paree, which once had belonged to Gus Winkeler. Bergl had survived several run-ins with the police, the Feds, and the gangster community, and the couple moved from Cicero to the suburb of River Forest, where they lived one block from Chicago crime boss Tony Accardo and three blocks from Sam Giancana. Joe Bergl and Dorothy had two daughters and a son, who was only 1½ when Bergl died in 1950.

Joe Jr. recalls some stories told by older members of the family about his father, who became Chicagoland's top Chevrolet dealer. One was that he had a lively sense of humor that inspired him, during a train trip to Florida, to spring a thousand-dollar bill on a dining-car waiter just to see his reaction and to amuse his friends. His grandmother remembers that his funeral cortege included fourteen carloads of flowers, and years later he discovered that his father's funeral-home guest book included the signature of Louis ("Little New York" Louie) Campagna. His mother told him that Campagna was just "one of the boys."

BOLTON, BYRON (ALSO BRYAN, BRIAN, OR BRYANT)

How Byron Bolton hooked up with Fred Goetz isn't known, unless it was through a mutual friend, Willie Harrison from St. Louis, who was also a friend of Gus Winkeler and Fred Burke. Georgette calls him Bryant.

Bolton had served as an enlisted man in the navy during the world war and by some accounts became a driver for Burke in St. Louis. Or he might have met Goetz in Chicago when Goetz was going by the name George Zeigler, a.k.a. Ziegler. (Georgette calls him George Goetz and says that Gus met him at a Cicero tavern.) Goetz did have friends in St. Louis, so Bolton's connection with that criminal community—where everybody seemed to know (or know of) everybody else—remains somewhat murky. Newspapers usually called him Byron and described him as a navy machine-gunner, as though that was a special rating.

Bolton's birth name was William Bryan Bolton, although he was also went by Bryon, Brian, Bryant, Monty Carter, and probably other names. He was close enough to Goetz that he sometimes lived with him in Chicago, and he enjoyed the protection of Goetz, who would send him to Arizona for his mild tuberculosis—or elsewhere to spare him

the wrath of Al Capone when he screwed up as a lookout for the St. Valentine's Day Massacre. (Chicago detectives had found a letter to him, and possibly a prescription medicine bottle, in one of the Massacre lookout rooms and tracked that to his family at a farm between Thayer and Virden, Illinois, where they found an empty crate that had contained submachine guns, but for some reason the trail stopped there.)

Byron Bolton in navy uniform.

BOLTON NAMES SELF AND 5 AS ST. VALENTINE KILLERS

$129,000 IN BANK NOTES, SILVER GANG'S LOOT IN MAIL TRUCK HOLDUP | HELPED KILL SEVEN! | 1, HUMPHREYS; 2, BURKE; 3, MADDOX; 4, BOLTON; 5. WINKLER; 6. GOETZ

Once Al Capone was in prison, Goetz and Bolton struck out on their own, and by 1932 they had hooked up with the Barker-Karpis Gang at Jack Peifer's Hollyhocks club in St. Paul. Gus Winkeler also was there for a 1931–32 New Year's Eve party, along with many other crooks of the day. Peifer (commonly spelled Peiffer in FBI documents) and one Harry Sawyer had taken up where Police Chief John O'Conner and Dan Hogan had left off (thanks to a car bomb), running a virtually crime-free city because it welcomed any gangsters who checked in with the cops, donated to the cause, and behaved themselves.

However, partly to discredit a new reform mayor elected in 1932, Sawyer and Peifer made exceptions for the Barker-Karpis Gang, setting up the high-dollar kidnappings of St. Paul's wealthy brewer William Hamm Jr. in June of 1933 and banker Edward Bremer in January of 1934.

A year later federal agents tracked part of the Barker-Karpis Gang to 3912–20 North Pine Grove in Chicago on January 8, 1935, killing Russell Gibson and capturing Byron Bolton. Bolton was rushed to St. Paul, and on January 23 his part in the St. Valentine's Day Massacre made front-page news in the *Chicago American,* which carelessly declared the Massacre "solved."

This was in fact a somewhat garbled second- or third-hand account that had two of the shooters mistaken, but it outraged J. Edgar Hoover that anyone in federal custody on a kidnapping charge would upstage him as having participated in gangland's "crime of the century." It may also have come as a surprise to Bolton, who insisted that he hadn't leaked it and who suspected that the tip-off to their hiding places, and possibly the newspaper story, had come from Frank Nitti's Chicago Syndicate.

Hoover immediately declared that the Bolton story did not hold "a grain of truth," and the press bought this, for the FBI would never lie; but a flurry of orders to St. Paul had its agents squeezing Bolton about the Massacre, and he was moved to spill what he knew. He elaborated at length on the crime, correcting substantial parts of the story, as did Georgette later when she was in Louisville, talking to FBI agents there.

Hoover neglected to retract his adamant denials, but later privately and reluctantly delivered an abbreviated version of Bolton's account to his Justice Department superiors, who still had the ridiculous notion that the Bureau should go after the other perpetrators for "flight to avoid prosecution." By this time, however, most were dead, were in prison, or had disappeared for good.

Meanwhile, Bolton testified for the government in both the Hamm and the Bremer kidnapping cases and was rewarded with prison terms of only three-to-five years, to be served concurrently, whereas Doc Barker and Alvin Karpis would go to Alcatraz for "life."

After Bolton's release he moved to California, and despite his old junkie habits and bouts with tuberculosis he died at his brother's place in 1977.

CAMPAGNA, LOUIS

Louis Campagna (Georgette calls him "Lefty Louie," although in Chicago he was better known as "Little New York" Louie) was born in Brooklyn about 1900 but left New York in his teens and settled in Chicago just prior to Prohibition. In 1918 he was convicted of robbing the bank in the west suburban town of Argo, and after his release he joined what Capone later began calling his "Outfit." There he rose through the ranks from gunman to confidant—as well as gunman.

Campagna was arrested in November 1927, when he led a contingent of Capone gunmen to the Chicago detective bureau at 625 South Clark Street with the intention of ambushing Sicilian gang leader Joe Aiello, who was temporarily in lockup but still competing with Capone for control of the Unione Siciliana (originally an organization intended to help newly arrived Sicilians).

Police were about to release Aiello when they recognized some Capone troops hovering around their building. They grabbed Campagna and deliberately locked him up in Aiello's cell—with an Italian-speaking cop, dressed as a bum, placed in an adjoining cell. He overheard Campagna making death threats to Aiello, and when Aiello was released he hurried to a waiting car and went into hiding.

"Lefty Louie" Campagna,
a.k.a. "Little New York."

When Aiello returned to Little Sicily he hooked up with Bugs Moran, whose North Side territory neighbored Aiello's to the west. Aiello already had put out the word that anyone who killed Capone would receive a "reward" of $50,000, but Capone's favorite gunman, Jack McGurn, sent at least five of the out-of-town bounty hunters home in boxes. Frankie Yale's support of Aiello's Unione Siciliana ambitions was one of the deciding factors in his murder by Winkeler, Goetz, and Campagna on July 1, 1928. They were led by Campagna rather than by McGurn, as most writers still believe, and it was the first time a Thompson gun was used in New York.

Local police found one such gun in an abandoned car and traced it to a Chicago dealer, causing New York newspapers to editorially worry that Chicago-style violence was coming to their city.

Georgette Winkeler doesn't include Fred Burke among Yale's killers, but after the St. Valentine's Day Massacre caused Chicagoans to enlist ballistics-expert Calvin Goddard and he compared Massacre bullets to the bullets recovered from Yale's body, he established that some of them came from a Massacre gun. So once the submachine guns were seized at Fred Burke's house in Michigan a few months later, Burke was blamed for Yale's death also.

With Capone's tax conviction in 1931, Campagna's loyalty shifted to Frank Nitti and then to his successors. He was convicted, along with other Chicago mobsters, in a Hollywood extortion case in 1943 but did not serve a long sentence. He eventually died of a heart attack in 1955.

CAPEZIO, ANTHONY "TOUGH TONY"

Capezio graduated from Chicago's juvenile "42" Gang and took up with Capone before he joined Claude Maddox as a partner in the Capone-allied Circus Gang on North Avenue. The Circus Café, where the gang headquartered, bordered the neighborhoods of both Bugs Moran, who ruled the North Side over to Lake Michigan, and Joey Aiello in Little Sicily. It amounted to a Capone beachhead in enemy territory, and it probably was the launching pad for the St. Valentine's Day Massacre. After that bloodbath Capezio was helping dismantle the Cadillac touring car in a nearby garage when he managed to get his cutting torch into the canister of gasoline attached to the car's firewall, causing a gasoline explosion. Well-singed by the flash fire, he hustled over to a clinic on North Avenue but then hurried back out when he realized that the cops and the fire department would soon arrive. (Apparently this earned him the nickname "Tough Tony.") Capone later made him manager of a brothel in the suburban town of Stickney.

After Capone went down, Capezio continued to prosper under Frank Nitti and Tony Accardo and became a principal in the Syndicate's wire-service takeover (for off-track betting) in the forties. He eventually died of a heart attack at the White Pines Country Club in Bensenville on July 7, 1955—not struck by lightning as some accounts have it.

Anthony "Tough Tony" Capezio

CAREY, BOB (A.K.A. ROBERT NEWBERRY, ROBERT CONROY, SANBORN)

Like Gus Winkeler, Fred Burke, and Ray Nugent, Bob Carey served in the army during the world war and evidently suffered wounds that left him with a slight limp that earned him the nickname "Gimpy." He, too, patronized the St. Louis Sharpshooter's Club, which evidently attracted more than its share of local hoodlums.

This group formed the nucleus of a loose-knit "crew" that included several other young hoods (probably veterans themselves) and who might be called "fun-loving" criminals, given to drunken parties and pranks as well as lawbreaking in the early twenties. All of them regularly tangled with the cops, but they also had friends on the police force, which at that time might have been characterized as a "police farce."

During the diaspora of the Egan's Rats in the middle twenties, Carey and Nugent followed Fred Burke to Michigan before joining up with Winkeler in Chicago, where they soon encountered Al Capone. Capone evidently was impressed with Winkeler, despite his outlaw history and his "snatch racket" operations with Burke. He was less impressed with Carey and Nugent, but later agreed to employ them as his "American boys" if Winkeler could keep them in line. Capone was personally opposed to kidnapping and insisted that they give it up, partly to get Burke on board as a shooter instead of a snatcher.

Bob "Gimpy" Carey,
a.k.a. Newberry, a.k.a. Conroy.

Following the St. Valentine's Day Massacre and a summer of hiding, Carey took up with a girl known as Rosemary Sanborn, or "Babe," who was no stranger to crime herself. They went their own way and began plying the "badger" game, in which men of prominence were lured to hotel rooms by Babe and secretly photographed in what the papers called "compromising positions." When one of the victims turned out to be a friend of Capone, he invited them to get out of town.

They moved to Washington, D.C., where pickings were good (including two U.S. senators), and then to New York City about April 1932.

Evidently Carey had experience in the printing business, and he set up a sizable press in an apartment at 220 West 104th Street, where he began turning out five-dollar bills. That was in late July, and he had not been in the business long before another tenant in the building, Alexander Gordon, noticed that "the Sanborns" were unusually quiet and not turning off their lights at night. Two days later he expressed his concern to a cop, and when no one answered a knock on the door the officer and Gordon found they could make their way along a ledge to an open window. (Such do-it-yourself techniques were not uncommon at the time.)

There they found the bodies of Rosemary, shot three times with her head in the bathroom doorway, and Carey, slumped over the tub with a bullet also in his head, from a .45 automatic found at Rosemary's feet. Police also noted the counterfeiting equipment and figured out that Mr. Sanborn was actually Robert Newberry, or maybe Robert Conroy, or maybe Robert Carey, who had both the police and the press confused over his various aliases. A Secret Service official declared the phony fives to be exceptionally good.

In any case, New York police wrote the two deaths off as a murder and suicide and closed the books. But in going through Sanborn's various aliases, they learned he also was a suspect in the St. Valentine's Day Massacre.

In her biography of Bugs Moran, *The Man Who Got Away*, Rose Keefe interviewed an elderly man who had been one of Bugs Moran's truck drivers. He said he happened to encounter his old boss at a suburban tavern in 1932, and Moran mentioned that he had just returned from a trip to the coast, where he had "taken care of Bob Carey." The name did not register with either the driver or Rose Keefe at the time, but she later learned that Carey had been one Capone's "American boys."

D'ANDREA, PHIL

Phillip D'Andrea was born in Buffalo, New York, probably in 1891, but followed his brother Anthony to Chicago, where he briefly attended law school. Anthony was a former priest turned crook who soon hooked up with Jim Colosimo, and with the advent of Prohibition brother Phil

Many of Chicago's ranking hoodlums joined police associations or departments in order to carry an identification card and star. D'Andrea had both, which did not spare him a six-month jail term for carrying a gun into a federal courtroom during Al Capone's trial for tax evasion. Capone himself had one in 1923, when he collided with a taxicab and threatened to shoot the driver. A few years later, when Rocco DeGrazia crashed his car west of Chicago, he declined to discuss either the police star he was carrying or the Thompson submachine gun that was lying on the back seat.

took to trucking booze. Meanwhile he had racked up several arrests for receiving stolen property, assault, and carrying weapons.

Despite D'Andrea's criminal record, Al Capone got him appointed a deputy court bailiff and teamed him up with gambler Billy Skidmore in the bail-bond business. He also worked as a bagman, gunman, and bodyguard for Capone. D'Andrea had a sizable house near St. Joseph, Michigan, that was used as a hideout for Chicago gangsters. It over-looked a golf course and was regularly used by Capone and his men.

D'Andrea's questionable credentials (he belonged to the Illinois Police Association, which pictured him in uniform, and he was a card-carrying member of the West Park Police Department) did not prevent his arrest on October 10, 1931, for carrying a gun into federal court dur-ing Capone's tax trial. That earned him a six-month jail sentence for contempt but did not prevent his becoming a power in the First Ward Democratic organization. He also served as president of Chicago's Italo-American National Union (formerly the Unione Siciliana) from 1934 to 1941.

After Capone's conviction, D'Andrea's loyalty shifted to Frank Nitti, and he helped advance such mobsters as Tony Accardo, Paul "The Waiter" Ricca, Charlie Fischetti, and Nick Circella. In 1943 he was con-victed in the same Hollywood extortion case that earlier had led Frank Nitti, in poor health, to take his own life.

D'Andrea died in Riverside, California, of natural causes on Sep-tember 18, 1952.

DILLINGER AND NELSON GANGS

It was Gus Winkeler's bad luck to be murdered on October 9, 1933, when Al Capone, the Beer Wars, and racketeering already were "history" in the public's mind, which quickly became focused on kidnappers, bank robbers, and a new breed of U.S. government crime fighters called "G-men."

Winkeler's death occurred only three months after President Roose-velt's attorney general had declared a national "War on Crime," implying that the U.S. Justice Department would now be cracking down not only on kidnappers and bank robbers but also on political and police corrup-

John Dillinger.

tion as well as any offense that could be construed as interfering with "interstate commerce."

This greatly overstated the authority of the federal government, but with Repeal in the works, and much talk of an "American Scotland Yard" and a "national police force" (to the consternation of J. Edgar Hoover), the public welcomed an exciting new game of Dick Tracy–style cops 'n' robbers, complete with such colorfully named lawbreakers as Pretty Boy, Machine Gun, and Baby Face.

If the Justice Department's crime-fighting prowess was exaggerated by Attorney General Cummings, the existing criminal community failed to appreciate how J. Edgar Hoover's public-relations efforts soon would turn his assortment of young lawyers, accountants, and investigators into scientifically trained, machine-gun armed, detective-magazine action heroes.

During this transition period Winkeler's partner, Joe Bergl, had been selling cars willy-nilly to gangsters, bank robbers, kidnappers, and any other unsavory character sent by another unsavory character. Winkeler had been trying to distance himself from murder and banditry as he rose to prominence as a nightclub impresario on Chicago's Near North Side, taking over much of Bugs Moran's old turf. And after Capone's tax conviction most of his "American boys" wandered off in other directions, some taking up with the yet little-known Barker-Karpis Gang, which had moved from armed robbery into kidnapping. With Capone in prison and Repeal in the works, the "March of Crime" seemed to be moving in a new direction:

- Wealthy brewer William Hamm Jr. was kidnapped in St. Paul on June 15, 1933.
- Two days later, on June 17, several officers, including a federal agent, were attacked and killed by machine-gun wielding outlaws in the Kansas City Massacre.
- A month after that, oil magnate Charles Urschel was kidnapped by Machine Gun Kelly in Oklahoma City.
- On September 26, Kelly was captured in Memphis—the same day that the future Dillinger Gang broke out of the Indiana state prison.
- On October 9 Gus Winkeler was murdered, but three days later a sheriff was killed by bank robbers freeing John Dillinger from a jail in Lima, Ohio.
- Two weeks after that Indiana's Governor Paul McNutt called out the National Guard to combat bank robberies.

· On November 15 Dillinger dodged police bullets as he escaped a
  trap at a Chicago doctor's office.
· On December 28, 1933, Dillinger was declared "Public Enemy
  No. 1" by Chicago police, which had created a public-enemy list
  of their own.

The so-called Dillinger Gang (as it was being called by Indiana police captain Matt Leach, hoping to cause dissention because Harry Pier-
pont was actually the leader) had zoomed into national prominence with
several dramatic bank robberies and police station holdups in the fall of
1933 before they were captured, without a shot, by a bunch of "yokels" in
Tucson, Arizona.

Dillinger was extradited to Crown Point, Indiana. Two months later,
with help from his "legal team" and some $15,000 in bribe money from
the little-known bank-robbery gang of George "Baby Face" Nelson (born
Lester Gillis) at the urging of former Dillinger fellow inmate Homer Van
Meter, he bluffed his way out of the Lake County Jail with a wooden
pistol, grabbed two machine guns and two hostages, stole the sheriff's
car, and motored out of town singing "Git along, li'l dogie, git along."

That made him a national celebrity, and only three days later Dil-
linger, Nelson, and their partners robbed the bank in Sioux Falls, South
Dakota. While Dillinger was on the run the FBI assembled a thirty-nine-
page document that listed more than 250 gang "contacts" for Dillinger
and Nelson, some of whom had taken up with girls from Winkeler's 225
Club and other classy nightclubs in Chicago's prosperous Gold Coast.
(Joe Bergl would later meet his wife Dorothy at the late Winkeler's Chez
Paree.)

When Nelson had managed his own escape in 1932 he was close to
the Touhys, who controlled DuPage County, and he already was well
acquainted with Capone mobsters Tony Capezio and Rocco DeGrazia,
both of whom had participated, one way or another, in the St. Valentine's
Day Massacre. Since then, Massacre participants Fred Goetz and Byron
Bolton had gone into business with the Barker-Karpis Gang, kidnapping
William Hamm in 1933 and staging their failed Loop mail robbery less
than a month before Winkeler was murdered.

After Dillinger's Crown Point escape on March 3, 1934, and his Sioux Falls bank robbery only three days later, he shot his way out of an apartment in St. Paul. In April he and rest of the gang slipped out the back of the Little Bohemia Lodge in northern Wisconsin while the G-men spent most of the night shooting the place up, mistakenly hitting three customers, one of whom died.

While the country's largest manhunt was in progress, Dillinger decided the safest place to hide was at his home in Mooresville, Indiana, where he was joined by family members and recklessly posed outside with his wooden pistol, a machine gun, and a smile on his face. Then he went back to robbing banks.

Dillinger's trick was to hide in plain sight. With Polly Hamilton, a new girl who worked at a Chicago sandwich shop, he celebrated his thirty-third birthday at the elegant French Casino, went to baseball games (once waving hello to his horrified lawyer, Louis Piquett), and enjoyed the rides at the Riverview Amusement Park. If anyone remarked that he looked a lot like Dillinger, he'd laugh and say something like, "Everybody thinks that."

Arthur O'Leary, assigned by lawyer Louis Piquett to keep an eye on the reckless Dillinger, recalled that when the Riverview Amusement Park's unexpected midday closing annoyed its customers, Dillinger assumed he'd been recognized by security personnel and whispered in the ear of a particularly aggravated woman, "They think they've got Dillinger cornered!" She began howling, which brought the cops. Dillinger and O'Leary jumped into a vacated police car and raced out one of the guarded gates yelling that they were going for reinforcements.

Dillinger's face was becoming so well known that he decided to undergo plastic surgery, which did not greatly alter his appearance. While recuperating he moved in with Anna Sage, who had operated brothels in Indiana and Chicago. She had an apartment near the Biograph Theatre on North Lincoln Avenue, and also had a sometimes-boyfriend, Martin Zarkovich, who may have known Dillinger through their mutual connections with the East Chicago mob. Hoping to save Anna from her scheduled deportation as "morally undesirable," Zarkovich alerted the Feds, making the ambush contingent on his participation. When Dillinger, Anna, and Polly left the Biograph on the night of July 22, 1934, he was cut down by the G-men, who also managed to wing two bystanders. Although Agent Samuel Cowley had been brought in to supervise the operation, nearly all the credit went to Special Agent in Charge Melvin Purvis, much to Hoover's annoyance.

With Floyd still lying low, the FBI targeted Dillinger's associate, Baby Face Nelson, who had taken it on the lam to California. At this point newspapers were not sure whom to declare "Public Enemy No. 1," since J. Edgar Hoover had refused to use that terminology.

On October 22, 1934, Pretty Boy Floyd surfaced near East Liverpool, Ohio, resuming his newspaper position as Public Enemy No. 1. He was killed the next day by local officers and federal agents, which promoted Baby Face Nelson back to the top of newspapers' public-enemy lists.

When Nelson, his wife Helen, and new partner John Paul Chase returned to the Chicago area that fall, they nearly fell into a federal trap that had been set at Hobart Hermansen's Lake Como Inn, where Nelson often stayed, a few miles west of Lake Geneva, Wisconsin. (Author Rose Keefe visited Lake Como and learned that Hobart's last name was not Hermanson, as commonly spelled, but Hermansen.)

After that he sped toward Chicago, and between Fox River Grove and Barrington, Illinois, he engaged federal officers in one of the most bizarre gun battles in outlaw history.

The Feds, racing north in a 1928 Model A Ford coupe on what was then Highway 12, turned around to chase a car they suspected was Nelson's, only to see Nelson do the same thing. Then, as they passed each other a second time, Nelson turned around again. In his new V-8 Ford Nelson easily pulled up behind the G-men and Chase let go with a Monitor automatic rifle (the civilian version of the BAR), shooting through his own car's windshield. The G-men fired back with pistols, and some lucky shots hit Nelson's radiator and fuel pump, which crippled his car and allowed the government men to reach a curve where they stopped, expecting to ambush Nelson as he sped by.

Meanwhile, Agents Herman Hollis and Sam Cowley encountered the running gun battle, turned their own car around, and saw that Nelson had made it only as far as the side road leading to Barrington's city park. They skidded to a stop fifty or so feet past the park entrance and jumped out with a Thompson and a shotgun.

Helen took cover in a weed-filled ditch while Nelson began shooting. Cowley ran toward a telephone pole and was killed with a shot through the head, but not before one of his .45 slugs had slipped under Nelson's bulletproof vest, hitting him in the stomach. Nelson yelled something like "I'm going to get those sonsabitches!" and marched straight into the shotgun fire of Herman Hollis, killing him also.

Nelson managed to back the federal car up to his own, helped transfer their guns, and escaped while several astonished spectators watched from the cover of ditches and a gas station. Mortally wounded, Nelson picked up his terrified wife but had to turn the driving over to his partner. They finally made it to a "safe house" owned by a friend in Wilmette, where Nelson died about three hours later.

With the help of the residents, Nelson's body was laid out next to St. Paul's cemetery in neighboring Niles Center (now called Skokie), where police found it the next morning. Chase meanwhile dumped the shot-up federal car near a railroad station, trained it into Chicago, and headed back to California, where he was later captured.

Which left the G-men to pursue the Barker-Karpis Gang. Some members were captured at an apartment on Chicago's Pine Grove Avenue in January 1935, which led federal agents to the Florida house where Fred and "Ma" Barker both were killed after a prolonged gun battle. Alvin Karpis was "personally" arrested a year later in New Orleans (after more than a dozen G-men were holding him at gunpoint) by J. Edgar Hoover, and that, for all practical purposes, ended the "War on Crime."

DEGRAZIA, ROCCO (A.K.A. ROCKY DEGRAZIO)

Although most newspapers accepted his birth date as 1900, DeGrazia was born in Italy on December 8, 1897. He emmigrated to the U.S. about 1920 and soon hooked up with the Torrio-Capone mob as a driver and gunman before rising to prominence as a gambling and loan-sharking figure. In the late 1920s he worked with Claude Maddox and Tony Capezio, who headed up the Circus Gang that operated out of the Circus Café on North Avenue. Maddox and DeGrazia harbored the shooters who took part in the St. Valentine's Day Massacre. In July 1932, DeGrazia suffered spinal injuries in a wreck near Bloomingdale, Illinois, but refused

to discuss the Thompson submachine gun found in the back seat
of his car or the police star he was
carrying at the time. After that he
tangled with the law on numerous
occasions, sometimes with Tony
Accardo and Sam "Golf Bag"
Hunt. In 1935 he was sentenced to
eighteen months in Leavenworth
for failure to pay income taxes. In
1946 he was picked up for drugs—
opium and morphine—which he
insisted were for use in doping
horses, although his brother Andrew was believed to be an addict.
Another brother, Anthony, served
as a Chicago police lieutenant un-

Rocco DeGrazia (a.k.a. Rocky DeGrazio)

til a 1959 vacation trip to Europe with Tony Accardo, mob boss of the
day, led to his suspension. The scandal attaching to that caused Rocco's
undertaking license to be revoked on the basis of "poor moral character"
and "hoodlum connections."

In later years he operated a lavish gambling club in Melrose Park
called the Casa Madrid. It was closed by authorities in 1961, although
mob bosses continued to meet there as late as 1969. After that he faded
into obscurity and died of natural causes on December 17, 1978.

DRURY, WILLIAM

William Drury entered the Chicago Police Department as a patrolman
in 1924, was transferred to the detective department a year later, and
soon emerged as the city's most conspicuous and flamboyant criminal-
catcher. Or at least harasser. He had received a commendation in 1927 for
nabbing a bandit who had foolishly tried to hold him up in his own car.

Drury's reputation as "watchdog of the Loop" later was tarnished,
but not much, when he told a grand jury that he knew nothing about any
gambling in his district, unaware that the state's attorney's men already

had found eight gambling dens in operation, apparently protected by Democratic precinct captains.

As a plainclothesman Drury drove an elegant car that the average cop could never have afforded, but he was not accused of taking bribes; and he was hell on such highly visible gangsters as Nitti and other mob colossi. Unlike Detective Captain William Shoemaker, Drury was the personal nemesis of Gus Winkeler who lost him in one car chase but later was busted for supposedly carrying a gun that Georgette, at least, thought was a phony charge.

This was at a time when Drury also was wearing formal outfits when hobnobbing with high-society swells and watching after their expensive fur coats; and he later headed up a detail of specially dressed World's Fair policemen who safeguarded the tourists.

At various times his activities got him fired, reinstated, and fired again, eventually he became a crime reporter for the *Chicago Herald-American*. He also opened a private-detective agency. Drury had worked up an impressive expose of Chicago political and police corruption for the Kefauver Rackets Committee in 1950 when, hours before his scheduled appearance, he was shotgunned to death as he backed his Cadillac out of his garage.

FLOYD, CHARLES "PRETTY BOY"

Pretty Boy Floyd was the first outlaw to make national news. On September 10, 1932, the *Literary Digest* called him "Oklahoma's 'Bandit King'" and reported, "He robs and laughs. Jeering the police, and even the Governor, he swoops down on a town, holds up a bank, and dashes away again by motor. In two years he has held up at least a score of banks. For his capture, dead or alive, there is an offer of a $3000 reward."

No matter that his catchy moniker wasn't coined by a sometimes-girlfriend Beulah Baird but by an early police error that mistook him for a Pretty Boy Smith (as discovered by researcher Mike Webb), it became his nickname and a historic shootout in Kansas City prevented him from going down as a footnote in outlaw history.

Floyd was basically a loner, although he often worked with others and ended up partnered with one Adam Richetti. He may have joined

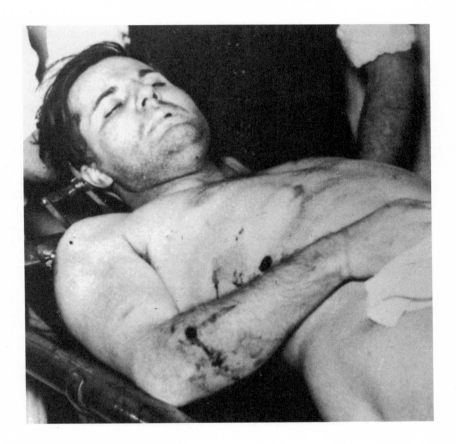

Charles "Pretty Boy" Floyd.

the Dillinger Gang for its last robbery at South Bend, Indiana, on June 30, 1934, where he was described by one gang member only as a "famous outlaw from the West." If so, he greatly antagonized Baby Face Nelson, until Dillinger warned Nelson that the man's partner was Floyd's gun-buddy Adam Richetti. Nelson supposedly threw a fit when the FBI got to Floyd first in October 1934, a month before Nelson killed two federal agents and was mortally wounded himself.

What put the G-men on Floyd's trail—and virtually launched what was then an almost powerless FBI—was his participation in the Kansas City Massacre of June 17, 1933, when those killed included a federal agent. After that, Attorney General Homer Cummings declared a national "War on Crime," which virtually forced Congress to make not only kidnapping but also bank robbery and attacks on federal agents "interstate" offenses.

The principal instigator of the Kansas City killings was lawman-turned-outlaw Verne Miller, who then rushed to Chicago and sought refuge with Gus Winkeler. Winkeler not only turned Miller down but secretly helped G-men try to locate him.

The other known participant in the Kansas City killings was Pretty Boy Floyd; he and his partner Richetti then tried to lose themselves in the northern part of the country.

A sheriff responding to a report of two men camping out near Wells-ville, Ohio, (they were awaiting repairs on their car) led to the capture of Richetti, but Floyd escaped into a wooded area. The sheriff called Chicago's FBI, who began their search around nearby East Liverpool. There Floyd was spotted at the farmhouse of Ellen Conkle while he was trying to arrange a ride, and when Pretty Boy took off running across a field he was cut down by East Liverpool police and by federal agents, who had become lost on unmarked country roads and were following the local cops back to town.

J. Edgar Hoover gave full credit to the men from the Chicago Bu-reau, which must have annoyed the East Liverpool Police Department. They did not want to contradict Hoover's version, however, considering that his G-men had become the country's new crime-fighting heroes, and the general public had no qualms about killing outlaws in any case. But many years later, after waiting until other local officers had died, Chester Smith, the East Liverpool officer who had knocked Floyd down with a bullet from his rifle, began telling another account to social and fraternal groups in his community. He said that when the badly wounded Floyd answered Melvin Purvis and other agents only with insults, Purvis told a G-man with a machine gun, "Fire into him."

That account had been long rumored and it was backed up by a sher-iff, but Smith, who probably didn't know one G-man from another, had been calling the machine-gunner "Hawless." (Purvis had been ordered out of town the next day, leaving Herman Hollis in charge.)

Local newspapers had been reporting Smith's account since the 1960s, Chester claiming that he did not want to take the "true story" to his grave. But in 1979 their articles were picked up by the wire services and made national news; *Time* magazine turned it into a short article critical of the FBI. That was when the name Hawless/Hollis all but scuttled Chester's story.

Another G-man, still living, wrote *Time* an outraged letter to the effect that Hollis, while in on the hunt, was not even at the scene when Floyd was killed. He also said that the bullets that killed Floyd came from federal guns and that the local police had no role in the killing: "The truth is he was shot by two of the four FBI agents present when Floyd aimed his gun at them and after he was shot two or three members of the East Liverpool Police Department who were in the immediate area at the time came up to us and offered assistance in directing us to the morgue in East Liverpool."

That left Chester Smith's account supported indirectly only by Ernest Sturgis, who was both the local mortician and the county coroner. On three documents pertaining to Floyd's death he wrote:

> "Gunshot wound through the chest and abdomen inflicted by police officers when attempting to escape."
> "Gunshot wounds, two through the chest and abdomen, and one through the forearm."
> "Four wounds, shot in stomach."

Ignoring these notations, most writers have since debunked Smith's account as simply untrue and have accepted the FBI version, although inquest testimony had Smith and another East Liverpool officer reaching Floyd first and disarming him before he could aim his guns at anybody.

Also puzzling is the fact that while the FBI went to considerable lengths to establish whose bullets did what in the Kansas City Massacre, the death of Dillinger, and the gun battle in which Baby Face Nelson killed two federal agents, no details of the Floyd shooting were discussed either at the local inquest or in the FBI's otherwise voluminous records.

GOETZ, FRED (A.K.A. GEORGE GOETZ, GEORGE ZIEGLER, GEORGE ZEIGLER, SIEBERT)

Fred Goetz was thirty-seven years old when he was shotgunned about 11 PM outside the Minerva Café in Cicero on March 20, 1934. That he died a short time later, on March 21st, confused both the newspapers and writers later describing the shooting.

Fred Goetz, a.k.a. George Zeigler,
a.k.a. Ziegler.

In his money belt police found several steel saw blades that they theorized were intended as escape tools in the event of his capture, along with a one-thousand-dollar bill. That supposedly was given to him as a consolation prize when a Reno gambling syndicate refused to launder the ransom money from a Barker-Karpis kidnapping. Most have speculated that the killing was ordered by Frank Nitti because Goetz was bringing too much federal heat down on the mob with his forays into kidnapping.

As Frederick C. Goetz (Georgette always calls him George Goetz), he had received an officer's commission in the Army Air Service during the world war and then enrolled in the University of Illinois, whose administrators said he played football, studied horticulture, and graduated in 1923.

While working as a lifeguard at the Clarendon beach in 1925 he was accused of luring an eight-year-old girl into his car with candy and molesting her, which papers commonly reported as attempted rape. Skipping bail on that charge, he took up armed robbery, bank robbery, and murder, frustrating the police by changing his name to J. George Zeigler (frequently spelled Ziegler) and collaborating with Chicago's John "Handsome Jack" Klutas, known as the College Kidnapper, as well as other criminals. These would include Fred Burke, a freelance gunman and robber then touring the Midwest, who was generally credited with introducing the snatch racket to Detroit, or at least making it a full-time business.

Goetz had his own St. Louis connections and could have known (or known of) Burke and Winkeler there, but Georgette believes that Gus met him at a Capone tavern in Cicero and he thereby became one of

Capone's "American boys." According to Byron Bolton after his capture in 1935, it was at Goetz's Wisconsin lodge in the fall of 1928 that plans were made to kill Bugs Moran in what became the St. Valentine's Day Massacre (which missed the man they were gunning for, but freed up the North Side for Winkeler's gentlemanly rise to power).

Goetz was one of the dozen or more gangsters and outlaws to whom cars were sold by Cicero dealer and Winkeler's partner Joe Bergl. He had joined up with the Barker-Karpis Gang when they pulled their dysfunctional Chicago Loop mail robbery in September of 1933, wrecking their getaway car, which landed both Bergl and Winkeler in trouble. With Goetz and Bolton, the Barker-Karpis Gang already had kidnapped wealthy St. Paul brewer William Hamm Jr. the previous June and took banker Edward Bremer in January of 1934.

Goetz, reincarnated as Zeigler, had prospered through crime but also operated a landscaping business (when anybody could find him) that provided a measure of respectability. He also joined more than a dozen country clubs, yacht clubs, and even the Illinois Police Association.

At the time of his murder police linked Zeigler through fingerprints to the man they knew as Fred Goetz, and they also discovered that he and his supposed wife, Irene Zeigler (nee Dorsey, a.k.a Goetz, although they never married), were then living a seemingly tranquil life as Mr. and Mrs. Siebert in an elegantly furnished apartment on South Lake Shore Drive. Their neighbors were amazed to learn that Mr. Siebert, ever friendly, well educated, interested in fine books, and a dabbler in the stock market, was also a bank robber, killer, and kidnapper. His landlady was likewise surprised. "They were fine people," she told a *Chicago Tribune* reporter. "Mr. Siebert seemed to me to be a very brilliant and handsome man. His wife was beautiful. She was tall, very blonde, and had gray-blue eyes. They always seemed to have plenty of money."

But after Goetz's death Irene took it on the lam. Some six months later she was located in a Modesto, California, hospital, claiming she was still too dazed by her husband's murder, which she had witnessed, to provide much information to authorities, and they let it go at that.

Irene, defying the usual "moll" tradition, later went to college, enlisted in the WACs during WWII, became an officer, and ended up a respectable housewife and shopkeeper in her hometown of Wilmington, Illinois, until her death in 1974.

GOLDBLATT, DAVID OR BENNY

David Goldblatt, whom Georgette sometimes calls Benny, was the black sheep of Chicago's Goldblatt's department store family. Instead of rising in those ranks he remained a street punk, hanging his hat in pool halls and speakeasies and getting to know such other young mobsters as Nails Morton and Hirshie Miller. According to researcher Jeff Gusfield, Goldblatt took up with Gus Winkeler sometime after Winkeler had eluded the Massacre-hunters and returned to Chicago, to work as his driver and bodyguard.

About this time Winkeler severed his official ties with the Syndicate, now headed by Frank Nitti, and began going "legit," at least to the extent of opening or reopening upscale nightclubs with private gambling operations that catered to the moneyed class in Chicago's Gold Coast neighborhood. Goldblatt had mixed loyalties that earned him and Ralph Pierce the enmity of Georgette Winkeler when Nitti began muscling in on the clubs. Georgette believed that Nitti ordered Gus's murder.

HARRISON, WILLIAM J.

Former St. Louis gangster Willie Harrison, who had known the Winkelers for years, married a woman named Ruth on December 16, 1931, the same day that Georgette and Gus, to fulfill his mother's wishes, also

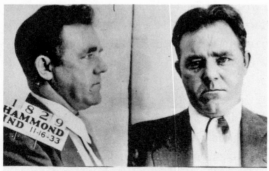

William J. Harrison

were married in the Catholic faith. Both ceremonies were performed by Father Edward Dwyer at Chicago's Notre Dame Church on West Madison Street. Harrison's marriage did not last long before he took up with a woman named Dickie May and then another named May Green, both of whom also visited the Winkelers with Harrison.

Harrison operated a saloon in Calumet City that had become a watering hole for his old gangster and outlaw friends. After 1932 he took up with the Barker-Karpis Gang, who evidently found him to be an unreliable alcoholic. He was shot to death on January 5, 1935, probably by Doc Barker, and his body found in a burning barn outside Ontarioville, Illinois.

HOLLENBERGER, FRANCIS X.

Everything known about Dr. Francis X. Hollenberger—if in fact he did have a Ph.D.—comes from the memorandum to J. Edgar Hoover sent by Special Agent F. E. Hurley dated January 31, 1935.

Evidently he was a "German spy" during the world war who had lived in Washington, D.C., before moving to Wisconsin, making promises of marriage to Martha Grabowski of Evansville, Indiana, and helping Georgette write a draft of her memoirs that she found much too detailed and insulting to federal and local officials. However, much of the research as to dates and some of the writing appear to be borrowed from his version, although she claimed to have written the manuscript herself.

His threat to expose Georgette's project to the Chicago Syndicate must have been accomplished one way or another, for the

The Mysterious
Dr. Francis Hollenberger.

mob evidently intimidated her publisher into breaking their contract when the manuscript was already prepared for publication.

There probably is a file on Hollenberger in some U.S. government agency, but it has never been found. Georgette warned that he was a Nazi sympathizer and, if necessary, should be approached only by an agent "who appears to sincerely praise Hitler."

HUNT, SAM "GOLF BAG"

Sam Hunt, when working for Johnny Torrio and later Al Capone, acquired the nickname "Golf Bag" Hunt because he regularly was arrested

Sam "Golf Bag" Hunt.

Police officer showing "Golf Bag" Hunt's method of carrying a shotgun.

for, or suspected of, using a golf bag to carry a shotgun, and that became his trademark.

Born in Birmingham, Alabama, around 1900, Samuel was arrested several times before finding his way to Chicago about 1920. There he soon gained the attention of the South Side mob and became fast friends with another hoodlum, Ralph Pierce. He was accused of several hits but seems to have dodged convictions until 1931, when he spent ninety days in Chicago's Bridewell jail on a weapons charge.

His major problem occurred in 1942 when, after four trials, he was finally acquitted of shooting the other driver following a traffic accident. He otherwise prospered through bookmaking, numbers, and other rackets before dying in 1956 of heart failure in Schenectady, New York, while visiting relatives.

KEMPSTER, BUCK

Oliver "Buck" Kempster had an interesting career as bodyguard to two Illinois governors and as a highway patrolman who was later given the job of liaison between the state and the FBI. He also was a friend of Gus Winkeler and, in his lawman capacity, introduced Winkeler to Special Agent in Charge Melvin Purvis.

Left to right: Buck Kempster, Tom O'Connor, "Pop" Lee, and Jack Britt.

Kempster was born near Sterling, Illinois, in 1900, and acquired enough clout to become a bodyguard of Governor Len Small. Small recommended him to the Illinois State Police when that group of only six men was first organized in 1922. During the twenties and early thirties, he caught, killed, or railroaded enough "suspects" into prison that he then became a personal bodyguard to Governor Henry Horner, who soon assigned him to act as the state's liaison with the Chicago office of the U.S. Bureau of Investigation. It was during this period that Kempster came to know Winkeler, as Gus was taking command of Chicago's Near North Side, now vacated by the Bugs Moran gangsters. Former Northsider Ted Newberry and Edgar Lebensberger were Winkeler's partners or fronts.

By 1932 Winkeler was trying to distance himself from his outlaw past and had worked with Chicago's "Secret Six" to clear himself of Nebraska robbery charges. Soon, with Kempster's support, he was helping the Bureau of Investigation track down Verne Miller, who had tried to contact him for shelter after the Kansas City Massacre in June of 1933. Kempster also kept Winkeler apprised of the Justice Department's operations.

Kempster was among the Bureau's personnel who, shortly after Winkeler's murder in October of 1933, assisted the Feds in their failed attempt to kill or capture Miller at the Sherone apartment-hotel, near Lake Michigan on Chicago's North Side. Miller escaped in an Auburn roadster into which Kempster put several machine-gun bullets, the first time a Thompson had been used by anyone but gangsters. Miller was himself killed by his gangland buddies, who no longer wanted anything to do with him and left his body in a Detroit ditch in November, the month after Winkeler's demise.

Prior to this period, Kempster was acquitted of protecting rumrunners on Illinois highways in 1931, took care of a wounded payroll robber in 1933, helped capture some small-time kidnappers that same year, and then was suspended from the state police after visiting "Three-Fingered Jack" White a few hours before he was killed in January 1934. About that time Kempster's duplicity became known to the Bureau, and he was sent packing.

Kempster was cleared of involvement in White's death and rejoined the state police, working his way up to captain. During World War II he made colonel and was instrumental in capturing a group of Italian counterfeiters. In the early 1950s, he retired to Florida, where he died in 1980.

LEBENSBERGER, EDGAR

Edgar Lebensberger was the son of a distiller who married the daughter of another distiller and gravitated in that direction, becoming friends (or friendly rivals) with North Side booze racketeer Ted Newberry. When Gus Winkeler began his own rise to power, both became part of his stable, as operators or partners in fashionable nightclubs in Chicago's Gold Coast and Near North Side. Lebensberger was the owner-apparent of the 225 Club at 225 East Superior Street, though he was frequently at odds with the Nitti Syndicate over profits and policies. His downfall took place on October 6, 1933, when he and others were dabbling in stolen bonds.

Edgar Lebensberger.

Federal authorities had been indicting those trafficking in negotiable securities stolen during the Loop mail robbery on December 6, 1932. Lebensberger found himself in that group, and he supposedly killed himself in his swanky apartment at 1268 Lake Shore Drive when he learned he was being indicted. While the police wrote it off as a "suicide while temporarily insane," a federal district attorney expressed doubts because of the placement of the head wound and the absence of powder burns.

Lebensberger and Winkeler had just leased the Opera Club at 18 West Walton Place, near the northernmost end of Michigan Avenue, Chicago's main street. Three days later Gus Winkeler would be killed.

LOOP MAIL ROBBERIES

Two major mail robberies occurred in downtown Chicago, locally known as the Loop because of the city's system of elevated trains.

The first, on December 6, 1932, set an all-time mail-robbery record when five bandits stole $250,000 (some papers reported the take as $500,000) in cash and securities and made a clean getaway.

During the second robbery, on September 23, 1933, the bandits crashed their getaway car and killed police officer Myles Cunningham in the course of commandeering another car, only to discover that their loot consisted of sacks of canceled checks.

Both robberies led to intensive investigations by Chicago police and federal agents, and both involved Gus Winkeler. The bonds stolen in 1932 began turning up among Winkeler's friends about the same time the 1933 robbery took place, adding to the confusion.

After the 1932 robbery the police found the abandoned getaway car that could not be traced but had a smokescreen device—one that might have been installed by Joe Bergl, a Cicero auto dealer whose partner was Gus Winkeler. When the stolen securities later made their way to Fred Goetz, an "American boy" who'd left the Capone reservation, and to Edgar Lebensberger, one of Winkeler's club managers, Gus told his wife Georgette that the robbery was the work of a gang operating out Minneapolis and St. Paul and that he had warned Lebensberger not to get mixed up in the stolen bond business.

After the 1933 robbery, some ten months later, the wrecked escape car was quickly traced to Joe Bergl, who had bulletproofed it, installed red and green headlights to resemble a detective squad, equipped it with a police-frequency radio, and also had added a smokescreen device. Under persuasive questioning, Bergl, whose car dealership was next door to Ralph Capone's Cotton Club, acknowledged that his partner was Gus Winkeler. Both were arrested in connection with the theft and for the murder of Officer Myles Cunningham.

Now facing murder charges, Bergl went into hiding, and newspapers speculated that he'd been killed. Another paper carried the banner headline, WINKLER SIEZED IN KILLING. After police raided Winkeler's suite on Lake Shore Drive he was taken into "technical custody" by federal agents on September 25, 1933. This may have been the occasion when Winkeler, already helping the Bureau in its search for Kansas City's Verne Miller, "gifted" Melvin Purvis with his custom-made .45 automatic.

The 1932 robbery might have been the work of other bandits, but over the next several months the net widened to include thirty or more persons involved in peddling the bonds. Suspicion apparently didn't fall on the yet-unknown Barker-Karpis Gang whom Winkeler had met during a "family reunion" of crooks at Jack Peifer's Hollyhocks club in St. Paul. But the 1933 mail robbery definitely was their work, and by now the gang included both Fred Goetz and Byron Bolton.

In any case, Winkeler and Bergl were linked to the bungled mail robbery and cop killing in September 1933. And Winkeler's club manager Lebensberger, with many others, were meanwhile being indicted for possessing bonds stolen during the earlier and successful mail robbery of December 1932.

The September charges were still pending when Lebensberger (despite Winkeler's belief that he could beat the 1932 rap) supposedly committed suicide on October 6, 1933. And Frank Nitti, knowing Gus had cooperated with the Secret Six and had been visiting the Bureau of Investigation, but not knowing what he might be spilling about one or both robberies or about the Syndicate, ordered Winkeler's murder three days later.

MADDOX, CLAUDE

John E. Moore, a.k.a. Claude Maddox, had left St. Louis in the early twenties and joined John Torrio and Al Capone. He was shot and wounded in 1924 when Chicago police were called in to quell the violence that accompanied a Cicero election. He later opened the Circus Café at 1857 West North Avenue, which amounted to a Capone beachhead bordering Joe Aiello's Little Sicily and Bugs Moran's territory that ran east over to Lake Michigan.

His partners in the operation were Tony Capezio and Rocco DeGrazia, and the "Circus Gang," as it was called, which later used the café as a launching pad for the St. Valentine's Day Massacre. Maddox also arranged for the rental of a garage in an alley be-

Claude Maddox.

hind Wood Street, only a few blocks away, where one of the phony detective cars exploded when Capezio got his cutting torch into the canister of gasoline on the Cadillac's firewall. Capezio was burned and ran to a North Avenue clinic, then ran back out when he realized that someone who had heard the blast would be calling the cops. This stunt earned him the nickname "Tough Tony." Helping him dismantle the car was Raymond "Shocker" Schulte, a.k.a. Charles Maginness, also from St. Louis.

Police easily tracked the anonymous renter to an address next door to the Circus Café, which they found deserted, but what they did find was a meeting room that contained several overcoats evidently left behind when the car blew, along with ammunition and the drum for a Thompson submachine gun.

When they later picked up Maddox he had the perfect alibi: the morning the call came in from the Massacre lookouts, he was in court on another matter, and Fred Goetz—at whose Wisconsin lodge the killing of Moran had been discussed—apparently had taken charge.

After Capone began his sabbatical in a Pennsylvania prison in May 1929, Maddox decided his future lay with Frank Nitti, and he became a major labor racketeer. On February 15, 1936, which newspapers tried to call the seventh anniversary of the Massacre, Maddox and Three-Fingered Jack White, another Nitti mobster, killed Jack McGurn in a bowling alley on Milwaukee Avenue, according to later FBI tapes. McGurn, an old Capone loyalist, had been relegated to the suburbs, was broke, and wanted back into the Syndicate.

Maddox remained in the rackets until his death from natural causes at his home in suburban Riverside on June 21, 1958.

MCGURN, "MACHINE GUN" JACK

Jack McGurn is not mentioned in Georgette's memoirs, nor are other Capone mobsters with whom she had no personal contact, but he supposedly had led the team that killed Frankie Yale and masterminded the St. Valentine's Day Massacre. Most writers don't question those versions, which deserve to be mentioned here.

McGurn was born Vincenzo Gibaldi in Licata, Sicily, in 1905 and soon immigrated to New York. When his own father, Tommaso, died of natural causes in 1911 (contrary to some writers, who claim he was murdered), McGurn was taken in by the DeMora family, who moved to Chicago. There his foster father opened a grocery and was expected to supply sugar and related items to local bootleggers. He was murdered in 1923, and young Vincenzo is supposed to have tracked down and killed the killers.

By that time he had changed his original name to Gibardi, and his revenge shootings in Little Italy may have attracted the attention of Al Capone. Or Capone, a boxing enthusiast, may have made his acquaintance at a prizefight, where Gibardi had since adopted the name Jack McGurn because of the sport's domination by the Irish.

In any case, McGurn became a Capone bodyguard and hit man—"a professional killer who killed professional killers," as Chicago researcher Mark Levell has put it—especially after Little Sicily's Joe Aiello made it known that anyone who killed Capone would earn $50,000. Aiello himself had become a contender for leadership of the Unione Siciliana, originally a service organization for Sicilian immigrants that later became a major source of home-cooked alcohol.

Capone's intelligence system was good enough that McGurn sent several of Aiello's bounty hunters home in boxes. He also was shot by Moran men at a Gold Coast hotel, and survived another attempt that riddled his car. By 1928 he was suspected of nearly any murder that could be construed as serving the interests of Capone, and his local notoriety was making him "too hot" to continue his wicked ways.

While McGurn no doubt knew that Capone was feeling obliged to waste Bugs Moran, who had since teamed up with Joe Aiello, McGurn holed up in the swanky Stevens Hotel on January 31, 1929, about the same time that surveillance of the North Clark Street garage began. He still was the Massacre's chief suspect when he and his "Blonde Alibi," Louise Rolfe, were found there two weeks later (coincidentally two floors below the suite that had been rented for the Massacre investigation). It was not until after the Massacre that McGurn acquired the nickname "Machine Gun."

In May 1929, Capone was summoned to the so-called national gangster convention in Atlantic City, after which he and his then-bodyguard Frankie Rio went to Philadelphia, where they obediently submitted to arrest for carrying guns. By the time they were released ten months later, Nitti had shaken off two or three rivals and taken control of Capone's Outfit, leaving the Big Fellow to deal with his tax problems.

Chicago police later decided they could not pin the Massacre on McGurn, but then he was hassled by federal government charges that he and Louise had been travelling together—unmarried—back and forth to Capone's estate in Florida. That violated the federal Mann Act, which originally was intended to combat interstate "White Slavery" but now was coming in handy to prosecute certain high-profile individuals.

McGurn and Louise were convicted of conspiring to commit that offense, but they appealed their cases all the way to the U.S. Supreme Court. And they won. The Court decided that the wording of the law did not contemplate a woman "debauching" herself and voided Louise's conviction. That left McGurn no one to have conspired *with,* which voided his conviction also.

By the time Capone went to prison in 1931 McGurn had no choice but to abandon his killing ways and virtually was forced to become a Chicago "sheik"—handsome, spiffy in his light blue outfits, supposedly good with the ukulele, and excelling at golf. Still a Capone loyalist, he was exiled by Frank Nitti to running handbooks in the suburbs, which failed to support his lofty lifestyle.

Around the mid-thirties McGurn sought reentry into the Syndicate. This annoyed Nitti enough that (according to later FBI tapes of another mobster's amused recollections) Claude Maddox and Jack White eventually were dispatched to kill McGurn in a Milwaukee Avenue bowling alley on the seventh anniversary of the Massacre, perhaps in the hope that it would be blamed on some relics of the Bugs Moran Gang. The shooters, or someone, earlier had left McGurn a comic Valentine card that depicted an unhappy couple outside their house with a "For Sale" sign. It read:

> You've lost your job; you've lost your dough;
> Your jewels and cars and handsome houses!
> But things could still be worse you know . . .
> At least you haven't lost your trousas!

Unfortunately, the shooters dawdled and didn't get in their shots until shortly after midnight, on February 15, 1936, to the frustration of local newspapers. (The name on McGurn's tombstone is Vincent Gebardi.)

Two weeks later, on March 3rd, Anthony DeMora, McGurn's half-brother, who Nitti feared might seek revenge, was killed in a Little Italy pool room.

MCLAUGHLIN, JOHN J. "BOSS"

John J. McLaughlin grew up on Chicago's West Side, engaged in ward politics, became city supervisor of West Chicago, served as a state representative for almost a decade, and earned his nickname "Boss" while

DAILY TIMES
CHICAGO'S PICTURE NEWSPAPER
2¢ Vol. 5. No. 202 CHICAGO, MONDAY, APRIL 30, 1934 36 Pages NIGHT EXTRA

'BOSS' M'LAUGHLIN SIGNS CONFESSION

Loop Bartender Also Admits Part in Bremer Case

WIN 11-YEAR FIGHT TO FORCE PHONE RATE CUT

John J. (Boss) McLaughlin today confessed that he had "handled" $53,000 of the $200,-000 ransom paid last February for the freeing of Edward G. Bremer, St. Paul banker. Melvin H. Purvis, chief of the lo-

The city of Chicago today won its 11-year fight to force reduction in charges made by the Illinois Bell Telephone Co. for coin box service. The reduction was ordered in 1923

MIXING 'EM. Theodore Janush, arriving today to open his tavern at 3000 S. Canal st., found bombers had done the job before dawn.

"Boss" McLaughlin.

operating a construction business during World War I. That had led to tangles with state authorities, and his political friends deserted him.

Those who stood by him were a few rungs lower than Chicago's politicians, and after paying a one-thousand-dollar fine for a Prohibition violation in 1923, he took to nightclub casino gambling. On October 6, 1933—the same night that Edgar Lebensberger died—he evidently learned that he also was about to be indicted for trafficking in bonds stolen in the unsolved Loop mail robbery ten months earlier. Three days later Winkeler would be killed.

Before the bond matter was resolved, McLaughlin was linked to ransom money obtained from the Barker-Karpis Gang. He was sixty-six when indicted on that charge, and the following May he confessed, motivated in part by the arrest of his seventeen-year-old son John Jr., who happened to be carrying eighty-five dollars of the ransom money, which he said had been given to him by his dad. McLaughlin was sent to Leavenworth Federal Prison for the possession of ransom money and he died there of bronchial pneumonia in December 1935. Two months later a federal judge dismissed the earlier stolen-bond charges against him and thirty-nine others.

MORAN, BUGS

The wipeout of Bugs Moran's mob ultimately paved the way for Winkeler to sever his official ties with the Chicago Syndicate and begin taking over the Gold Coast and Near North Side's nightclub and casino operations, fronted by (or in partnership with) such men as Ted Newberry and Edgar Lebensberger.

Georgette's belief that Moran was threatening the Capone empire may have been based on some knowledge of Chicago gangland politics when the Winkelers were on the run after the St. Valentine's Day Massacre. Or she may have known more about Moran's ambitions than other writers believe. Moran's men had shot McGurn and McGurn had shot at them, and in 1928 they killed Tony Lombardo and Patsy Lolordo, who enjoyed Capone's support to head the Unione Siciliana.

Author Rose Keefe learned that Moran's name originally was Adelard Cunin, born in St. Paul on August 21, 1891. He had mischievoused his way through burglary, robbery, safecracking, and jails until he found a home, as it were, at McGovern's Liberty Inn, 661 North Clark Street. There he met a small-ish singing waiter named Dean O'Banion, also a born trouble-maker who during the early years of Prohibition had become the city's first "famous" gangster. He operated out of Schofield's flower shop at 738 North State Street, only two blocks from the Liberty Inn and just across the street from the Holy Name Cathedral. (Leg-end has it that O'Banion either was an altar boy or sang in the choir there.)

O'Banion on the North Side and John Torrio on the South Side originally had partnered in the purchase of several breweries ostensibly turning out "near beer," which according to the Prohibi-tion law required the brewing of real beer that had to be "dealco-holized" down to one half of one percent alcohol. One of these was Sieben's Brewery, and O'Banion, claiming he was leaving the racket, lured Torrio there on an inspec-tion tour that turned out to be a half-million-dollar swindle. By prearrangement police raided the place, arresting Torrio and others, which meant jail time for Torrio on a second Volstead Act conviction.

Bugs Moran.

No doubt chuckling over this coup, O'Banion easily resolved his own legal problems over the raid and then left for a vacation at fellow mobster Louie Alterie's dude ranch in Colorado, from which he returned armed to the teeth with ordnance that included Chicago's first three Thompson submachine guns. Before he had a chance to use them, however, he was shot to death in his flower shop—the famous "handshake" murder—on November 10, 1924.

This opened Chicago's so-called Beer Wars. O'Banion's wild-man successor, Hymie Weiss, soon shot up the car of Al Capone, who was hardly known at the time and not even riding in it. Then Weiss, Vincent Drucci and Bugs Moran shot but failed to kill their main target, Johnny Torrio, in the front yard of his South Side apartment building near the lake. Torrio, who was more a businessman than a killer, decided that a citywide shooting war was about to begin, and retreated to New York as gangster emeritus. He left his operations to his own wild man, Al Capone.

Thanks to a new and one-term reform mayor, William Dever, Capone was forced to move his headquarters from the South Side's Metropole Hotel to the Hawthorne Hotel in neighboring Cicero in 1925. The following year a vengeful Weiss led a caravan of cars down Cicero's main street and shot up the Hawthorne. There were no fatalities (Capone even paid for the injuries suffered by a pedestrian), and twenty-one days later, on October 11, 1926, Weiss and his bodyguard, Patrick Murray, were killed in Capone's own carefully planned machine-gun ambush next door to O'Banion's old hangout, across from the Holy Name Cathedral. Capone had since obtained submachine guns of his own, and the cathedral later covered the bullet damage to its cornerstone with a wide walkway.

The North Side leadership then passed to Vincent "The Schemer" Drucci, but before Capone had to deal with him Drucci was killed during a struggle with arresting officers on April 4, 1927, and an equally volatile Bugs Moran took over.

It was Moran's teaming up with another Capone opponent, Joe Aiello, that had led to the killing of Brooklyn's Frankie Yale in 1928, Capone's one-time employer, by his "American boys." Moran missed out on the St. Valentine's Day Massacre only by minutes and had gone into hiding, but he later ventured back to Chicago's northern suburbs, where he tried to install slot machines. His criminal career continued to spiral downward until bank robberies landed him in Ohio's state prison and then in Leavenworth, where he died on February 25, 1957.

NEBRASKA ROBBERY

Gus Winkeler's car-wreck injuries, his friendship with Burke, his bank-robbing reputation, and a mistaken ID from bank personnel made him enough of a suspect in the Lincoln National Bank robbery of September 17, 1930, that Nebraska authorities (wanting to lock up nearly anybody) picked him. They also suspected others connected with the Harvey Bailey crew, and when they learned that Winkeler was hospitalized following the car wreck in Michigan in 1931 he was charged with that crime while they continued looking for others.

It was the biggest bank robbery of the times—maybe the biggest ever—and it made national headlines. The take was over $2,000,000 in 1930 dollars, or over $25,000,000 currently.

It would turn out the authorities had no real case against Winkeler—not without stacking the deck to get a conviction—but they were obviously counting on his using what clout he had within the bank-robbing community to get the loot returned. And that was what he managed to do—with considerable help from Capone. This was an accomplishment that involved good luck, good timing, Capone's $100,000 bail, and a measure of "honor among thieves," despite Georgette's opinion to the contrary.

Winkeler cut a deal with the Chicago Crime Commission's so-called Secret Six (the commission's unofficial action arm), with Nebraska's state prosecutor, and with Lincoln bank officials, all of whom seemed fairly certain that Winkeler would come through. And he did, through friends of Harvey Bailey who were in on the job.

Georgette's revelation about his contacts with the Secret Six—that he walked into their office in the Loop and simply plopped a suitcase on a table—went unreported in favor of a better story, fed to the press, which had the suitcase left under a lamppost by a mystery man in the middle of the night.

Winkeler's dealings with the Secret Six apparently worried Frank Nitti, who was virtually running the show following Capone's post-Massacre sabbatical in a Pennsylvania prison.

And Harvey Bailey had the bad luck to be camping out with some of the kidnappers of Oklahoma's Charles Urschel, sleeping next to Machine Gun Kelly's Thompson, when several members of that gang were arrested in Texas by federal agents in July of 1933. Convicted with the others for a crime in which he took no part, Bailey ended up in Alcatraz.

NEWBERRY, TED

Ted Newberry grew up on Chicago's Northwest side during the early years of Prohibition and acquired a booze franchise from North Side mob leader Dean O'Banion. After O'Banion's murder in November 1924 Newberry maintained good relations with other members of the gang, especially Bugs Moran, with whom he shared a thoroughly warped sense of humor. The two would discover somebody hoofing it alongside the road, offer him a ride, and then go into a lunatic act extolling the merits of murder until their backseat passenger said thanks, but he'd just re-membered that he needed to ... whatever. This, according to author Rose Keefe, would crack up Newberry and Moran, who inherited control of the North Side mob and probably never suspected that Newberry might later become a "spy" for Capone.

Georgette doesn't mention that Newberry, like Moran, was late for the February 14th meeting when the St. Valentine's Day Massacre took place or that he soon was welcomed into the Outfit where he received one of Capone's diamond-studded "AC" belt buckles.

After Capone went to prison at the end of 1931, Newberry and Gus Winkeler renovated the Chez Pierre nightclub into the Chez Paree at Fairbanks and Ontario, but Newberry ended up owing the Syndicate for booze he hadn't paid for. As Georgette explains, Newberry's plan to have Frank Nitti killed became known to a Dr. David Omens at a party, and (this may not have been known to Georgette at the time) Newberry was offering to pay the killer $15,000.

Mayor Anton Cermak, elected in 1931, already had failed to interest the Touhy mob in wrecking the Syndicate, without interference from Chicago police, and so he must have welcomed the news, presumably from Detective Sergeant Harry Lang, that Newberry also wanted Nitti knocked off because the Syndicate was muscling in on his North Side casino operations.

Nitti's downtown office at 221 North La Salle was raided on December 19, 1932, and after Detective Lang plugged Nitti with three bullets he gave himself a flesh wound, claiming Nitti had fired first. But other witnesses said, and other officers admitted, that Nitti was unarmed at the time.

Ted Newberry.

When Lang himself was prosecuted, a fellow officer said that Newberry had met with Lang minutes before in the lobby of Nitti's building. But during Lang's turn at bat he testified that he was acting on orders of Mayor Cermak, who, he said, feared he was marked for death by "Little New York" Louie Campagna.

Before Nitti recovered from his December 19th wounds (and refused to prosecute), Newberry was "taken for a ride" on the night of January 6, 1933. His body was found near Chesterton, Indiana—possibly as a favor to Chicago cops, who did not have jurisdiction outside the city.

The following month Cermak himself was mortally wounded by an assassin presumably shooting at newly elected President Franklin D. Roosevelt in Miami, Florida.

On the same day that Lang accused Mayor Cermak of ordering him to kill Frank Nitti—
September 26, 1933—Machine Gun Kelly was arrested in Memphis and the future
Dillinger Gang broke out of the Indiana state prison.

NITTI, FRANK

Georgette doesn't mention that the Massacre earned Capone a summons
to the country's presumably first "gangster convention" at Atlantic City
in May 1929, after which he and bodyguard Frankie Rio submitted to
arrest in Philadelphia for carrying guns—something Capone never did
when he had bodyguards. But once he and Rio were locked up for ten
months, Chicago newspapers felt free to stop treating him with appre-
hensive respect and start attacking him in editorial cartoons, meanwhile
speculating wildly and often wrongly on who would or could take over
his Outfit. For even in Pennsylvania Capone was treated like visiting
royalty in matters of carpeting, furnishings, a telephone, and a cell whose
door usually was unlocked. So while the papers assumed he would be
preoccupied with tax problems and maintain a lower profile, they also
assumed he would still be in control. In fact, while Capone, enthroned
in the Lexington Hotel, still was the "Babe Ruth" of American gangsters,
Nitti was running the show.

Detective Named in True Bill; $15,000 Killing Fee Reported

Newberry Wanted 'Enforcer' Killed, Says Officer.

ALLMAN ACTS

Suspends Policeman Charged With Wounding Nitti.

Detective Harry Lang was suspended yesterday by Commissioner Allman pending an inquiry by the police trial board.

Here Are Detectives' Conflicting Stories

Nitti Fired, According to Lang; Had No Weapon, Says Officer.

five minutes before the raid, Lang met Ted Newberry, North Side gang chief, who was ousted by the Capone outfit, in the lobby of the building where Nitti was shot.

BY LANG (before the grand ju... a piece of paper, ...ntaining ..., when I ...h him to ob... ...ng the fight, ...un and fired, . . .

The report was that Newberry gave $15,000 to kill Nitti, according to Miller's reported testimony.

Although Nitti survived Lang's bullets, Newberry lived exactly nineteen more days. His body was found in a ditoh near Bailleytown, in northern Indiana.

Nitti's testimony before the grand jury was reported confined to the statement that he knew Newberry

Frank Nitti still eluded the Chicago Crime Commission's "Public Enemy" list until 1933, when he was finally recognized as Capone's successor.

Nitti was born Francesco Raffele Nitto in the southern Italian town of Angri on January 27, 1886, and after his father's death he traveled steerage-class to Brooklyn with his mother and a sister in the summer of 1893. He was almost thirteen years older than Capone but lived in the same neighborhood and almost certainly came to know the Capone family. He ran in the same juvenile gang circles as Capone, and he probably knew Johnny Torrio, who had formed the John Torrio Association, and Frankie Yale, who later hired young Al to work at his tavern, the Harvard Inn.

The year 1913 found Nitti in Chicago. He was reputably barbering in Little Italy, and there he developed a working relationship with a variety of hoods who introduced him to fencing stolen property and working as a "booze broker" during a wartime version of prohibition enacted to save grain. By 1920, when national Prohibition went into force under the Volstead Act, his circle of friends included one-time Brooklynite turned Chicago vice lord and restaurateur Big Jim Colosimo, who had imported John Torrio a decade earlier to deal with Black-Handers. Torrio dealt with three by shooting them in a Southside railroad underpass. Also by 1920, young Al Capone, facing a possible murder charge, had fled from New York to Chicago to work for Torrio.

Torrio was suspected of having Colosimo murdered for obstructing his rise in the promising bootlegging business, where he successfully allocated territories to various gangs without bloodshed. When gangland disputes began to menace the Pax Torrio after 1923, Nitti weighed his options and signed on with Torrio, partly for his own protection. The following year, the city's only headline gangster, Dean O'Banion, swindled the lower-profile Torrio in a Sieben's Brewery deal. His "handshake" murder at his North State Street flower shop opened what soon became known as the Chicago Beer Wars, and both Torrio and Capone started making news.

Only when the St. Valentine's Day Massacre in 1929 led to Capone's prearranged arrest on a weapons charge in Philadelphia did Nitti even

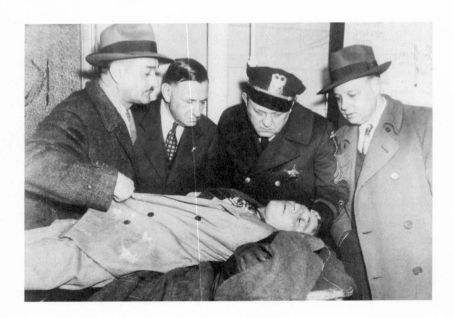

begin to attract much notice by the police. Once Capone was convicted, Nitti, after some internal squabbles with potential rivals, began reassembling Capone's "Outfit" into a "Syndicate" dominated by Italians. He did not even make the Chicago Crime Commission's "Public Enemy" list until 1933.

Capone's "American boys" had already left the reservation, two of them hooking up with the Barker-Karpis Gang; and with a few exceptions for those who had joined Nitti in other forms of racketeering, the others fell to Nitti's guns.

In 1943, facing prosecution in a Hollywood extortion case, Nitti, in poor health and presumably drunk, staggered to some nearby railroad tracks and shot himself in the head. The first bullet knocked off his hat. Another did the job.

NUGENT, RAYMOND "CRANE NECK," "GANDER"

John Raymond Nugent was born about 1895 and grew up in Cincinnati's rough West End neighborhood, where he devoted himself to everything from youthful delinquency to burglary to robbery to bootlegging to murder.

He may have served in the same division as Fred Burke during the world war when Burke was doing his thing in a Renault FT-17 two-man tank, one of the first of the new turret models. After Nugent's discharge he and another war buddy, Bob Carey, ended up in St. Louis with Burke, who had meanwhile gotten to know Gus Winkeler at the

local Sharpshooter's Club. Somewhere Nugent had picked up the nickname "Gander," perhaps derived from the expression "to take a gander" (as in male goose), which somehow became mistranslated into "Crane Neck," which hardly suited his otherwise normal physique.

Whatever the case, Nugent and his friends tangled with the law regularly but began scattering north after Egan's Rats self-destructed as a gang about 1925, a dozen going to prison when one "ratted" out the others

Ray Nugent.

following a mail robbery. The survivors stayed in touch, with Nugent returning to Cincinnati, where he had a wife, Julia, and two children. Bob Carey, whose aliases included Conroy and Newberry, renewed his connections with Burke, but after pulling a robbery in Detroit he rejoined Nugent in Cincinnati.

For a while Nugent prospered as a bootlegger but would also sign on for armed robberies, and he had no qualms about murder, either in the line of duty or in the course of arguments. On the night of April 2, 1927, Nugent, Carey, and others were drinking with the local bootlegging chief and his cronies when a fight erupted. One of the gang hit Nugent with a chair and, as author Daniel Waugh (*Egan's Rats*) put it, Nugent demonstrated why one should not bring furniture to a gunfight.

Nugent soon became known to Cincinnati police as a rumrunner, armed robber, and killer, and both he and Carey moved on to Chicago to meet up with Gus Winkeler, who had made his own way there in 1927 and was helping Fred Burke operate his Detroit snatch racket.

When one of the snatch victims turned out to be a friend of Al Capone, who objected to such kidnappings on principle, Capone discouraged it by hiring the three—and then Burke himself—as a special-assignment crew unknown to either the Chicago police or his gangland opposition, one that Georgette Winkeler would call Capone's "American boys."

This worked well enough for the killing of Capone's one-time employer Frankie Yale in Brooklyn on July 1, 1928, when Yale's booze supplies faltered about the same time he took sides with Capone rival Joe Aiello. Seven months later the "American boys" perpetrated the St. Valentine's Day Massacre, which became a nationally headlined if wrongly reported bloodbath, and everybody scattered while Chicago police rounded up "the usual suspects."

After the Massacre, Nugent made a stop in Cincinnati to kill the man who had killed one of his friends, and then headed for Florida, where he connected with Ralph Capone and opened a tavern. His mistake was in buying beer that did not always come from breweries controlled by Al Capone, and in 1931 he mysteriously disappeared.

His body was never found, and in 1952 a judge granted the petition of his wife, Julia, to have him declared legally dead in an effort to collect some $1,500 owned him from his army service in WWI.

O'HARE, EDWARD

Edward J. O'Hare was a St. Louis lawyer credited with promoting the "rabbit" that greyhounds still chase around a track. Dog-race betting was legal in Missouri but not in Illinois, at least not when gambling was involved. This invited Al Capone to open the Kennel Club, as such operations were generically called, and hiring O'Hare to operate it. Then O'Hare got religion and secretly provided the Treasury Department with information that prosecutors would use to convict Capone of tax evasion in 1931.

The religion O'Hare got was his son, Edward H. "Butch" O'Hare, who would attend Annapolis and become a navy flier, shooting down enough Japanese planes during the early part of World War II to earn himself a Medal of Honor. He was killed in combat in 1943. To honor a bona fide war hero, and despite his father's former mob ties, Chicago's O'Hare International Airport was named after him in 1949.

During the thirties, however, Eddie O'Hare continued to operate dog tracks in Chicago and to open them in other states in the mistaken belief that he could do business with gangsters without becoming a gangster himself. And while his perfidy in the Capone case was suspected, it had not excluded him from a role in the Chicago Syndicate, but he wasn't trusted, either.

On November 8, 1939, eight days before Capone's release from prison, O'Hare had been receiving ambiguous threats (which he wrongly assumed were coming from Capone) and was showing enough signs of agitation that he had a .32 pistol on the seat of his car as he drove up Ogden Avenue toward the Loop. When a suspicious sedan pulled up next to him he hit the gas and so did the other car. Both were traveling at least fifty miles per hour when two shotgun blasts hit him in the head and the neck. His coupe left the street and crashed head-on into a steel utility post.

PACELLI, WILLIAM, AND DANIEL SERRITELLA

The Pacelli and Serritella mentioned in Bolton's interrogations and in Hoover's 1936 memo were two of Chicago's most illustrious and durable politicians. Before William Pacelli became a state representative and

Daniel Serritella a state senator, both were city aldermen or committee-
men and cronies of Al Capone, whose power flourished under Mayor
"Big Bill" Thompson.

Serritella, as a member of Thompson's cabinet and his city sealer,
responsible for supervising weights and measures, was accused of bilking
Chicagoans out of many thousands of dollars, but both he and Pacelli
stayed in politics and the rackets despite sporadic efforts of reformers.

If, as Bolton later claimed, Detective Chief John Stege actually was
on Capone's payroll, it probably did not behoove Stege to turn over too
many rocks lest he find that Pacelli and Serritella had been in on the
meeting with Capone, Winkeler, Bolton, Goetz, and others in late 1928
when it was decided that Bugs Moran had to go.

PATTON, JOHNNY

Even in his later years, Johnny Patton was called the "Boy Mayor of Burnham" because he had opened a saloon there at the age of sixteen, was
elected mayor in 1906 at the age of twenty-two, and during Prohibition
had welcomed Al Capone and company to make his little suburb south
of Chicago a goldmine of illegal saloons, gambling parlors, bookie joints,
and bawdy houses.

At the same time, he kept these operations off the main street and
provided Burnham's citizens with good schools, good streets, and low
taxes. A typical Patton election was held in 1917 and the "Boy Mayor"
received 179 votes against 30 for his opponent. This was considered re-
markable, as Burnham had only 134 registered voters at the time, and
only 100 had voted in the previous national election.

Patton held his job as mayor for the next forty-three years, all but
ignored by the Cook County Sheriff's Department despite accusations
that he received stolen property from freight-car robberies and protected
illegal whiskey shipments. Burnham became the suburb where Capone's
Outfit guys could either enjoy themselves in comfort or hole up if the
heat was on. One snag did occur: after playing golf with Mayor Johnny,
Capone, climbing into a car to leave after the game, had a pistol go off in
his back pocket. He was quietly hustled to a hospital in Indiana, where
he signed in under an assumed name to have his wounds treated.

Following World War II, Mayor Patton finally was counterattacked by a new generation of ex-GIs. Before the 1949 elections, he deemed it wise to announce his "retirement from public life."

PIERCE, RALPH

Ralph Pierce had hooked up with the Capone Syndicate during the heydays of Prohibition but obviously did not make a favorable impression on Georgette when Nitti appointed him Gus's unwanted "bodyguard."

Pierce was born June 12, 1903, in Newcomerstown, Ohio, and by 1926 had been arrested for auto theft, gambling, extortion, rape, assault, kidnapping, and murder, but he never spent time in jail. He was not well known to the press, which couldn't think of how to identify Pierce except as a "Capone advisor" or something equally vague. When Capone went to prison in 1931, Pierce chose to remain with Frank Nitti, managed much of the Syndicate's gambling operations, and expanded into general racketeering.

By the early 1940s he had casino interests in Las Vegas. but was acquitted in the Bioff-Brown movie extortion case that led Nitti, already in poor health, to commit suicide.

Pierce remained active in the Syndicate well into the 1960s, when the reigning bosses were Sam Giancana and Tony Accardo.

PURVIS, MELVIN

Georgette Winkeler wrote her first letter to Melvin Purvis in the mistaken belief that the federal government would or could deal with local racketeering (at the time, interstate car theft, kidnapping, bank robbery, and capturing federal fugitives were among the few crimes over which the Justice Department had jurisdiction). Purvis immediately forwarded the letter to Director Hoover, who already had "disowned" him to the point that Purvis was preparing to resign from the Bureau. That alone might have caused her, in later interviews with the FBI, to think of him as "stuck up."

Purvis, born in Timmonsville, South Carolina, in 1903, had practically bullied his way into the Bureau of Investigation in 1927, where he

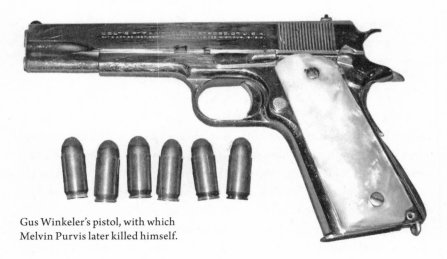

Gus Winkeler's pistol, with which
Melvin Purvis later killed himself.

soon found himself the Golden Boy of Hoover, who appointed him special agent in charge of the Bureau's office in Chicago in 1932. Purvis did
his part in the Kansas City Massacre of 1933, but in rushing to trap the
Dillinger Gang at Wisconsin's Little Bohemia Lodge in April 1934, his
inexperienced men embarrassed Hoover by letting the outlaws escape
(through no fault of Purvis) and shooting three innocent customers who
failed to hear or heed orders to stop. That same night he lost a federal
agent to Baby Face Nelson when Nelson was making his escape. It was
the last time Hoover would call a press conference at which he expected
to announce the capture of the Dillinger Gang.

Hoover later dispatched an experienced gunman, Herman Hollis,
to participate in the ambush of Dillinger outside Chicago's Biograph
Theatre on July 22, 1934, but Purvis received most of the credit, much
to Hoover's displeasure. After Purvis hurried to East Liverpool, Ohio,
to participate in the killing of Pretty Boy Floyd on October 23, Hoover
ordered him to shut up, get back to Chicago, and leave Herman Hollis in charge. But the following November 27, when Baby Face Nelson
killed both Herman Hollis and Sam Cowley in a bizarre running gun
battle, Purvis rushed to the scene at Barrington, Illinois, and further upset Hoover when he was widely quoted as taking a blood oath to avenge
their deaths.

By this time Hoover's Golden Boy had become persona non grata,
and he was sent on meaningless trips around the country to evaluate

other Bureau offices. Hoover's earlier letters, which had been intimate and nearly flirtatious, gave way to terse and often critical directives, and by the end of 1934 Purvis could see that his days at the Bureau were numbered. The following July he turned in his resignation.

In the years to follow other federal agents were ordered to sabotage any of Purvis's efforts to remain in law enforcement, obtain security-management jobs, or even consult on crime movies. However, they couldn't stop him from endorsing Dodge automobiles and Gillette razor blades, or from signing on with Post Toasties to replace their full-color comic page featuring an "Inspector Post" with his own "Melvin Purvis Junior G-Men," which soon flooded the country with "Melvin Purvis Junior G-Man" badges, detective instructions for youngsters, siren rings, and other trinkets that are now collectors' items.

In 1942 Purvis joined the army with enough hoopla that Hoover couldn't overtly block his commissioning, although he did convey his disapproval by advising Purvis's military superiors to investigate his character. When he was released from service in 1946 Hoover, incredibly enough, was still intent on undermining any effort he might make to return to police or security work. Thanks to his pre-war "Junior G-Man" fame and income from a radio station, he purchased a fine home in Florence, South Carolina, where he lived until February 29, 1960.

That day, while his wife was outside in the yard, he started to climb a pull-down staircase to the attic, where he intended to clean the nickel-plated, pearl-handled Colt .45 automatic that had once belonged to Gus Winkeler, intending to loan it to a friend for a display. He was apparently unaware that his son and a friend had used it for target shooting a few days earlier, firing tracer rounds (which would never be the bullet of choice for shooting one's self). The still-loaded gun fired, its bullet striking him in the jaw. Purvis had been experiencing depression and treating it with alcohol, and possibly for those reasons his death was considered a suicide.

A few days later his wife, Rosanne, sent a terse telegram to J. Edgar Hoover:

WE ARE HONORED THAT YOU IGNORED MELVIN'S DEATH. YOUR JEALOUSY HURT HIM VERY MUCH BUT UNTIL THE END I BELIEVE HE LOVED YOU

RIO, FRANKIE

Born in Italy about 1895, Frank Rio, or Reo, emigrated to the United States as a child and soon enough went into business as a delinquent, petty thief, and burglar, and from there progressed to jewel and fur thefts, until he was arrested as a suspect in bank robberies. He also possessed some $40,000 in bonds from a Union Station mail robbery in 1921, but he evidently beat those raps.

By this time he had attracted the attention of the Torrio-Capone mob and supposedly shielded Capone from the guns of Hymie Weiss, who led a motorcade that riddled the Hawthorne Hotel and an adjoining restaurant in 1926. Weiss was thoroughly machine-gunned from a next-door window outside the late Dean O'Banion's flower shop twenty-one days later.

In May 1929, Rio joined Capone for a Philadelphia prison sentence, further establishing his loyalty in what probably was an effort by Capone to abide by a decision of a "national gangster conference" at Atlantic City, and perhaps to escape the wrath of those remnants of the Bugs Moran Gang who had not been killed in the St. Valentine's Day Massacre.

Rio's influence diminished once Capone went to prison in 1931 and Nitti took over the Syndicate. He died of heart failure at his home in suburban Oak Park on February 23, 1935.

STACCI, DOC (AND OTHER GANGSTER HANGOUTS)

Doc Stacci operated the O.P. Inn in Melrose Park and had an interest in other taverns in the western suburbs of Chicago. His places were gangster and outlaw layovers like Louis Cernocky's Crystal Palace and Louie's Place at Fox River Grove, Jimmy Murray's Rainbo Barbecue restaurant just north of Chicago, Hobart Hermansen's Lake Como Inn near Lake Geneva, Wisconsin, and Emil Wanatka's Little Bohemia Lodge in upper Wisconsin. All were friends or acquaintances of one another.

Chicago also had underworld doctors such as David Omens and Otto von Borries, who were the health-care providers for local mobsters, and Joseph P. Moran and Wilhelm Loeser, who specialized in outlaws. And for car repairs and modifications, hoods had the garages of Joe Bergl

in Cicero and Clarence Lieder in Chicago, to name the two most prominent, and Capone's men commonly kept cars at "Clark's garage," probably that of James P. Clark in Cicero.

Gun dealers included Peter Von Frantzius and Louis Scaramuzzo,
who had their own shops, as well as Al Dunlap, who was an authorized
Auto-Ordnance dealer of Thompson submachine guns as well as publisher of the professional police journal *The Detective*. James "Bozo"
Shupe and Frank V. Thompson were straw-man purchasers of Thompsons that usually made their way to the Chicago underworld.

The attorneys who specialized in crooks would include too many to
list, but the one mentioned by Georgette, Abraham Lincoln Marovitz,
represented her in civil actions to recover Gus's property. He had his
share of mob contacts, including Frank Nitti after he was shot, but in
later years Marovitz became a respected U.S. district judge whose office gradually filled up with busts, early photographs, letters, and other
Abraham Lincoln memorabilia.

In short, the underworld in Chicago, as well as in other cities, had
what amounted to a support group who mostly avoided jail time, leaving
that to a few saloon-keepers.

Doc Stacci paid dues to the local and county police and didn't get
himself into serious difficulty until the Kansas City Massacre of 1933
when federal agents traced telephone calls and decided he was a major
player in the botched effort to free bank robber Frank Nash. Along with
several others tried in 1935, he went to prison on a two-year sentence,
as did Elmer Farmer, who operated a tavern in Bensenville and whose
connections with the Barker-Karpis Gang would land him in Alcatraz.

THOMPSON SUBMACHINE GUN

The Thompson submachine gun was conceived by General John Talia-ferro Thompson during the First World War in the belief that Allied soldiers needed the firepower of a handheld, fully automatic weapon to break the stalemate of trench warfare.

Prototypes were being tested at the time the Armistice was signed, but the funds already spent on the gun's development compelled the privately owned Auto-Ordnance Corporation to put it into commercial production in 1921—15,000 Thompsons, made by Colt's—intended only for military and police use and for "the protection of large estates." (An early advertisement depicts such an estate owner, in full cowboy regalia of the day, using a Thompson gun to riddle a bunch of Mexican banditos, which was not that outlandish considering that Pancho Villa had raided Columbus, New Mexico, in 1916.)

Until that time no one had heard of a Thompson submachine gun. The "sub" was coined by Thompson himself because it did not fire the rifle ammunition needed for Brownings, Maxims, and other heavy machine guns, but rather used the army's standard issue .45-caliber pistol cartridge.

The gun was demonstrated for the U.S. and several foreign armies, donated to the New York Police Department, and purchased by a few private security firms to intimidate striking miners in such places as Kentucky and Colorado, but it was not discovered by Chicago bootleggers for another three years. They were the ones who turned it into the gangster equivalent of the cowboy's six-shooter.

After Northsider Dean O'Banion swindled Southsider Johnny Torrio in a brewery deal, O'Banion decided that would be a good time to vacation at the dude ranch owned by fellow hoodlum Louie "Two-Gun" Alterie in Colorado. On his way back to Chicago O'Banion stopped in Denver and loaded up on ordnance, including three Thompsons, which the *Rocky Mountain News* called "baby machine guns." So evidently he was expecting trouble, but he had been back in the city only a few days when Torrio had O'Banion killed—the famous "handshake murder"—in his North State Street flower shop on November 10, 1924, setting off five years of Chicago's Beer Wars.

Visitors at Louie Alterie's dude ranch in Colorado, where Dean O'Banion acquired the first Thompson guns brought to Chicago. (O'Banion holding cap, his wife Viola, and Louis Alterie.) *Photo courtesy of Rose Keefe.*

The Tommygun's first use did not take place until the following September 25. The Southside Saltis-McErlane Gang, now affiliated with the late O'Banion's Northsiders, tried to kill rival Spike O'Donnell at the corner of Western Avenue and 63rd Street, the busiest intersection in Chicago's West Englewood neighborhood. It was a drive-by shooting; they missed their intended target, but took out the windows of a Walgreen's drugstore. The large number of empty .45 shell casings mystified Chicago police until October 4, when a black touring car sped down South Halsted Street and riddled the headquarters of the Ralph Shelton Gang at the Ragen Athletic Club, which was the usual hangout for young hoodlums who mixed workouts with holdups. The bullets hit and killed one Charles Kelly, presumably the Thompson's first victim.

Initially puzzled by all the shots that had been fired at O'Donnell and ascribing them to .45 automatic pistols, this time the police figured out what all the bullet holes meant. According to the *Chicago Daily News:*

A machine gun, a new note of efficiency in gangland assassinations, was used to fire the volley from a black touring car, killing one man and wounding another in front of the Ragen Athletic club . . . at 5142 South Halsted St. last Saturday night.

Captain John Enright of the stockyards police said today his investigation satisfied him that a machine gun had been used, and that the same gun had been used in an attack on Spike O'Donnell. . . .

"The bullets were fired from a machine gun," Captain Enright said, "because we find that more than twenty bullets were fired into the clubhouse. Witnesses say they came in too rapid succession to be revolver shots. However, we are basing our theory on something more than that. . . . So far as their being bullets of the same kind as were fired at 'Spike' O'Donnell, I compared them with bullets which Englewood police picked up at the time and they are identical."

Despite the machine gun, the story was buried on page 5. And the wire services wrote it up as a short human-interest item—the latest wrinkle in Chicago's gangland warfare.

If McErlane's early attacks were poorly reviewed by both the police and the press, he finally attracted attention as Chicago's Tommygun pioneer on February 9, 1926. The shooting, despite the usual poor marksmanship, earned the *Chicago Tribune*'s front-page banner headline the following morning and started the Thompson on its road to ill fame:

MACHINE GUN GANG SHOOTS 2

Thirty-seven bullets from a light automatic machine gun were poured into the saloon of Martin (Buff) Costello, 4127 South Halsted Street, last night, by gangsters striving to assassinate two rivals for the highly profitable south side traffic in good beer.

The Costello saloon machine-gunning convinced Capone that he was lagging behind in the underworld arms race, and the next day he dispatched three of his men to the South Side sporting goods store of Alex Korecek. Korecek took one look at his customers and agreed to order three Thompson submachine guns. Two months later Capone killed three men and wounded two in the first sensational "machine-gun massacre" of the twenties.

During the early evening of Tuesday, April 27, 1926, Capone's crew (possibly led by Capone himself) felt compelled to waste some Klondike O'Donnell men who were poaching in Capone's Cicero territory. They had stopped by a saloon called the Pony Inn at 5613 West Roosevelt Road when the Capone men loosed more than a hundred rounds into the interlopers, the building, and the cars parked in front of it. Unfortunately for Capone, one of those killed was Assistant State's Attorney William McSwiggin, known as the "hanging prosecutor," who just happened to be partying that night with his bootlegger friends.

Since bootleggers were supposed to shoot only one another, the killing of McSwiggin, a public official, made national headlines. Marcellus Thompson, son of General Thompson and general manager of the Auto-Ordnance Corporation, rushed to Chicago and offered his assistance in tracking down the Tommygun discarded by the killers. Its sale was traced to Alex Korecek, who by now was wishing he'd never gone into the gun business. One reporter described him as "speechless with fear," and when a writ of habeas corpus came out of nowhere requesting Korecek's release, the reporter asked who filed it. Korecek replied, "I don't know, but I know he wasn't any friend of mine!"

Korecek managed to survive both the cops and Capone, and Capone of course survived the police investigation.

Not long after that the late O'Banion's successor, Hymie Weiss, staged what must have been the mother of all drive-by shootings when he led a caravan of cars along Cicero's main street and riddled Capone's headquarters at the Hawthorne Hotel. He didn't kill anyone, but twenty-one days later Capone set up an elaborate machine-gun nest that killed Weiss and his bodyguard Patrick Murray as they stepped out of a car in front of the Holy Name Cathedral, across the street from the late O'Banion's headquarters. The war was on, much to the dismay of the Auto-Ordnance Corporation.

It turned out that the Thompson was too large a gun to qualify as a concealed weapon and was therefore legal to own, for nobody had thought to prohibit machine guns as such. That same year *Collier's* magazine published two alarmist articles denouncing the Thompson gun, one author going a little overboard: "This Thompson submachine gun is nothing less than a diabolical engine of death . . . the paramount example of peacetime barbarism . . . the diabolical acme of human ingenuity in man's effort to device a mechanical contrivance with which to murder his neighbor."

That same year, 1926, bandits with Thompsons robbed a mail truck in New Jersey, which inspired the postal authorities to supply the U.S.

Marines with some two hundred Thompsons to guard the mails. Police departments in many cities also started buying Thompsons, but not in large numbers. In 1928 the U.S. Navy adopted the gun as an auxiliary weapon, but in relatively small numbers. That also was the year that Al Capone's "American boys" killed Brooklyn mobster Frankie Yale with Thompson guns, the first time such a weapon had been used in New York, causing the press to worry that Chicago-style violence was reaching their city.

Which it did. In 1930 "Mad Dog" Coll missed his intended target in front of the Helmar Club in Uptown Manhattan but managed to spray a group of children, killing one. He was dealt with by other gangsters, probably Dutch Schultz's, in a telephone booth at a drugstore in lower Manhattan.

By this time "motorized bandits" had discovered that submachine guns were just what they needed to make the proper impression on bank employees and kidnap victims, which soon saddled one low-rent bootlegger and armed robber named George Barnes (a.k.a Kelly) with the moniker "Machine Gun Kelly," for he was carrying one when he went big-time and kidnapped Oklahoma City oilman Charles Urschel in 1933. By 1934 all the famous outlaws of the day were using the weapon to intimidate their victims, or to kill them if they were police returning fire.

In 1930 the Auto-Ordnance Corporation discontinued all sales to wholesale and retail dealers, with exceptions for the military and for police departments ordering guns on their official letterheads. The company had become a skeleton operation that still had some five thousand Thompson guns in inventory when it was purchased by Russell Maguire in 1939. At this time General Thompson wrote a sad note to Theodore Eickhoff, the supervising engineer who had left Auto-Ordnance in the middle twenties: "I have given my valedictory to arms, as I want to pay more attention now to saving human life than destroying it. May the deadly T.S.M.G. always 'speak for' God and Country. It has worried me that the gun has been so stolen by evil men and used for purposes outside our motto, 'On the side of Law and Order.'"

That note was penned on August 1, 1939, and a month later the German Wehrmacht invaded Poland. Suddenly every Allied army began clamoring for submachine guns, and in buying Auto-Ordnance Maguire had acquired not only the remaining stock of Thompsons for the wholesale price of the guns but also the machine tools for their manufacture. He rushed most of the existing guns to Britain and France while tooling up for their mass production. He ultimately sold more than two million before the end of the war, becoming both wealthy and famous as America's "Tommygun tycoon."

TOUHY VS. FACTOR

As can be inferred from Georgette Winkeler's statements to her FBI interviewers, year 1933 was not a good one for Roger Touhy.

Touhy had led the mob that controlled beer and slot machines in DuPage County, which neighbored Cook County on the west. Touhy already had ignored the entreaties of Capone, whose trucks needed to traverse Touhy territory when bringing booze into Chicago. He not only refused to cooperate, but to impress visitors from what Capone then called his "Outfit," Touhy would festoon his headquarters with weaponry, including Thompson submachine guns borrowed from the county police. Later, having no inclination to engage in a shooting war, he had declined an offer from Chicago's Mayor Cermak, who had beaten Big Bill Thompson in the elections of 1931, to take on the Nitti Syndicate with no interference from the police.

But Touhy's legal and other problems did not begin until 1933, when Capone, now imprisoned at Atlanta, believed him to be responsible for kidnapping Jerome Factor, the son of his friend Jake "The Barber" Factor. Georgette Winkeler also assumed that to be the case, for Capone contacted Gus, and with a little help from

Roger Touhy.

the syndicate the boy was soon released; but given Touhy's antipathy toward Cook County hoodlums in general, this might have been the work of some lesser gang.

That same year federal prosecutors tried but failed to convict Touhy of kidnapping William Hamm Jr. (who in fact was snatched by the little-known Barker-Karpis Gang). Then "The Barber" himself supposedly was kidnapped by the Touhys and (again supposedly) released upon payment of $70,000 ransom.

That case ended up in a state court, and FBI agents, paraphrasing Georgette in 1936, said they were told that "she was absolutely positive that the Touhy mob did not kidnap Jake Factor, as the boys sat around her apartment and laughed over the fact that the Touhy mob was so strongly suspected." She added that it looked like Factor would be staying in this country after all.

In fact, Jake the Barber already had been scheduled for extradition to England to face charges of financial misdeeds, but the British evidently backed off when, this time, Touhy was convicted and sentenced to ninety-nine years in the state prison at Joliet.

After nearly twenty-five years Touhy's case was reviewed by a federal judge, who held that the Factor kidnapping was bogus from the start, based on the perjured testimony of Jake Factor and Captain Daniel "Tubbo" Gilbert of the Cook County Police, among others. Toward the end of Touhy's prison ordeal he collaborated with prominent journalist Ray Brennan on an autobiography titled *The Stolen Years,* published in 1959.

The state set him free on November 16 of that year, and two weeks later he was shotgunned to death on the front porch of his sister's house. Touhy was quoted as saying as he lay dying, "The bastards never forget!" which turned out to be the invention of a Chicago journalist who needed some "last words."

WHITE, WILLIAM "THREE-FINGERED JACK"

Once associated with Klondike O'Donnell's "West Side" gang, William "Three-Fingered Jack" White was suspected of a payroll robbery in 1926 and other criminal pranks before he shifted his allegiance to Al Capone.

He then moved into labor racketeering in a big way, earning himself second place on the Chicago Crime Commission's "Public Enemy" list in 1933, the first year that it included Frank Nitti.

White remained close to Gus Winkeler before Nitti began his house-cleaning. Besides not liking Winkeler's continuing loyalty to Al Capone and his increasing independence, Nitti suspected that he was getting too cozy with the FBI and ordered him killed on October 9, 1933. White himself was killed on January 23, 1934, by two presumed friends who had stopped by his Oak Park house for drinks shortly after he had been visited by Buck Kempster, the state's liaison man with the Justice Department, and federal agent Melvin Purvis.

FRANKIE YALE

Brooklyn mobster Frankie Yale was killed with submachine guns—the first time such a weapon had been used in New York. One of the guns, left in a car abandoned near the East River, was traced to a Chicago gun dealer, and New York police were quick to declare that Chicago-style gang violence was spreading to their city.

Most books accept the claim (still made by writers citing earlier books and newspapers) that the murder was the work of Jack McGurn, who had spent his childhood in New York before moving to Chicago. However, Georgette Winkeler attributes the killing to her husband and Fred Goetz, whom she usually calls George (as in his alias, George Zeigler). She says they were led by Lefty Louie Campagna (usually called "Little New York Louie" in Chicago), who was familiar with New York and often visited family members living in Brooklyn.

Capone, a former Brooklynite himself, had worked for Yale as a bouncer/waiter in a joint ironically called the Harvard Inn. That was where Capone acquired his facial scars about 1917 when his joking remarks about a young woman customer led her brother, Frank Gallucio, to attack him with a knife.

Yale called for a sit-down at which Capone apologized, and Gallucio had no choice but to accept. When Capone later became a suspect in other crimes, he found it convenient to move to Chicago and soon became an aide to Colosimo's John Torrio (originally brought in from

New York to eliminate Colosimo's Black Hand threats) at a nearby dive called the 4 Deuces, at 2222 South Wabash.

Once Prohibition set in, Yale remained a principal supplier of booze to his colleagues in Chicago, and he almost certainly killed two prominent Chicago mob figures, Jim Colosimo in 1920 and Dean O'Banion in 1924, as favors to Torrio and Capone, for he was in the city on both occasions. Then gang politics put him on the wrong side of the Chicago Outfit. When Capone was trying to take over Chicago's Unione Siciliana by proxy, Yale's regular supplies of East Coast liquor unaccountably found themselves being hijacked. This aroused Capone's suspicions, and when Yale took sides with Capone's rival, Joey Aiello, who not only had put a bounty on Capone's head but had teamed up with Bugs Moran, Capone sent his "American boys" to kill him on July 1, 1928.

Georgette does not mention Fred Burke in connection with the killing of Yale, but when some of the bullets from Yale's body were found to have come from one of the machine guns used in the St. Valentine's Day Massacre and later seized at Burke's house, he was assumed to have been one of the shooters.

INDEX

WILLIAM J. HELMER is author or coauthor of *Dillinger: The Untold Story* (Indiana University Press, 1994), *The Complete Public Enemy Almanac*, *Public Enemies* (the original), *The St. Valentine's Day Massacre*, *Baby Face Nelson*, and *The Gun That Made the Twenties Roar*, as well as numerous magazine articles on the gangland era.